Other Relevant Writing by David Coates

The Labour Party Collection

The Labour Party and the Struggle for Socialism (1975)
Labour in Power? (1980)
The Crisis of Labour (1989)
New Labour into Power (2000) # **
Paving the Third Way: The Critique of Parliamentary Socialism (2003) **
Blair's War (2004) #

Issues for Labour

Socialist Arguments (1983) # **
Socialist Strategies (1983) # **
The World Order: Socialist Perspectives (1987) # **
Features of a Viable Socialism (1990) #
Economic and Industrial Performance in Europe (1995) **
Working Classes: Global Realities (2000) # **

The Context of Labour Politics

The Context of British Politics (1984)
A Socialist Anatomy of Britain (1985) # **
*The Economic Decline of Modern Britain: The Debate between Left and
    Right (1986) # ***
*The Economic Revival of Modern Britain: The Debate between Left and
    Right (1987) # ***
Running the Country (1991/5)
The Question of UK Decline (1994)
UK Economic Decline: Key Texts (1995) # **
Industrial Policy in Britain (1996) **
Models of Capitalism: Growth and Stagnation in the Modern Era (2000)
Varieties of Capitalism, Varieties of Approaches (2005) **

jointly authored/edited   ** edited collection

Prolonged Labour

The Slow Birth of New Labour Britain

David Coates
Worrell Professor of Anglo-American Studies
Wake Forest University

First published 2005 by
PALGRAVE MACMILLAN
Houndmills, Basingstoke, Hampshire RG21 6XS and
175 Fifth Avenue, New York, N.Y. 10010
Companies and representatives throughout the world

PALGRAVE MACMILLAN is the global academic imprint of the Palgrave Macmillan division of St Martin's Press LLC and of Palgrave Macmillan Ltd.
Macmillan® is a registered trademark in the United States, United Kingdom and other countries. Palgrave is a registered trademark in the European Union and other countries.

ISBN-10   1–4039–9359–9 hardback
ISBN-13   978–1–4039–9359–5 hardback
ISBN-10   1–4039–9360–2 paperback
ISBN-13   978–1–4039–9360–1 paperback

This book is printed on paper suitable for recycling and made from fully managed and sustained forest sources.

A catalogue record for this book is available from the British Library.

A catalogue record for this book is available from the Library of Congress

10   9   8   7   6   5   4   3   2   1
14   13   12   11   10   09   08   07   06   05

Printed and bound in Great Britain by
Antony Rowe Ltd, Chippenham and Eastbourne

For Eileen and Jonathan
with love

Contents

Preface

Books are written for specific purposes and to a specific design. This one is no exception. It has been written in order to establish the record of New Labour in power during its first two terms, the better to enable those who read it to make an informed judgement on the adequacy of that record. In the cut and thrust of politics on a daily basis, it is often difficult to locate either the patterns of policy or their cumulative impact over time. Yet just such a location is essential if the daily political battle is to be understood in full; and so there is always an important role – in the literature on current politics – for carefully-constructed stocktakings of progress to date. This book was written as such a stocktaking.

It has been written to a design that separates the telling of the record from the assessment of its adequacy, and to a specification that – in the laying out of the record – privileges the reproduction of the actual words of the key players involved in the policy-making process, and the content of the key policy documents which that process has generated. It has been written in that form in the hope that its readers will be able to come to a judgement on the adequacy of New Labour as a government that is independent of that of its author. I have a view, of course, and that is laid out in the last section of the book; but that is not important here. What is important is that an accurate record of New Labour's achievements be established fully and quickly for all of us, so that the judgements that we are all periodically called upon to make can be as well-informed as it is possible for them to be. To that end, the book does not, except inadvertently, interweave the story and the assessment. At least it does not do that until its closing chapters. There are some splendid books around already that mix analysis and description in that alternative way.[1] Their strength is that they give their reader a clear sense of the authors' understanding of New Labour. Their weakness is that they *give* it to their reader, normally without creating in the process an independent base from which the reader can then evaluate the adequacy of the particular understandings that are structuring the material being read. This book attempts to create for its readers that independent base.

No presentation of the historical record can, however, be entirely neutral, and this one is not. It sits in a series of studies of the Labour Party that I have written down the years, and in that sense is, for me at least, part of a private dialogue with my own past. There are definitely differences between this Labour government and previous ones which I, among others, was rather slow to spot, and which now oblige all of us to approach it with fresh eyes; but there are also similarities between this Labour government and previous ones which are often denied, the understanding of which is actually advanced by the remobilization of insights from the past. Whether the balance of the 'old' and the 'new' in this study of New Labour is adequately struck is something else that will have to be left to the judgement of its readers!

In making that judgement, it is worth noting from the outset the genuine danger that exists whenever the term 'New Labour' is used as a noun rather than as an adjective: the danger of implying a unity of understanding and purpose to an entire government that in reality has often been divided by faction and driven by circumstance. What follows here will on occasion run that risk: because what is novel about this Labour government, relative to Labour governments in the past, does appear to be the degree to which there is an underlying unity to the way in which its key architects understand the world and their role within it. The text that follows will note the factional divisions and mention the personalities, but it will not focus on them. It will focus instead on the trajectory of the policies that those divided personalities have generated, and on the logics associated with their 'third way' take on the nature of the modern world. So if the soap opera of New Labour in power is your interest, then this is not the book for you; but if the long-term consequences of New Labour in power concern you, then it most certainly is.

Studies like this are only possible because of the work of others, and writing them necessarily involves the accumulation of considerable intellectual and personal debts. The intellectual ones accumulated here come in three main forms: to the political journalists whose daily telling of the comings and goings of New Labour personalities provides a vital first level of political understanding; to the social commentators whose articles and books structure those comings and goings, and give them meaning and significance; and to the academic specialists whose writings on different aspects of the New Labour project help to situate it in the wider order of things. In the first of those three categories, I am particularly indebted, as the notes will show, to the work of Andrew Rawnsley and James Naughtie; in the second to Will Hutton, William Keegan, Madeleine Bunting, Jeremy Paxman, Polly Toynbee, David Walker and Larry Elliott; and in the third to the academics whose work can be found in the various collections and conferences organized by Steve

Ludlam, both with his colleagues at Sheffield University and through the PSA Labour Movements Study Group.

What this book attempts to add to the political journalism on New Labour in power is a greater analytical depth and historical background than the requirements of a daily newspaper column normally allow or invite. What it hopes to add to the social and academic commentary is a greater coherence and range of coverage and explanation than is often possible in texts addressed to just part of the New Labour agenda or in collections written by many hands. But synthetic and analytic work of this kind can only be written because of the prior existence of journalistic and academic material of the very highest quality; and this book was so much easier to write than it might otherwise have been because there is so much of that high-quality work around. Indeed, my admiration of the journalism provided by the BBC, by newspapers like the *Guardian* and the *Observer*, and by magazines like the *New Statesman*, continues unabated, and it is a personal pleasure to be able to record that admiration (and debt) here. It is a personal pleasure too to be able to say much the same thing about the quality of work produced by friends and former colleagues in the various departments of politics and government that are tucked away in that remarkable string of Northern English universities that stretches from York and Leeds to Manchester and Sheffield. The notes to the various chapters will show how deep and wide my debt to them actually is. New Labour in power has been well served by many of the journalists and academics who monitor its progress; and I, watching the story unravel from afar, have also been a major beneficiary of that monitoring.

Books like this are also only possible because of the direct help of talented people. Ben Halfhill acted as senior researcher on this project, as earlier he did on *Blair's War*, my co-written commentary on aspects of New Labour foreign policy to which this volume is an intended companion.[2] Ben was there at the outset of the writing, and at the end, and was throughout an industrious and invaluable supplier of primary and secondary material in volume. At the outset of the research, Greg Pollock briefly played a similar role. As the writing developed, I benefited enormously from conversations with Joel Krieger, and with Greg Dyke, Will Hutton, Colin Leys, Alan Simpson and Clare Short: plus my son Edward, my brother Barrie, and my particular version of Woodward and Bernstein's 'Deep Throat' – my secret source, close to the centre of power, who must remain forever anonymous! Wake Forest University provided the funds that made the research possible. Colleagues in the Department of Political Science provided the break from teaching that allowed the writing to happen. Leslie Gardner was a great ally and friend in moving this project from conception to contract; and Eileen and Jonathan provided the love which daily makes life worthwhile, and which kept the research and the writing in its proper place. My debt to all of them is huge, and to Eileen and Jonathan is quite literally beyond measure. I can only hope that, for them, this book acts as a modest payback for at least some of the countless ways in which they touch my life and give meaning to my existence.

Wake Forest University
November 2004

Part 1
The Promise

1
The Legacy

When the dust had settled from the general election of 1997, it was possible for the very first time in modern British electoral history – or at least it was possible if you picked your route with care – to drive from Land's End to John O'Groats without passing through a single constituency held by a Conservative MP, bar one. When all the election results were in, the one unavoidable blot of blue on your otherwise pink road map was an isolated Tory stronghold in the Yorkshire Dales. The isolation of that Ryedale constituency stood as stark testimony to the scale of the cull of Conservative MPs effected by the UK electorate in May 1997. Never since 1836 had the UK's traditional governing party been so decimated and discarded. Never since 1945 had a Labour government come to power amid such excitement and with such promise. 'Dilute that excitement with whatever doses of scepticism you feel appropriate', Andrew Rawnsley told us as the results came tumbling in, and yet there was still 'no question that on Friday morning Britain woke up a different country. It may be a trick of the light,' he wrote, 'but it feels like a younger country.'[1]

Yet countries, of course, do not age. Only their inhabitants do. It is the people, not the land, whose moods and optimisms shift with the electoral tides; and those shifts are invariably incremental and often invisible. They are captured at moments of electoral change, but they are not created by them. The general election of 1997 was one such moment of realignment. It is one we remember now because of the scale of the change it signalled. Equipped with the wisdom of hindsight, that sea-change has an element of inevitability about it; but we need to remind ourselves at the very outset of this exercise that when it happened, it came as an enormous surprise to virtually everyone caught up within it. To quote Tony Benn: in 1997 the New Labour leaders 'went to the beach to have a paddle and were hit by a tidal wave'.[2] They found themselves in power in the wake of an almost two-decades-long period of Conservative ascendancy that had for much of its length looked impregnable. They found themselves in power in possession of a political space far wider than they – and in truth any of the rest of us – had anticipated as the election loomed. And they found themselves in power amid a generalized excitement and inflated set of expectations that were generated by the scale of the result itself. What they did with that space, and to what degree they met those expectations, is the subject matter of all that will follow here.

The excitement that was so general among Labour's supporters on that May morning in 1997 is, of course, far in the past now. It is largely forgotten and overshadowed by all we have subsequently experienced and learned of the complexities of New Labour in power. Yet if we are to judge the Blair governments aright, we need to start, not with our knowledge now of the complexities that would come, but with our (and their) ignorance and innocence as the story began. We need to start back in 1997. We need to start where they did, and as they did, on that bright and apparently young morning. We need to begin with a mind set firmly back in the mid to late 1990s, equipped only with the political memories of the decades before. 'The past,' L. P. Hartley once wrote, 'is a foreign country.'[3] Since it is, we need to begin this assessment of the performance of New Labour with a small amount of foreign travelling of our own.

The economic legacy

When the scale of the political victory in 1997 became obvious, it invited comparison to an earlier Labour Party victory of equal magnitude: that of 1945. But though the scale of the political landslide was similar in the two cases, the economic context within which it occurred was not. For between the two elections, the UK had participated to the full in the general economic changes that had transformed living standards in the core capitalist economies. Between 1945 and 1997, the UK economy's own position within that core had also changed in a series of significant ways; and the UK electorate had already lived through two sustained (though ultimately unsuccessful) state-led attempts to improve that position. The Blair government, unlike the Attlee one, came to power, that is, in the wake of a set of fundamental changes in the character and performance of the UK economy. It also came to power in the wake of first an Old Labour and then a Thatcherite assault on the inadequacies of that performance. In fact it would not be too much to say that the

Blair government came to power precisely because key sections of the UK electorate were in a mood for an assault of a different kind. There was a definite constituency in 1997 for a new and a *third* way; a constituency that existed only because its Thatcherite predecessor had ultimately proved, for many people at least, to be both economically ineffective and socially unacceptable.

An economy transformed

The economy that New Labour inherited was simultaneously prosperous and in trouble. It was prosperous. Living standards were higher in the UK in 1997 than they had ever been; and compared to 1945, of course, stratospherically so. So if the UK economy in 1997 was still in decline, it was only in a decline relative to the superior performance of its competitors, and not in one relative to its own past. On the contrary, the UK economy had grown steadily at an average rate of 3% a year between 1950 and 1973, at 1.5% a year in the 1970s and at 2.1% a year through the 1980s; and a long-term growth performance of that kind had been more than enough to leave each generation of the post-war British 'roughly twice as well off as its parents and four times as well off as its grandparents'.[4] It was true that the economy had gone through two deep recessions under the Conservatives since 1979. The 1979–81 recession had in fact been the deepest experienced by the economy in the century as a whole; and the 1990–94 one, though milder, had actually been the longest in the entire post-war period. But by 1997 even that was three years over, and commentators were again beginning to argue that, even if the long-term international decline of the UK economy had not actually been reversed, it was now at least probably behind us.[5]

The Attlee governments had inherited an economy based on the old Victorian industries of coal, cotton and rail. The Blair government did not. The textile industry had been run down in the 1950s, and the railways a decade later. Coal too had shrunk. In 1956, the industry had employed 694,000 people to produce the coal on which 95% of the economy then depended for their primary fuel.[6] Outside the agricultural sector indeed, there was no single larger occupational group in the UK in the mid-1950s than the miners; and as late as 1974 those miners had enjoyed sufficient numbers and economic centrality (still meeting 55% of the UK's fuel needs in 1970) to disrupt a government and trigger a general election. Even as late as 1985 there had still been 184,000 workers in the coal industry: but they were not there by 1997. For by then the Thatcher government had broken the militancy of the National Union of Mineworkers in a year-long strike, and had effectively shut the industry down. The day Tony Blair replaced John Major as Prime Minister, the labour force that remained in the UK's recently privatized coal mines was fast shrinking to its millennium total of a mere 13,000.

In fact, by 1997, the centre of gravity of the post-war UK economy had shifted not once, but twice. Its first shift had been the standard Fordist one.[7] Investment and employment had moved in volume and with speed from the labour-intensive low-productivity industries of the UK's Victorian heyday into the new capital-intensive and highly productive *light-engineering industries* of the post-war consumer boom, and into industries geared to maintaining the UK's global role as a major military power. Investment and employment had moved into airplane production and munitions, and into industries producing washing machines, fridges, telephones, televisions, motorbikes and – overwhelmingly – cars. By 1971, 505,000 people worked in car assembly, and the car industry had become the economy's largest export industry.[8] The production of cars alone had been the source of fully a third of the economy's entire economic growth in the 1950s and 1960s.[9] In 1966, the year that employment in manufacturing industry peaked in the UK, more than one worker in three (and some 8.5 million in total) worked directly in the manufacturing sector.

But again, not by the time New Labour came to power: for by 1997 all that too was a fading memory. By 1997, the UK was predominantly a *service economy*. It was in terms of the percentage of GDP generated by each main economic sector. As late as 1979 manufacturing had contributed 30% of UK GDP: by 1997, that figure was down to 21% and falling. It was also in employment terms, for by 1997 deindustrialization had taken a heavy toll of manufacturing jobs. As New Labour came to power, employment in car assembly plants was down by more than 50% on its 1970s peak; as a manufacturing sector that in 1961 had employed 44% of all full-time workers had shrunk to one employing only 22% of them. In the year 2000, 76 workers in every 100 in the UK worked in the service sector: and twice as many people worked in retailing and banking as in the entirety of British-based manufacturing.[10] The UK economy had long ceased to be 'the workshop of the world' by the time the Attlee government inherited it in 1945: but immediately after the Second World War it was still a major manufacturing force. By the time it was Blair's turn to preside over growth and employment, UK-based manufacturing had lost much ground: to the point indeed that by 1983 the UK had for the first time since the industrial revolution become a net *importer* of manufactured goods, and had remained so ever since.

Moreover and not surprisingly perhaps, given sectoral readjustments of this rapidity and scale, by 1997 at least 6% of the available UK workforce was not in paid employment at all. Unemployment, and the fear of it, left a shadow down the entirety of the 1990s, put there by the longevity and depth of the recession through which the economy had moved from 1990 to 1994. The official figure for unemployment in the UK had averaged around half a million through the 1950s and nearly 1 million in the 1970s. But it had settled around 2.7 million through the 1980s; and had then peaked for the 1990s at 2.9 million in 1993. That was one worker in ten; and the official unemployment figure in May 1997 was still 1.7 million. Viewed with a wider lens, the problem ran deeper still. The economic activity rates that measured the proportion of the available labour force actually in work – at just under 80% – remained stubbornly low through the 1990s: suggesting a haemorrhaging out of the official statistics of significant numbers of older workers in particular. Indeed as late as 1999, 2.3 million men of working age were economically inactive in the UK. The 1979 figure had been just 400,000.[11]

Over the Thatcher period as a whole, there had been a substantial diminution in the number of full-time jobs generated by the UK economy. In 1971, out of a total employed labour force of 21.6 million, 18.3 million people had been in full-time employment. A half-generation later, in 1993, the figure for full-time employment was only 15 million;[12] and that in an economy where – in international and comparative terms – wage rates were slipping and the length of the working day, though formally declining slightly, was actually being stretched by the amount of overtime regularly being worked. In 1960, per capita income in the UK exceeded that in West Germany, France, Italy and Japan: in the latter case by a factor of nearly three. By 1998, per capita income in the UK had slipped below that delivered by each of these key competitor economies, particularly the German.[13] In the 1990s British workers put in ever longer hours at work to compensate for this shortfall. As the Employment Policy Institute put it as New Labour settled into office, 'the working week for the average full-time male worker' in the UK had 'lengthened by two hours to 47 hours in the decade to 1998', and 'at 43 hours, the average full-time female worker was working three hours longer in 1998'[14] than she had a decade earlier. In consequence, in Andrew Rawnsley's 'younger country' the average British worker was actually putting in 175 more hours of work each year than his/her German equivalent, and 186 hours more than their Swedish counterparts. For all the years of market-oriented Thatcherite reform, the welfare capitalist economies of Germany and Sweden were still significantly more successful than the British in 1997 on virtually any measure of economic performance: and that superiority was evident in the extra four or five weeks of leisure that German and Swedish workers enjoyed when set against the more meagre vacation allowance of their harder-pressed UK equivalents.[15]

An economy in need of reform

This is not to say, of course, that British workers were denied their vacations. They were not. In fact, in the 1980s and 1990s, many of them took a regular two-week summer vacation, and increasingly they took it abroad; so coming face to face with the growing gap between the performance of the economy on which they relied and those of its more successful Western European competitors. For it was not simply in relation to hours and wages that the economy inherited by New Labour was underperforming internationally. It was underperforming right across the board.

The rate of deindustrialization in the UK in the years from 1971 was more severe than elsewhere in the advanced capitalist world. The number of people working in manufacturing between 1979 and 1990 fell in the UK by 30%. That compared 'with 17% in France, 11% in Italy, 5% in the US, no change in Germany and an *increase* of 13% in Japan'.[16] The resulting loss in the share of world trade in manufactures had been similarly sharp. The UK's hold on world trade halved between 1962 and 1991, and settled at anywhere between 7.5% and 9.6%, to leave the UK as a whole with a negative balance on its manufactured trade for every year after 1982.[17] That trade shortfall reflected the extent to which the productivity performance of the economy, both on the labour side and on capital, continued to lag behind that achieved in more successful economies elsewhere,[18] and in consequence average living standards, though rising in the UK as we have seen, grew more slowly than in Western Europe as a whole. By 1992 they had fallen to 89% of the OECD average.[19]

It was not all gloom and doom, of course, even in comparative terms. The UK economy did have its pockets of strength. There just weren't very many of them. When Michael Porter, the Harvard business guru, counted them in 1990, he found 'the largest concentration of British competitive advantage', in his judgement, to be 'in consumer packaged goods'. Another important cluster was 'financial or financially related services'; and yet a third

> looming large in export volume, [was] petroleum and chemicals, including paint (where ICI and Courtaulds [were] world leaders).

Significant clusters [were] also present in pharmaceuticals, entertainment and leisure products...publishing...aircraft, defence goods, motors and engines, and textiles (largely fibres). Other pockets of advantage [he reported, lay] in radio transmitters and radar apparatus, electrical generating equipment, glass and scrap metal.[20]

Other commentators pointed similarly to strengths in chemicals and pharmaceuticals; aerospace and defence industries; food, drink and tobacco; and financial services.[21] Significantly missing from their lists, however, as from Porter's, were motor vehicles, machinery and most textiles, which collectively were responsible between 1978 and 1989 for three-quarters of the deterioration in the UK's trade balance.[22] Foreign investment did generate improved performance in motor vehicles and electronics in the 1990s: but even these remained islands of improvement in a manufacturing sector which generally had lost competitive ground in the 1980s, when, as Porter noted, 'far more competitive industries in Britain lost world export share than...gained it'.[23] And yet the UK remained hungry for manufactured goods: to the point indeed that the imbalance between manufacturing and services, though large, could not cross-compensate. For 'given the composition of UK exports,' the House of Commons Select Committee on Trade and Industry reported in 1994, 'every 1% decline in exports of manufactures requires more than a 2½% rise in exports of services to compensate'. Yet 'only about 20% of service output can be exported'.[24]

None of this, of course, went unnoticed. It certainly did not go unnoticed by the various committees and Government departments that were periodically charged with the task of documenting and rectifying this pattern of relative decline. In fact there was a remarkable unanimity and consistency in the findings of the main reports shaping Government policy during the Thatcher and Major period.[25] The first such report, from the House of Lords in 1985, was highly critical of what it took to be the Thatcher government's 'neglect of manufacturing'. It rejected the view that the UK's imbalance in trade would correct itself 'automatically and in time'. On the contrary, it told an initially sceptical government that this reflected a 'lack of overall competitiveness and consequent reduction in capacity of manufacturing industry as a whole' which was both structural in origin and long-term in nature. The Committee looked to the government to put that right: first by recognizing that the problem existed, and then by initiatives aimed at increasing both the price and non-price competitiveness of UK-based firms. A stable currency, low interest rates and a business-friendly tax code were high among the Committee's recommendations for action in 1985. So too were the encouragement of closer, and longer-term, bank–industry relations, and the reduction of foreign sourcing of components by major UK-based companies.[26]

These were recommendations designed to enhance productivity and to stimulate much-needed investment in the UK's manufacturing base that were echoed nearly a decade later when, with a new Prime Minister and a deputy keen to correct the 1980s neglect of the manufacturing base, the Major government published in quick succession two equally damning stocktaking reports on the economy's strengths and weaknesses.[27] Given their authorship, both the later reports understandably claimed significant improvements because of government policy since 1979:[28] but they also pointed to long-term and structurally-rooted sources of economic underperformance with which public policy had as yet failed to deal. Their problem specification was largely unchanged from the mid-1980s: it was one of diminished international competitiveness, reflected in persistent deficits on the balance of payments and rooted in systematic underinvestment relative to competitors.[29] If there was a difference in these reports, it lay in the growing awareness in the 1990s – in government circles and beyond – of just how wide that shortfall in investment over time in the UK had actually been: not just a shortfall in investment in manufacturing plant and equipment (though both new reports were obliged to concede that) but also a shortfall in investment in people and their skills.[30] The performance of the UK economy, both reports conceded, showed a persistent inability to narrow the productivity gap with world leaders (in this instance, with the US in particular);[31] and did so both because UK-based workers had less capital equipment at their disposal than the best equipped of their overseas competitors, and because they lacked levels of general skill and formal training of an internationally adequate standard.[32]

By the time New Labour came to power in 1997, that is, the post-Thatcher Conservatives had found their own route to a 'third way' understanding of the importance of investment in human capital as the route to international competitiveness. In that sense, as Robert Reich, Clinton's first Secretary of State for Labour put it, by 1997 'we are all third wayers now'. And if they were not, the Labour Party and its allies in opposition had reports of their own to reinforce the message;[33] and the Select Committees on Trade and Industry in both Houses of Parliament were equally active and critical. 'Taking the last two decades as a whole', the Commons Select Committee on Trade and Industry reported in 1994, 'the UK is the only major industrial country whose manufacturing output has remained virtually static.... Not until 1988 did UK manufacturing output recover its level in the peak year of 1973, and in 1992 it was less than 1% higher than in 1973, whereas output increased by 27% in France, 25% in Germany, 85% in Italy and 119% in Japan during the same period.'[34] Clearly this level of underperformance was something that could not be allowed to continue.

So the Major governments had struggled with, and now New Labour inherited, a set of embedded economic weaknesses. Long years of underinvestment in capital and in people had left the UK economy with a set of gaps dividing it from its major competitors: an investment gap, a skills gap, a productivity gap, a trade gap, and now a prosperity gap. Those same years of neglect had left governments in the 1990s facing not one economy but two: facing a shrinking manufacturing sector, large parts of which were losing competitive advantage, and a growing service sector which contained new and influential centres of world excellence. The Conservatives left New Labour with an economy expanding again after the recession of the early 1990s. That much was positive in the legacy. But they left them too with an unfinished agenda of structural reform, and with yet more evidence of just how difficult that agenda was to implement. The legacy gave New Labour its opportunity and its task. It also provided it with its constraints. So it was a janus-faced economic legacy that New Labour inherited: but then Labour only ever defeats a sitting Conservative government when the economic constraints are tight, and poison chalices invariably come janus-faced. In that sense, though the detail of economic life for New Labour in 1997 was very different than it had been in 1945, the underlying dilemmas were still remarkably similar.[35]

The social legacy

In social terms, of course, 1997 was definitely not 1945. By 1997 we all had our images of the 1945 electorate. They were invariably images in black and white. The past had no colour because of the way it had been recorded, and that lack of colour intensified the difference. But the differences were still huge, whether accurately captured or not. The Labour government in 1945 inherited a society at war. It was one used to the discipline of a collective military effort, its people sealed from the full force of market processes by labour direction and the rationing of consumption. The Labour government of 1997 inherited a society at peace. The restrictions of wartime were all long gone. If they figured at all in the society's collective memory at the century's end, they did so only in the recollections of the very old. By 1997 you had to be at least 50, and male, to have experienced even the vestigial national service of the 1950s.

New Labour inherited a society in which the vast majority of potential voters were used to the high and rising standards of personal consumption of the long post-war boom. In 1997 people bought and spent freely, and they spent in volume: using a system of credit cards unknown in 1945 and personal bank accounts that at the end of the Second World War had been the status symbol of the few. They spent on commodities unimaginable a generation before, and on things which in 1945 had been beyond the grasp of most of the Labour electorate. By 1997, the majority of Labour voters expected to own their own home, to drive their own car, to take their own vacation, to settle each night in front of their own multichannel television set, and to be free to settle their own private earning and spending priorities. By 1997 too, the capacity of most potential Labour voters to sustain the lifestyle that they desired required that both adult members of the UK's conventional nuclear families brought in a wage or salary, for by then one of the new ways to be excluded from this generalized affluence was to be trapped in a single-parent family unit split asunder by divorce. And by 1997, there was a lot of divorce. Four marriages in ten ended that way in 1997. In 1947 it had been less than one in ten.[36] Whatever 1997 was, in social terms it was not 1945 at all.

A society transformed

As the old industries of the UK's Victorian heyday faded in the post-war period, the men and women who had worked in them had been obliged to work elsewhere. To remain in those industries, or to remain where they had once been, was to miss out on the rising productivity (and so on the growing wages and living standards) of the New Britain. The old working class was slow to vanish entirely. Its members remained locked in the river valleys of the English North and on the coalfields of the Celtic fringe, as industrial power shifted south into the English Midlands in the 1950s and 1960s, and then later into the Scottish lowlands and the English South East. A new working class emerged around those Midland and South Eastern industries: a new working class which, in the Midlands and the car industry, remained unionized and Labour, but a new working class which everywhere was more private and family-focused in its ambitions and social habits than had been the Northern and Celtic working class of the generations before. In 1945 Old Labour had appealed to a generalized sense of solidarity in a working class which had sustained a distinct sense of community: with its own traditions of working men's clubs, workers' libraries, Saturday football and May Day parades. It had been, in a real sense, a class apart from the middle-class world of the then small English suburbs. The rise and fall of the new manufacturing industries, and the Thatcherite assault on trade unionism, had changed much of that. So New Labour, by contrast, faced a working class whose members largely shared the concerns of middle England. It faced a working class less likely than in 1945 to be unionized, more likely to own its own home and transport, more likely to enjoy untrammelled access to credit (and so to consumption), and less comfortable with self-definitions that emphasized features of its shared proletarian condition. Such individualized ambitions and sensibilities had never been entirely absent from the agenda of previous generations of the UK working class: but by 1997 they were central to that agenda in ways that had not been true before.

In part, that was because, alongside this changing working class a new and wider middle class has also emerged in the post-Attlee years. In fact, two new middle classes had emerged in volume. One – based in the private sector – had emerged as the managerial hierarchies of the great Fordist industries had expanded in the 1950s and 1960s to cope with the new problems of administrative co-ordination created by the growth in size of companies and markets. The UK social structure acquired, over the half century that followed the end of the Second World War, a new strata of technocrats: men (and they were mainly men) who supervised production, planned marketing, supervised accounts and managed corporate divisions. Such men did not actually own the companies they helped to run. They still earned a wage (which they normally called a salary). But it was a wage that was inflated to match their managerial function and elevated industrial status, and accordingly they acquired with it many of the attitudes and self-definitions traditionally associated with the owners of capital. By 1997 the UK had had its managerial revolution. A whole generation of self-made managers had embedded itself. It had embedded itself industrially, setting itself apart from ordinary factory and office workers by differentiations in pay, hours, conditions and facilities. It had embedded itself socially, setting itself apart from ordinary workers by the quality and location of its housing, and by its propensity for the consumption of private education and health care. And it had set itself apart politically, by giving the Conservative Party its loyalty as the party of business.

That new private sector middle class had been staffed by the brightest boys of the first post-war generation of English workers, filtered out from the rest through the new selective education system set up in 1944 and organized around the 11+. Initially (and that means until the mid-1960s) this was a middle class that in the main was recruited directly from the new grammar schools. The brightest and the best went straight into industry at 18, trained there and were promoted internally. But progressively from the 1960s, that route of short-term social mobility was itself abandoned, replaced instead by the 'milk round': the selection of bright graduates generated by and through the expanded university system that emerged in the wake of the Robbins Report. With the rise of education and the new universities, the UK acquired a second middle class: one based not in the private sector but in the public. By 1997 New Labour faced, as the Attlee government had not, an electorate in which the largest group of unwavering Labour supporters worked in the schools and offices of the greatly expanded welfare state. Those supporters worked as teachers. They worked as social workers. They worked as nurses. They worked as hospital administrators. Not all of these new public service semi-professionals were Labour supporters, but the majority of them certainly were; and they too took home a salary, lived in the suburbs, and owned their own cars. In fact, one of the great differentiators between these two new middle class blocs by 1997 was precisely car ownership. In general, the private sector-based middle class received their cars as part of their package of benefits. They paid tax on those cars but they did not actually own them. The public sector middle class, in general and by contrast, did: and of course, because they did, they tended to drive smaller and older cars. The class structure of the UK changed dramatically in the years between Attlee and Blair, but the nuances of the new social structure now faced by New Labour were as class-inflected as they had ever been.[37]

So when New Labour surveyed its potential electorate in 1997, it faced a mixture of the old and the new. There were definite continuities with the past. In Scotland and Wales in particular, the older industries remained entrenched, and older class patterns and attitudes remained entrenched with them. The small business sector and the traditional professions: they too were still in place, and still largely closed to the Labour Party in electoral terms. But the old was overlaid with the new; and the old and new alike enjoyed a prosperity that was historically unprecedented. With that prosperity, and with the confidence in consumption that accompanied it, other cultural changes had come as well. Traditional patterns of deference had all but ebbed away by 1997. The monarchy was significantly less popular than it had been in 1945 (or indeed 1953), and religious commitments (and the social impact of the clergy) had been largely marginalized: except in the new ethnic communities and in Northern Ireland, where a different politics still prevailed. A new youth culture was now a whole generation old. Indeed the youth culture of the 1960s had been transformed into a middle-age commodity and repackaged by 1997: no longer radical, but challenged itself by the musical preferences and lifestyle of the baby boomers' own children. And by then the patriarchal and racist elements of the culture that had been widely taken for granted in 1945 were no longer acceptable in public discourse. By 1997 there was a new political correctness. Patriarchy and racism were still there: but in a much more subterranean form.

For by 1997 the public world of gender and immigration had been reset in the UK by a half-century of major social change. Women had entered the public domain on an unprecedented scale in the years after 1945. Women, of course, had always provided the bulk of the unpaid labour on which UK society rested. They had always borne and raised the children, fed the men and cared for the sick and the old, and most of that was still firmly intact in 1997, for all the talk of 'new men' and the resetting of gender divisions.[38] But those same women had increasingly joined the paid labour force as well, so taking on a double burden of work. In 1951 only 26% of married women in the UK worked outside the home. By 1991 that figure had risen to 71%.[39] By 1995 the proportion of young men and women in higher education had passed parity. By then, for every 100 men with higher education qualifications in the UK, there were 115 women. The numbers of men and women in employment were also approaching parity as New Labour took office, though women continued to be disproportionately employed in part-time work, as men were not.[40] At work, women still met a series of glass ceilings – barriers to equal access to high wages and promotion – but at least by 1997 the immediate post-war notion of a society built around the male breadwinner was well and truly gone.[41] New Labour in 1997 inherited a society in which, in affluent households, two-income families were increasingly the norm, and in which women – and to a lesser extent, their men – therefore juggled the conflicting demands of family and work.[42] It also inherited a society in which, as a new group among the poor, there were at least a million homes in which divorce and desertion had left women raising children alone. For both these reasons, New Labour also inherited a society in which the gender gap in voting (the one which, by predisposing women to vote Conservative, had once kept the Labour Party out of power) no longer operated.

The UK was also, by 1997, far more of a multicultural society than it had been in 1945. Before the Second World War, the UK had experienced only two major immigrations in the modern period: one from Ireland from the 1840s (a migration that was formally internal to the UK until 1922) and an Eastern European Jewish migration from the 1890s. After 1945, however, it experienced a third. For with full employment, many UK-based firms (particularly in the older industries now in decline) turned outwards for new sources of labour, and waves of migrants arrived (initially single men in the main, followed later by their families) mainly from the Caribbean and South Asia. Political persecution added Ugandan Asians to the mix in the late 1960s. By 1997 two or three generations of such immigrant families were settled in the UK, and ethnic minority numbers were rising faster than natural population growth for the first time since the war. By then, the 4 million members of ethnic minority communities in the UK made up 7% of the total population, but they were not randomly scattered through that population, either socially or geographically. On the contrary, immigrant communities had largely been ghettoized by the strength and ubiquity of English racism, predominantly obliged to settle and work in decaying sections of the industrial towns and cities of the English Midlands and the North, and initially locked there (and in equivalent areas in the capital) in conditions of urban poverty. Over time, however, these ghettoized communities had developed their own internal social differences, as an immigrant business and professional class had emerged and flourished, particularly so in the various Asian communities now established in major English cities. With that class differentiation, the solid propensity of the newly-arrived to vote Labour had begun incrementally to weaken, but the deep-rooted racism of sections of Labour's potential electorate had not. So New Labour entered office facing a difficult cocktail of issues set in motion by the way in which urban decay and immigration, class and race had all interlocked in the years of the Thatcherite ascendancy. New Labour may have inherited a young country in May 1997, but it also inherited one riddled with tensions of gender change and ethnic division.

A society in need of reform

In fact, the social agenda waiting for New Labour ran wider even than this, and was a considerable one. It was an agenda partly rooted in the problems of affluence, and partly in the problems of the poor; and it was one that had been intensified by the particular balance struck, in the Thatcher years, between what J. K. Galbraith long before had labelled as 'private affluence and public squalor'.[43]

New Labour inherited a social fabric in which the results of systematic underinvestment by public bodies over a long period of time were increasingly difficult to ignore. This was particularly so in the areas of education and health care, housing and transport. As early as 1991 the European Commission had issued figures showing capital expenditure rates on education per head of the population in Germany and France running twice as high as in the UK;[44] and through the 1990s a whole string of reports had documented significant shortfalls in the quality of the education and training being provided by those undercapitalized schools, when compared to the performance of equivalent institutions elsewhere in the advanced capitalist world.[45] Likewise, the health system was in serious difficulty. New Labour inherited growing public disquiet with the length of hospital waiting lists, the quality of medical service and the regional disparities in its availability: all this at the heart of what for half a century had been the unchallenged flagship of the welfare state that the Attlee government had created. Moreover, New Labour inherited a public sector labour force whose job conditions and employment security had been systematically eroded by the privatization initiatives of the Conservatives, and whose wage range remained limited when set against that available in the private sector. Demographics too were not helping New Labour here. Instead, an aging population, a low productivity manufacturing base and an electorate trained by Thatcherism in the desirability of low rates of personal taxation were by 1997 combining to present the incoming government with a welfare dilemma of unprecedented proportions.

If that was not enough, New Labour also inherited serious weaknesses in the UK transport systems and housing market. The public provision of low-cost housing had been stopped by the Conservatives in the 1980s, and towards the end of that decade declining interest rates and a slowly growing housing stock had triggered an explosion in house prices. Between 1990 and 1997 the average price of a house in the UK rose by more than 33%. That house price explosion had been particularly marked in the English South East where, during the recession in jobs and house prices of the early 1990s, many homeowners had found themselves trapped into negative equity. But only temporarily, for by 1997 the house price explosion was on again: with, in consequence, in significant sections of the country, whole tranches of low-paid workers unable to afford the cost of housing. A nurse's pay was not significantly higher in London than it was in Newcastle; but by 1997 the average price of a house in London was fractionally under twice its price in the English North. There was probably not a single nurse in London by then who could afford, on her NHS salary alone, to buy even the most modest house close to her place of work.

The resulting retreat into the suburbs, and the associated lengthening of people's daily commuter runs, then added a generalized transport crisis to the emerging housing one as New Labour came to power. The typical British commuter added a remarkable 17% to the length of his/ her daily commute during the 1990s:[46] partly by travelling further, and partly by travelling more slowly on public systems that were overcrowded and along road networks that were increasingly jammed. In 1950 there had been just 2 million cars on UK roads. By 1997 that number was approaching 24 million, and 120 people were being killed or injured on UK roads every day. It was generally understood in government circles by then that road traffic in England was likely to grow, unless regulated, by at least 28% between 1996 and 2011, and that growth rates of those proportions raised the possibility of generalized gridlock around major UK cities within a lifetime. (The Commission for Integrated Transport later suggested that, in the absence of government regulation, road congestion would add as much as 70% to the length of rush-hour journeys within two decades.) For by 1997, Britain's transport infrastructure, New Labour's transport watchdog would later report to ministers, was suffering from 'two generations of neglect': neglect which had left the UK with 'the worst transport record in Europe, with the most congested roads, highest prices and neglected networks starved of investment'.[47]

These resource pressures applied to all of us in varying ways by 1997, and coloured daily life everywhere, but they were particularly acute in certain regions and among certain groups. Regional disparities in the quality and cost of social capital were a particularly marked feature of the Conservatives' legacy to New Labour. The housing stock left behind from the Victorian creation of Northern towns and cities remained in generalized need of renovation by 1997. In fact, across whole swathes of the English North West and Midlands, an aging housing stock, a scarcity of new building land and an associated propensity to squeeze new and small houses between old and dilapidated ones, had combined by 1997 to leave those parts of the UK with a dense patchwork of inadequate housing. A special report commissioned by the *Guardian* later reported:

> Nowhere is this seen more clearly than in the northern conurbations. Despite the welcome city centre developments in places like Leeds and Manchester, go half a mile away from the new penthouses, restaurants, offices and multi-screen cinemas and you will be in the land of the forgotten – the endless rows of impoverished (private) terraces and half empty council housing…where unemployment levels are horrendous, where houses sell – if at all – for less than £10,000,

where crime or the fear of crime traps people in their homes...where drugs are common currency.[48]

These 'forgotten' houses were increasingly the dwellings of the poor: isolated from a more affluent Britain by the middle-class flight into the suburbs. Travel in 1997 through the Lancashire cotton towns and then out into the Cheshire countryside, or leave inner London in search of the commuter towns served by the M25, and you could not avoid seeing the new and socially unequal society that New Labour would inherit. And it was unequal: more unequal by 1997, in fact, than at any time since records began in the 1880s.

It was regionally unequal, and increasingly so. The GDP/head in the English North East was only 80% of the national average in 1997. The GDP/head in London, by contrast, exceeded the national average that year by 25%. On unemployment, on wealth and poverty, on health and the length of life, on education and on skills, regional inequalities intensified after 1979, so that New Labour inherited a genuine and an entrenched North–South divide. It also inherited a large and widening disparity in incomes between the different participants in the UK's hierarchically-organized labour markets and welfare distribution systems. Between 1979 and 1993 the poorest fifth of the UK's population had seen its income rise by at most 6–13% (the income of the bottom tenth had actually fallen by 17% during that period), against a rise of more than 60% for the richest fifth of the population.[49] Andrew Rawnsley's young country, that is, had a huge underclass of the poor on that May morning in 1997, as well as a more visible strata of the yuppy rich.

It was an underclass made up of people on low incomes, and of people dependent on state benefits: both the adults themselves and their children. In April 1997, when the average hourly wage rate for male workers in the UK had reached £8.24, there were 1.5 million workers earning less than £3.00 an hour, and 6 million (one worker in four) earning less than £4.50.[50] Moreover and as early as 1991, the income of 3.4 million state pensioners in the UK had slipped below the official poverty line of half average income, as had that of 2 million recipients of other state benefits (for disability, single-parenting and long-term unemployment). In consequence, the Child Poverty Action Group (CPAG) as early as 1987 had been able to locate 10 million people living at or just above Supplementary Benefit level in the UK. By 1990, one-third of all UK workers earned less than the decency threshold set by the Council of Europe; and by 1994 one child in three in the UK (4.1 million in total) was living below the official poverty line. In 1979 poverty had been the condition of only one child in ten. In the Thatcher years, income inequality had grown faster in the UK than in any comparable industrial country. In just two decades of predominantly Conservative rule, the proportion of the population with access to less than half the average income had actually trebled.[51]

The result was that New Labour inherited a patchwork Britain. It inherited a country, part of whose social geography looked Second World rather than First: a society of run-down and crime-ridden housing estates, closed factories and long-term unemployment. Yet New Labour also inherited a country, part of whose social geography stood at the tip of that banana-shaped wedge of land – stretching from London in the north through the eastern parts of France, the Low Countries and the western part of Germany, down into northern Italy – where living standards were as high as anywhere in the Western world.[52] Market forces and individual self-interest continued through the 1990s to set those two worlds increasingly apart. New Labour faced more than a two-speed economy. It also faced the two-speed society which that economy had created and sustained, and it would have to design policies to deal with them both.

The state we're in

There are times when political projects work and times when they do not; times when their advocates set the pace and the agenda, and times when advocacy has to be replaced by denial and defence. There are times, that is, when the tide turns, and the mid-1990s was one such time. Through the 1980s Thatcherism had carried all before it. Thatcherite specifications of the UK's ills had prevailed in public discourse, and the persistence of those ills had successfully been laid at the door of an older Labour Party, condemned for squandering the fruits of power in the decades before. But by the early 1990s these Thatcherite attacks on Old Labour were beginning to wear thin. By then the Conservatives had themselves been in office for far too long to be able credibly to pass responsibility back in this fashion, and the centre-left was beginning to find its voice again as the impact of Thatcherite policies on UK institutions and social practices became far too visible to ignore. The first of those centre-left voices to make its mark, and thereby signal the change, was that of Will Hutton. There was a 'Will Hutton moment' in the mid-1990s. It was a moment that helped to shape both how New Labour and its supporters came to understand the economic and social legacy awaiting them in 1997, and how they came to see the possibilities that the legacy created for them.

It was Will Hutton, more than anyone else, who pressed the panic button in the 1990s that challenged the by then long-established complacency of the centre-right. Against the right's idolization of Margaret Thatcher and her programme, it was Hutton who argued that, on the contrary 'Britain's national affairs [were] reaching explosive levels of stress'.[53] 'Britain cannot,' he wrote 'in the autumn of 1996, be described as a country at ease with itself.' True, economic recovery was underway and incomes were rising: but that 'was scant consolation'. For 'beyond our front doors lies an increasingly menacing social jungle that promises to become more menacing still': a social jungle in which 'the prospects of living in a "good" society seem to recede daily'.[54] Two decades of Thatcherism, Hutton argued, had left deep scars in UK institutions, deep divisions in UK society and extensive sets of unreformed practices whose removal required new and qualitatively different political leadership. Examine *The State We're In*, he had insisted in his widely read book in 1994,[55] and the need for a break with the neo-liberalism of the British right was everywhere evident.

The social legacy of Thatcherism, for Hutton, was at once ideological and structural. It was ideological in that Thatcherism had weakened communal values and aspirations, replacing them with a rampant individualism underpinned by authoritarian policies. 'What began as a reasoned attack on over-powerful and obstructive trade unions and inefficient public ownership', had hardened, he wrote, 'into an ideology as pernicious, in its way, as communism'.[56] The Thatcherites had created a society – or at least they had tried – in which it was 'everyone for themselves': a society in which problems of social deprivation were defined as the product of individual failure, not social process, and a society in which the consequences of inequality were as likely as not to be addressed by repression rather than by social reform. The social legacy was also structural, in that the policies of 'free market and strong state' advocated by Margaret Thatcher's Governments had divided the society into three quite different bands. They had created a 40:30:30 society, in whose labour markets a privileged 40% experienced rising incomes and high levels of job security, 30% experienced far less security in both employment and wages and a bottom 30% were locked into various forms of social disadvantage. 'Record levels of inequality', in Hutton's view, 'had gone to the marrow of the British soul.'[57] Thatcherism had not created one Britain but three: a country scarred by 'inequality that you can see by driving through the poor and rich parts of any town'. And these structural and ideological legacies of Thatcherism were linked here – for Hutton at least – by the adverse impact on morality and the quality of life produced by the interplay of widespread poverty, job insecurity, high housing costs, low wages and long working hours. 'What is more likely to cause the parenting deficit which so threatens families?' Hutton asked. 'A decline in moral values, or parents working crazy hours to generate the income to service mortgages?'[58]

Hutton tied that growing social and moral malaise to twin features of the legacy that the Conservatives would later leave to New Labour. He tied it to a political system that was overcentralized, that lacked a written Constitution to set effective limits on the power of the Executive, and that lacked a voting system to ensure the representativeness of the Executive so empowered. And he tied it to the unreformed model of capitalism then prevalent in the UK: to one from which institutions of co-determination were absent, and to one in which short-term financial interests and institutions had a disproportionate and deleterious impact on the level and quality of investment and R&D in the UK manufacturing base. 'Britain has become an economic backwater where long-term gain is sacrificed to quick profit', he wrote in 1994; 'in the configuration of Britain's peculiar market capitalism...firms are not allowed the financial headroom to grow organically and husband their human resources'. On the contrary, 'the combination of powerful savings institutions under pressure to deliver high returns to savers, an antique system of company law that enshrines shareholders' rights, and an over-dominant Stock Market, compels British companies to accelerate the downsizing of their operations'. In their enthusiasm for unbridled capitalism, the Conservatives under both Thatcher and Major had left this particular and problematic configuration intact. They had forgotten that 'the operation of the unchecked market has an inherent tendency to produce unreasonable inequality, economic insecurity and immense concentrations of private, unaccountable power', and they failed to see that 'to protect itself, society must have countervailing powers built into the operation of the market, otherwise the market cannot deliver its promise'.[59] So at least Hutton argued – and his argument struck deep chords.

Will Hutton became very well known in the UK in the mid-1990s as the advocate of stakeholding: pushing for the reform of political and economic institutions to increase the sensitivity of their decision-making processes to the legitimate concerns of all the groups that had a stake in the decisions being made. There was a 'stakeholding moment' too in the rise of New Labour, to which we will come in the next chapter. But the particular solution he advocated for the ills of Thatcherite Britain is less important to our purposes here than was his presence as a cataloguer of things yet to be done. For if Andrew Rawnsley found the UK a younger country on that May morning in 1997, it was in no small measure because Will Hutton had established in the minds of many Labour voters, prior to 1997, the many-sided weariness of its older and Conservative-dominated predecessor. Births always need midwives. In Will Hutton, without knowing it, New Labour found its own.

2
The Instrument

The Labour government that picked up Will Hutton's challenge on that May morning in 1997 came to its moment of power down a long and troubled history of its own. The arrival of a new government is always of this fashion. New governments invariably enter office engaged in a dialogue with more than the opportunities of the moment. They also enter office engaged in a dialogue with moments from their own past. Electorates tend to see just the novelty of the hour. Their thoughts, as well as their hopes, are predominantly directed towards the future. Politicians, by contrast, are obliged to read that novelty through a party lens of their own. Their hopes are also directed to the future, but they read that future as a moment in a longer story.[1] New Labour certainly came to power in 1997 in that mental condition. It entered office conscious that throughout the party's entire history, Labour governments had never managed to survive through more than two full electoral cycles. It entered office also conscious that from the previous four general elections no Labour government had emerged at all. Tony Blair and his colleagues came to their moment of power, that is, poised to make a new history for themselves and their party, but they did so against the background of an 'old' party history that was littered with the ghosts of governmental and electoral failure.

New Labour's excitement and pride in at last achieving office was palpable on that May morning. It was palpable in the tone, as well as in the content, of the new prime minister's announcement, made from the steps of 10 Downing Street, that 'the Queen had graciously invited him to form a new administration of government'. But excitement and confidence were, and are, not the same thing; and there was little in Labour's past that could legitimately prevent that excitement from being tempered, at least in the minds of the more reflective of the new ministers, by a generalized anxiety about the possibility of failures to come. For there was so little in the party's history of office – certainly so little in the party's history of office since the 1960s – to give them much hope that this time things could be different. Only the size of the parliamentary majority that the new government possessed was as unique as it was unexpected. Clearly, the immediate electoral ghost had been laid, and laid unambiguously. That much was certain. What was less certain, on that May morning in 1997, was whether the governmental ghost could be laid in an equally uncompromising manner. Presumably the entire New Labour Cabinet hoped that it could be; but they must have sensed that, if that hope was to be realized, their performance in office would have to be equally unexpected and unique.

The forging of New Labour

Yet even to have arrived at this moment was a major achievement for a generation of Labour politicians, the vast majority of whom had never been in office before at all. For 1997 marked for the Labour Party the end of the wasted years, the end of what had seemed for a while in the late 1980s to be an unbreakable and interminable period of Conservative political dominance. So long indeed had that period of dominance been by 1997, that the last time Labour had been in office, the new prime minister had not even been in Parliament. Since the fall of the Callaghan government 18 years before, the party had tried first one tack and then another in a seemingly vain attempt to dislodge Margaret Thatcher and her acolytes. The Party had tried going left, and it had tried going right, but the result had been on each occasion disappointingly the same. When Margaret Thatcher had first taken the country to the right after 1979, in as doctrinaire a period of monetarist politics as the UK had ever experienced, the Labour Party had just as decisively moved its programmes to the left. The result, in 1983, had not exactly been Labour's finest moment: on the contrary, the result that year had constituted the party's worst electoral performance in terms of votes won since 1935, in terms of poll share since 1918, and in terms of votes per candidate, since its very first election in 1900. In the 1983 election the Labour Party outside London had been virtually obliterated south of a line from the Wash to the Severn. Amazingly only three Labour MPs had been returned to Westminster from constituencies outside London in that entire area. The party's candidates had run third in a staggering 309 constituencies out of 650. In fact, in some of those, its candidates had polled so badly that 119 of them had actually lost their deposits, to leave the Labour Party under the new leadership of Neil Kinnock requiring a staggering 12% swing in public opinion to return to office. Only the vagaries of the UK's 'first past the post' electoral system had saved the Labour Party in 1983 from descending to a point of parity with the rising force of the Liberal/SDP Alliance. In 1983 the Labour Party took 27.6% of the popular vote, and 209 seats. The Alliance took almost the same percentage of the vote, 25.4%, but tragically for them, only 23 seats.

The road back to electoral victory by Labour a decade and a half later had been a long and bitter one, and had involved a string of crushing defeats for the Labour left. Even before John Smith's untimely death accidentally had propelled a young and untried Tony Blair into the party leadership in 1994, his predecessors (first Neil Kinnock, then John Smith himself) had incrementally reset power relationships within the party, to free the leader to shape policy in a significantly greater way than hitherto. The Leader's Office had been created and developed. The National Executive Committee had been restructured and emasculated. The weight of union bloc votes at party conferences had been significantly reduced. A form of party government that historically had been based on affiliated organizations had incrementally been reset into one based on direct individual membership, and policies dear to the left (but not apparently dear to the electorate) had been progressively abandoned. By 1992 the Labour Party was no longer opposed to the UK's retention of nuclear weapons. By 1992 it was no longer opposed to membership of the European Community. By 1992 it was no longer even committed to the full and immediate repeal of the Conservatives' policies on public ownership and industrial relations 'reform'. Tony Blair had been instrumental in the achievement of the latter, but the rest were not directly of his doing. For after four electoral defeats in a row at the hands of the Conservatives, the party he inherited in 1994 was already primed to meet their political opponents on grounds of the Tories' choosing, not on those of Old Labour. What Blair's coming did was then to ratchet up that break with Labour's past, and to produce a leader keen to repackage that break as the party's key electoral asset.

With Tony Blair as party leader, the already quickening pace of internal party reform intensified. He entered the leadership convinced that the full transformation of the party's constitution and programme was a vital prerequisite to the transformation of the party's electoral performance, and in consequence set about changing the Labour Party with a renewed urgency. Within a year he had persuaded the party to replace the old Clause 4 of its constitution with a new statement of party values and aims.[2] He and his allies then progressively gutted the party conference of any real decision-making power, and very quickly began to put what Neil Kinnock later described as 'a huge distance in reality and in public perception'[3] between the policies they advocated and those canvassed in previous elections by both the Labour left and the old Wilson/Callaghan centre. To that end, he and they began to call themselves *New* Labour, and to invite an electorate which was by then increasingly disenchanted with the policies and personal foibles of the Conservatives to think of their New Labour alternative as a form of politics that would be significantly free of such imperfections. 'New Labour' is now an established part of the UK's political lexicon, but in 1995 it was not. That year, when Tony Blair spoke to the party conference, he used the term 37 times in a single speech, just to make sure that everyone got the message![4]

The rise of New Labour was more than an exercise in repackaging. It also involved major changes in policy. Blair and his team wanted to put clear political distance between what they were offering as 'New Labour' and what the Conservatives repeatedly labelled as Labour's 'core' policies: namely those adopted by the party prior to the disastrous electoral showing of 1983. They also wanted to establish clear political space between themselves and the failed Labour governments of the 1970s. They wanted to do that on the full range of the party's agenda: on economic, social, foreign and even constitutional policy – and they did.

So in relation to the economy, which for most of the electorate in 1997 was the key concern, New Labour rapidly positioned itself well to the right of the party's policy stance in 1983. In 1983 the party had presented itself as enthusiastic for state ownership and control, and hostile to private ownership and market forces. New Labour, by contrast, presented itself as possessing exactly the reverse set of enthusiasms. Through the language of its new Clause 4, it signalled its commitment to the creation of 'a partnership between government and industry, workers and managers – not to abolish the market but to make it dynamic and work in the public interest, so that it provides opportunities for all'. Additionally, through their regularly stated lack of enthusiasm for any industrial policy that involved the state selection and funding of 'national champions', the New Labour leadership even put clear water between themselves and the more moderate 'corporatist' policies of the Wilson and Callaghan governments to which the 1983 radicalism had been the left-wing response.[5]

Where the 1983 party had promised a five-year national plan and the return to public ownership of all the firms and industries privatized by the Conservatives, New Labour promised none of those things. Where the 1983 party had intended to deliver its radical 'alternative economic strategy' in a close partnership with the trade unions New Labour, by contrast, professed no enthusiasm for such a relationship at all. Instead it actively distanced itself from the trade unions and from the traditional role of union leaders within the party's policy-making process. 'Fairness, not favours' was to be the New Labour way with the unions, as though in the past it had been something else. The Blair team denied that they were actively anti-union in a Thatcherite sense, and Blair himself occasionally made clear his willingness to work with the unions in the pursuit of industrial competitiveness. But from the very beginning there was no empathy between the Blair team and its trade union equivalent, of the kind that had been central to previous generations of Labour politics; and the Blair people certainly had no intention of reversing the Conservative industrial relations legislation, as their predecessors had promised. On the contrary, as Blair told the TUC immediately on taking office, an incoming Labour government under his leadership was determined to 'keep the flexibility of the present labour market', and was keen to ensure that there would be no return, as he put it, 'to the days of industrial warfare, strikes without ballots, mass and flying pickets, secondary action and the rest'.[6]

The 1983 party had also been heavily committed to the redistribution of wealth and power, and to the provision of an extensive and largely unreformed set of welfare services. New Labour entered office committed to none of these things. In 1983 the party had proposed to increase public spending (and to borrow extensively to finance this spending), to tax the rich, to raise child benefit, to tie pensions to inflation/average earnings (whichever was rising faster), to phase out health charges and to extend the range of disability benefits. New Labour, by contrast, explicitly sought to distance itself from this 'tax and spend' agenda. It promised to adopt the spending ceilings of its Conservative predecessor. It refused to increase income tax for the duration of its first parliament, and it contemplated a major review/reform of the entire welfare and benefit system. New Labour entered office, as we will see, with its own ambitious welfare programme, but it did so convinced that it had reached the limits of the public's willingness simply to fund an unreformed welfare system through ever higher taxes. In consequence, New Labour came to power committed to a new deal for the unemployed that would move them from welfare to work, and to a major overhaul of the modes of provision of both health care and educational excellence.

The 1983 party had also been opposed to membership of what was then the EEC and to the UK's retention of nuclear weapons. Its election manifesto had committed a future Labour government to the full repeal of the 1972 European Communities Act and to the establishment of a non-nuclear defence policy for the UK. No such commitments informed the election manifesto of 1997. On the contrary, New Labour went to the country promising constructive leadership within the European Union and a strong defence stance within NATO. Against the Conservative Party's increasingly strident opposition to greater European integration, New Labour made clear in 1997 its commitment to the rapid completion of the Single Market and to the acceptance of the Social Chapter, while indicating its continued opposition to the idea of a European federal superstate and its caution in relation to immediate European monetary union. And while the 1997 manifesto was as keen as the 1983 one had been on international negotiations to reduce nuclear stockpiles, it signally declined to follow the 1983 initiative of unilaterally cancelling the Trident programme. Instead it offered a strategic defence and security review (which would allow British nuclear weapons to be included in any multilateral arms reduction talks), the banning of production and trade in anti-personnel mines, and a foreign policy in which human rights, environmental concerns and the combating of global poverty all moved up the priority agenda.

New Labour presented itself in 1997 as a major reforming force on the UK centre-left. It presented itself as a party that was still firmly rooted in the values of the Labour tradition, but one whose re-renewed radicalism came from its willingness to forge new modes of delivering those values, modes appropriate to the realities of the modern age. For all its claims to newness, the emphasis placed by the leadership of New Labour on the underlying continuities of its policy proposals was a strong one. For from the very beginning of his push for power, Blair was adamant that 'the Labour Party got into problems, not when it stuck to its abiding commitments to equality and social justice, but when, like many left-of-centre parties, it started to confuse [its values and principles] with particular means of implementation, which might be relevant for a particular time but which then have to change from generation to generation'.[7] As he put it when steering the reform of Clause 4 through an initially sceptical party conference:

Our values do not change. Our commitment to a different vision of society stands intact. But the ways of achieving that vision must change. The programme we are in the process of constructing entirely reflects our values. Its objectives would be instantly recognizable to our founders.[8]

But the claim for radicalism and novelty was equally strong. For New Labour saw itself in those years as possessing an unprecedented sensitivity (relative, that is, to previous Labour Parties) to the need for strong communities, conventional families and widespread respect for law and order. New Labour leaders talked a language of stakeholding, duty and responsibility in ways that previous Labour leaders had not, and were in consequence drawn towards active policies on youth crime, school truancy, even inadequate parenting, which had been missing from the policy portfolios of earlier Labour administrations. This New Labour Party also possessed an unprecedented scale of commitment (again when measured against past Labour governments) to a major package of constitutional reforms: not just to the reform of the House of Lords and to Scottish and Welsh devolution (as was the Labour Party in the 1970s) but also to a Freedom of Information Act, to the incorporation into UK law of the European Convention on Human Rights, and to the possibility of major changes to the rules governing the electoral system. The party that went to the country in 1997 seeking a fresh mandate may have been Old Labour in its values, but in many of its policies it was not Old Labour at all.

The novelty of New Labour[9]

After Tony Blair took the party leadership in 1994, a huge amount of effort went into the redesign and repackaging of the Labour alternative to nearly two decades of Thatcherite ascendancy, and into the presentation of that alternative as something that was quintessentially 'new'. Yet in truth the attempt to sell Labour programmes as new was itself rather old. The Labour Party had certainly tried it at least once before, at the end of an equivalently prolonged period of Conservative political ascendancy in the 1950s. As noted earlier, Hugh Gaitskell had tried to revise Clause 4 in 1959, after the Labour Party had lost three elections in a row; and later, after his unexpected death, with a new young leader again thrust into the limelight, Labour had offered that generation of jaundiced Conservative voters a new vision, a new Britain, just as Tony Blair did to their equivalents after 1995. Harold Wilson packaged his as *The New Britain: Labour's Plan Outlined*. Tony Blair, a generation later, packaged his as *New Britain: My Vision of a Young Country*, but in truth the vision and the packaging were much the same. It is worth pondering, for example, whether this was Wilson or Blair, promising, if elected, to mobilize the entire nation in the nation's business...to create a government of the whole people...to replace the closed, exclusive society by an open society in which all have an opportunity to work and serve, in which brains will take precedence over blue-blood, and craftsmanship will be more important than caste. Labour wants to streamline our institutions, modernize methods of government, bring the entire nation into a working partnership with the state.

In fact, it was Wilson, speaking in 1964,[10] but it could have been Blair 30 years later, promising 'a genuine modern civic society for our own time, based on merit, commitment and inclusion', or insisting that a New Labour government would quickly 'decentralize and make accountable the institutions of political power in Britain'.[11]

Because for all the language of novelty, there was actually very little that was particularly new about such a set of commitments. The objectives and revivalist aspirations that had stood centre-stage in the party's election manifestos for at least the previous nine Labour campaigns were all remarkably similar. As we have just seen, the 1964 Labour Party had entered office committed to 'mobilize the entire nation in the nation's business'. A decade later, the Labour Party had promised to 'heal the savage wounds inflicted...in recent years, and to turn the hopes and exertions of our people in a new direction, the better for the nation as a whole'.[12] Labour in opposition after 1979 had regularly offered its programme as the key (as it put it in 1983) to getting 'Britain back to work, to rebuild[ing] our shattered industries, to get[ting] rid of the ever-growing dole queues'. After 1964 the Labour pitch on the economy was invariably of this kind.[13] In 1987 the party had offered the electorate a choice between its 'programme of work for people and the Tory policies of waste of people: between investment in industrial strength and acceptance of economic decline', between a Britain with 'competitive modern industries, and a Britain with a low tech, low paid, low security economy increasingly dependent on imports'. In 1992 the Party actually called its manifesto, *'It's time to get Britain working again'*: and offered the electorate the by-then standard choice between 'a Conservative Government paralysed by recession and a Labour government determined to get on with building recovery'.[14] The big change in 1997 was less that the goals of economic policy were different, but that this time Labour won the opportunity to pursue them.

Beyond the novelty of the result, of course, what was new in 1997 was the limited nature of the range of policy instruments that New Labour leaders proposed to deploy for the achievement of these long-established and distinctly 'old' Labour objectives, particularly in the sphere of the economy. As is now well documented,[15] the novelty of New Labour in 1997 lay primarily in its refusal to deploy many of the standard policy instruments of Old Labour. The 1979 party had proposed to use planning agreements, and a price commission. It had contemplated import controls, a tripartite standing pay commission and a major extension of industrial democracy. In 1997, New Labour did not. The 1987 party was wedded to the creation of a British Investment Bank and the repatriation of British savings and investments overseas. It had also committed itself to the repeal of the Conservatives' labour laws. New Labour, by contrast, insisted that 'some things the Conservatives got right. We will not change them.'[16] Even the 1992 manifesto, produced after a considerable realignment of policy in what now we would label as a Blairite direction, had committed a future Labour government to the creation of a National Investment Bank; but that too proved to be a commitment too far for New Labour in 1997.

In its reluctance to adopt old policy instruments, the 1997 New Labour manifesto created the very clear impression that previous Labour Party economic packages had been a barrier to entrepreneurship and a burden on 'purpose and energy'. Indeed, Tony Blair actually dismissed many of these abandoned Labour Party policies as 'the politics of envy...outdated dogma and doctrines' for which he personally had no time. In his introduction to the 1997 manifesto, he was quite clear that 'we need more successful entrepreneurs, not fewer' and that we 'want a society in which ambition and compassion are seen as partners, not opposites...a country with drive, purpose and energy'.[17] So, in contrast to Labour Parties in the past, New Labour went to the country in 1997 claiming that it could achieve its economic (and by implication, its social) objectives by avoiding public ownership (1974), state control/direction of private industry (1983), extensive state investment in industry (1974, 1983), the creation of a state investment bank (1983, 1987), and the extension of industrial democracy (1974, 1983, 1987). Instead it sought to raise the trend rate of growth and strengthen the productivity performance of the UK's wealth base, by building (in its words) 'on the British qualities of inventiveness, creativity and adaptability', by combining 'a skilled and educated workforce with investment in the latest technological innovations, as the route to higher wages and employment'.[18] In 1997, the New Labour leaders, like Labour leaders before them, wanted to make the UK an economy in which both local and overseas investors would place their capital, but this time they thought they could achieve this best by establishing a close and enabling partnership with UK-based industry and by prioritizing the achievement of competitiveness on the basis of 'higher quality, skill, innovation and reliability'.[19]

The particular New Labour fusion of old goals and new methods reflected more than the electoral pressures that had built up over four unsuccessful general election campaigns. It also reflected intellectual realignments by the party's leadership prior to 1997. Two intellectual shifts were of particular significance for what was to follow. The first was a wholehearted (and in many ways even enthusiastic) adoption of a neo-liberal understanding of the imperatives associated with changes in the global economy: a positively Thatcherite reading of globalization.[20] The second was an associated openness to the new growth theory associated with the writings of Lucas and Romer, and a concomitant specification of a distinct but limited set of state responsibilities and entry points for policy intervention.

Both those intellectual shifts were evident in policy statements delivered by key figures in the New Labour pantheon prior to 1997, most notably in Tony Blair's widely cited speeches on his East Asian tour in January 1996 and in the earlier presentations by both Blair and Gordon Brown to the conference on 'New Policies for a Global Economy' held in September 1994. In those venues and others, the New Labour leadership insisted 'that the driving force of economic change today is globalization',[21] which is creating 'an increasingly integrated world economy' whose changes can be neither evaded nor resisted, but instead have to be 'mastered and exploited' to enable 'people to prosper with change'.[22] Those changes were variously understood by Blair and Brown as involving the enhanced mobility of technology and capital, the global sourcing of companies, intensified international competition, a new wave of technological change, new patterns of paid work and gender roles, greater consumer power, the transformation of communications and culture, and the 'expansion of taste, choice and knowledge' across national boundaries.

In such a world the old distinction between state and market was seen by the incoming New Labour leadership as outdated and debilitating: and because it was, the policies of Conservatives and previous Labour governments were rejected by them as no longer appropriate to the times. As Gordon Brown had it in 1994: a 'crude free market dogma' (the Thatcher version), failed to meet the requirements of the moment because it lacked a proper economic understanding of what was going on, and consequently 'did not encourage long term relations and commitments' and gave 'no incentive for people to invest in the future'. Likewise, the 'Old Labour language – tax, spend and borrow, nationalization, state planning, isolationism, full-time jobs for men while women stay at home' was 'equally inappropriate' to a world which now required state initiatives that sought not to replace private market forces but rather to work in partnership with them. The job of the modern state, in the New Labour lexicon from its earliest articulations, was to co-ordinate investment in knowledge, skills and infrastructure. It was to act – in Gordon Brown's telling phrase – as 'the *lubricant in the engine of the...economy*, oiling its wheels and allowing it to run faster and more smoothly without the damage and regular breakdowns we have seen so often in the recent past'. 'Without coordinated action', Brown told his 1994 audience, 'we cannot expect to see the kind of investment in industry and in skills and in infrastructure that we need. Everyone is worse off. And the Government is forced to tax and spend to deal with the casualties of change rather than deliver policies which allow people to benefit from change.'[23] Even before he took charge of the Treasury, Gordon Brown believed that a New Labour government working in partnership with private industry could break out of that cycle: and he increasingly presented the Conservatives as the party that had let industry down, and Labour as the party that could work with industry in that lubricating role.[24]

Such a government needed to be guided in its lubricating role, so the argument ran, by two things missing during the Thatcher years: a 'clear diagnosis of the underlying structural weakness of the British economy' and 'an explanation, rooted in political economy' of why that weakness had proved impervious to previous attempts at state-led reform.[25] Gordon Brown once famously claimed to have found both those requirements in 'post-Keynesian neo-classical endogenous growth theory' (the 'new growth theory') and in the writings of a string of economists from Krugman, Freeman and Katz in the US, through Reich and Summers, to Gregg and Machin in the UK.[26] These new intellectual sources equipped the New Labour leadership with the confidence fully to embrace free trade (and to reject protectionism or competitive devaluation) as adequate responses to intensified international competition. It gave them the confidence to eschew public ownership and to embrace the growth potential of only lightly state-regulated private enterprise. It strengthened their determination to focus macro-economic policy on the creation of financial stability by prioritizing the control of inflation and the containment of public spending. It persuaded them to focus their industrial policy on the encouragement of small business, the attraction of foreign direct investment, and the strengthening of investment in research and development. And it predisposed them to put educational reform at the heart of that industrial policy – to make re-skilling their central labour market concern – while they combined retention of the Thatcherite industrial relations changes with new initiatives on the minimum wage and on the movement of people from welfare to work. Overall, as Gordon Brown said, it gave them the theoretical understandings through which to assert 'a new view of the state and its relationship to the market economy', and the capacity to build what as early as 1994 he signalled would be New Labour's view of what constituted 'a proper relationship between public and private sectors': namely a public sector 'acting with private agents to ensure that the market economy works in a long-term, dynamic manner to ensure prosperity and opportunity for all'.[27]

So well before New Labour came to office, the party leadership's understandings of how economic and industrial policy would be reset were clear and explicit. Their thinking on social policy and the enhancement of community was less developed, but in relation to the economic growth on which social reform depended, they were clear. They intended to encourage progress in four areas: *investment in industry*, through tight and disciplined tax policies geared to 'keeping inflation low and as stable as possible';[28] *investment in infrastructure*, through the extension of public–private partnerships in areas as diverse as training, education, defence, transport, housing and regional policy; *investment in employment opportunities*, through active labour market policies to move people from welfare to work; and *investment in people*, with lifelong learning initiatives, better industrial training and higher school standards. Though much was made, in the run-up to the election, of New Labour's commitment to 'the golden rule' of fiscal prudence and of its enthusiasm for welfare reform and a new deal for the unemployed, 'investment in people' was invariably the policy area highlighted as paramount. 'Education, education, education' was the mantra adopted by Blair at the 1996 party conference as the key to economic success as well as to social justice, a mantra that required not simply the maintenance of the UK's already outstanding higher education sector, but also the spreading 'of educational excellence throughout the population'.[29]

By the time of the 1997 election campaign, there was a discernible coherence to much of what New Labour was by then promising, a coherence rooted in a distinctive understanding of how modern nations supposedly worked. They worked well – according to New Labour – if they were based on a dynamic economy and a developed civic society. They worked badly if economic dynamism was blocked and if social cohesion was undermined. A dynamic economy required the encouragement of enterprise, the development of skills, and an active partnership between business, workers and government. A strong civic society required stable families, strong communities and well-resourced public services. It also required a widespread respect for law and order. In a New Labour understanding of the world, economic dynamism was a likely casualty of over-regulated product and labour markets, and of inadequate systems of education and training; and social cohesion was a likely casualty of persistent poverty, social exclusion and widespread criminality. For New Labour, as it approached power in 1997, economic dynamism and social cohesion went together, and each could only be enhanced by policies which recognized that 'the role of government has changed: today it is to give people the education, skills, technical know-how to let their own enterprise and talent flourish in the new market place'.[30] It is hard to imagine Labour leaders making this assertion with such force back in 1964 or 1945, but they certainly made it repeatedly in 1997, and with that repetition came an unprecedented level of electoral success.

New Labour's 'third way'

The confidence with which the New Labour leadership approached the electorate in 1997 stood in stark contrast to the lack of confidence with which that approach had been made by previous Labour Party leaderships at each election since 1979. True, the Bennite left had been certain of the wisdom of its programme in 1983, but clearly at that point significant elements of the party's electorate had not. Confidence and electoral wisdom had not coincided on that occasion, and did not easily do so again for more than a decade. After the 1983 failure – on the basis of an election manifesto that was quickly dubbed 'the longest suicide note in history'– party leaders in 1987 and 1992 had seemed unsure of both the content and the superiority of their alternative to Thatcherism. Not so in 1997. By 1997 New Labour had found its voice again, and it had done so because by then the party leadership had come to believe that what they now offered to the UK electorate constituted a veritable 'third way' to the failed policies of both their Old Labour ('first way') and Thatcherite ('second way') predecessors.

The search for such a 'third way', and for the big idea at its core, had occupied the party leadership consistently since 1983, initially without success. Their inability speedily to find a coherent alternative to Thatcherism had been the product in part of their incapacity to weaken more traditional forces and visions within the party, but it had also reflected widespread uncertainty within party leadership circles about precisely which alternative 'vision' they should adopt. That vision had to connect with models of successful capitalist economies and societies

– there was an issue of which capitalist model, if any, to favour – and that was never an easy thing to handle in a party of the left.[31] The vision had also to connect to (and make sense for) both core electorates open to radical programmes and to marginal voters open to far less. In the specifics of the 1980s and 1990s, any new Labour Party vision, that is, had to address the 'supply side' issues that Thatcherism privileged while remaining distinctly left-wing, radical, or even socialist in ambition. Such a vision was not easy to put together.

Yet even so, it did not take long after 1983 for its general shape to become clear. Under first Kinnock and then Smith, the leadership began systematically to develop what Noel Thompson later called 'a supply-side socialism which aim[ed] to increase the flow, enhance the quality and improve the use of factor inputs: the primary objective being to increase productive efficiency, reduce unit costs and, crucially, enhance Britain's international competitiveness'.[32] Initially, some sections of the post-1983 party leadership toyed with the idea of achieving this by resetting policy in a more continental social democratic mode, promising social compacts of the German or even Swedish varieties. When first John Smith and then Bryan Gould held the industry portfolio in Kinnock's early Shadow Cabinet, such an outcome had seemed a definite possibility. Then later, when the key industry portfolio had been handed over to the more traditionally left-wing Robin Cook, there had been some exploration of Will Hutton's notion of 'stakeholding', with its radical commitment to an extensive democratization of UK industry and the state.[33] But in the event, as first Kinnock gave way to Smith and then to Blair, and as Gould and Cook were eclipsed by Brown, the weight of the party leadership was thrown elsewhere. It was thrown behind a non-radical version of stakeholding. It was thrown behind a non-statist version of 'supply-side socialism'. It was thrown behind what both Blair and Brown liked to present as a fusion of the best of the competing European and American models: 'an opportunity', as Blair later put it, 'to combine values traditionally associated with Europe – fairness, solidarity – with the economic dynamism traditionally associated with the US'.[34] The result was a significant shift in language and priority. Noel Thompson again:

> What strikes one the most powerfully when reading the...economic literature of the Labour Party is the magnitude of the shift in policy emphasis that has occurred in recent years and the extent of the hegemony of the supply-side philosophy. A new economic discourse dominates. The socialist project is now articulated in the language of competition, efficiency, productivity, economic dynamism, profitability

and, above all, that of individual choice and self-fulfillment in the context of a market economy. Of course...it could be argued that such a discourse is not new. Elements of it can be found in the technocratic enthusiasms of the Wilson years and, to a lesser extent, in Webbian Fabianism....What is different, though, is the extent to which this language now infuses all discussions of economic questions – often to the exclusion of those ideological markers which traditionally indicated that what was being read was the literature of a putatively socialist party.[35]

Much of the intellectual content of this emerging 'third way' between Europe and the United States turned out to be home-grown,[36] but the origins of the programme were always more international than that. There was a strong American influence on the thinking of the young and inexperienced New Labour team from key figures in Bill Clinton's first administration, not least from the already widely read centre-left intellectual, Clinton's Labour Secretary, Robert Reich.[37] There was also an Australian input, from the then Labour Prime Minister Paul Keating. There were the suddenly fashionable communitarian writings of Amitai Etzioni, and there were the writings of Anthony Giddens himself. In fact, so distinct and coherent a network of thinkers and policy-makers did this 'third way' world become by the late 1990s that its leading figures took to meeting annually both during and after the Clinton presidency. From their meetings, working papers and conference reports then emerged that claimed to deepen and develop a project that was very much still in its period of formation. For there was never a moment when this 'third way' thinking was finished. It was certainly not finished in 1997. Nor really was there ever a moment when the substance of 'third way' thinking was fully clear. It was not that kind of intellectual project.[38] But unfinished and unclear as it was, the very existence of a 'third way' agenda marked a step-change for the centre-left from their situation in the 1980s, when all the intellectual running had been made by neo-liberal networks of the centre-right.[39]

The critics of the 'third way' did not care for all this ambiguity of course, but its advocates often presented the unfinished and innovative nature of third-way thought as one of its greatest strengths. They often presented it less as an ideology, more as a rhetorically defined space whose 'defining frameworks [were] broad enough to accommodate...quite basic disagreements on values and policy – disagreements that cut across opposing public philosophies in the true sense of the word'.[40] 'The third way', as Anthony Giddens later told his critics, 'is simply a label for

the renewal of social democracy: centre-left parties across the world…
[revising] their doctrines in the light of social and economic changes:
the disappearance of socialist utopias, globalization, the development
of a service economy, and aging populations'.[41] To its critics from the
outset, the 'third way' was simply 'left-wing governments introducing
right-wing policies',[42] governments that were simply 'smaller, cleverer,
fiscally sound and friendly to business',[43] but to its advocates it was
nothing of the kind. For them, the 'third way' represented a new blend
of free markets and social democracy, a new way to achieve a market
economy without a market society, a new politics for a centre-left that
could no longer rely on Keynesianism but was still determined to avoid
the divisive social consequences of the neo-liberal alternative.

And in truth, though still only emerging as a political project, the
broad outlines of a 'third way' take on the role of the modern state were
clear by 1997, and were influential in strengthening the confidence, and
sharpening the profile, of New Labour as it came to power. As Tony Blair
put it much later, New Labour came to power in 1997 armed with its big
idea – 'a progressive political party, saying you can combine economic
efficiency with social justice'[44] – and confident in that assertion because
it had a relatively coherent and developing body of thought behind it.
So confident in fact that by 1998 the new Labour Prime Minister was
prepared to draft a Fabian pamphlet with *The Third Way* as its title, and
A New Politics for the New Century as its subtitle, and even colleagues in
the party leadership who had initially been sceptical of all this newness
were quickly on record as believing that the third way was 'a political
project as distinct from the individualist politics of neo-liberalism as it is
distinct from the corporatist ethos of old-fashioned social democracy'.[45]
Some of that confidence and assertiveness was clearly time-serving and
window-dressing, as opportunistic as it was disingenuous; but much of
it was not. New Labour came to power in 1997 led by a team of genuine
believers: led – in Sarah Benton's wonderful image from the time – by
the 'St George of New Labour…a chivalrous knight on a moral crusade
to slay the last dragons of Thatcherism'.[46]

Tony Blair's New Labour team certainly arrived in power committed
to the view that developments in the global economy and in national
social structures and attitudes precluded old-style Labour solutions to the
long-established agenda of UK politics. It arrived in power committed
to the view that trust-based capitalisms work better than purely market-
based ones, arguing that both sides of industry needed to work together
in partnership to produce necessary technological change. New Labour
came to power preferring policies that privileged equality of opportunity

over equality of outcome: arguing that with the latter 'the result was a neglect of the importance of rewarding effort and responsibility, and the association of social democracy with conformity and mediocrity rather than the celebration of creativity, diversity and excellence'.[47] It arrived in power committed to the communitarian argument that economies and societies flourish best when the social bonds within them are firmly rooted in notions of mutual responsibility and duty: arguing that 'too often rights were elevated above responsibilities', and that 'the responsibility of the individual to his or her family, neighbourhood and society cannot be offloaded on to the state'.[48] And in consequence New Labour certainly arrived in power committed to what were recognizable even then as 'the main outlines of the third way'.

> The restructuring of the state and government to make them more democratic and accountable; a shake-up in welfare systems to bring them more into line with the main risks people face today; a stress upon high levels of job creation, coupled to labour market reform; a commitment to fiscal discipline; investment in public services (but only when conjoined to thorough-going reform); investment in human capital as crucial to success in the knowledge economy; and the balancing of rights and responsibilities of citizens.[49]

Indeed as we have already had cause to observe, in an article widely cited at the time, Robert Reich claimed that if those were the core ideas of the 'third way', then the New Labour leadership were not alone in their convictions: that in some real sense by 1997 we had all become third-wayers. According to Reich at least, this was in part because, in the package of beliefs that was said to make us so, there remained large elements of the Thatcherite 'second way' thinking that had held such general sway in elite circles in both London and Washington for so long. Third-wayers, according to Reich, agreed with Reagan and Thatcher on the importance of 'deregulation and privatization, free trade, flexible labour markets, smaller [welfare] safety nets, and fiscal austerity', but they did so with one crucial difference. 'The distinct theme', Reich told his American audience in 1999,

> ...uniting Blair, Clinton, Schroeder and Jospin is that the economically displaced must be brought along. Rather than distribute income to them (as was the strategy of the First Way), the idea is to make it easier for them to obtain good jobs and thus become economic winners. The central faith of the Third Way – a faith based, admittedly, more on

hope than experience – is that the economic growth spurred by its free market policies can be widely shared if those who are initially hurt by them are given the means to adapt….Importantly, it is a moral precept as well as a policy idea: work is the core responsibility. If people are willing to work hard, they should have a job that pays enough for them to live on. In order to qualify for such a job, they should have access to adequate job skills…governments should not try to block change. They should not protect or subsidize old jobs in old industries or keep unemployed people on the dole. Instead, governments should embrace economic change, but – and here's the sharp break from Reagan and Thatcher – they should do it in a way that enables everyone to change along with the economy. Such broad-based change will not happen automatically. Financial capital adapts much more easily to changed circumstances than do people. People often have the wrong skills, or no skills, or they're in the wrong places, or they're burdened with costs and responsibilities that make it hard for them to work. So it follows that government must be actively involved – helping people over the fence.[50]

The claim for Jospin here was a little wayward – the French Left was never 'third way' in a Blair and Schroeder sense – but what Reich said certainly held for the rest. There were a lot of 'third way' ideas and people around in the corridors of power by the late 1990s: not just in London but across Western Europe and North America too. There was a Canadian 'third way' to match the Washington one, and a German 'third way' to match the UK's own. And in that ubiquity lay the real source of New Labour's confidence as it entered office. It came to power, not alone, but as part of a general tide.

3
The Moment of Power

New Labour went to its moment of electoral glory in 1997 behind a manifesto that carried the title *New Labour: Because Britain Deserves Better*. It went to its moment of power armed with what its leader defied anyone to say was 'anything other than a radical programme'. But it was a programme that stood, he told the opening press conference of the election campaign, 'in the radical centre of politics: modern, forward-looking, utterly in tune with the times and instincts of today's Britain'.[1] And in electoral terms, it clearly was. For by any standards, Labour's electoral performance in May 1997 must stand as one of the most remarkable of the democratic age.

When all the results were in, Labour had broken a whole sweep of electoral records. The party had a working majority of 179 seats: its greatest ever. Its total number of MPs (419) was the largest the party had ever returned, and the largest by any party since 1935. New Labour brought a record number of women into parliament (101) in 1997, and more MPs with ethnic minority backgrounds – nine – than ever before. Blair's party won 145 more seats than had Neil Kinnock's in 1992 – no other Labour Party had ever managed such a step-change in the space of one parliament – and the electoral swing to it (10%) was twice that achieved by Margaret Thatcher in her watershed election of 1979. The Conservatives, by contrast, broke all the negative records on the night. Their percentage of the popular vote in 1997 was lower than that achieved by the Tories in any election since the party's formation, and the number of their MPs in the House of Commons was as small as any returned under Conservative colours since 1906. For the first time in their history, the Conservatives returned not a single Member of Parliament from Scotland and Wales. They became once more an entirely English party, and they held on, even in England, only to 17 seats in urban areas.[2] They were marooned in the suburbs and rural constituencies of a land over which, only three elections before, they had been entirely transcendent.

In consequence, New Labour entered office with an extremely *wide* electoral base: wide geographically, wide ethnically and wide socially. The process of class de-alignment in voting, which for two decades had hit Labour hard, now hit their opponents instead. When the dust had settled, it was clear that New Labour had out-performed their opponents on social territory hitherto unsympathetic to them: among middle and senior managers in private sector firms, among older women based at home, and even among those 18–24-year-olds, 'Thatcher's children', who had been born and raised in an entirely Conservative Britain. Labour's vote had grown since 1992 in the river valleys of the North, where the residues of Victorian industry remained, and it had grown in the more prosperous new industrial belts of the Midlands and the South East. It had grown among people working in manufacturing, and in the new service sectors. It had grown among women, both those who worked outside the home and those who were home-based. It had grown among new immigrant groups and among the traditional professions, among those who owned their own homes, and even among those who owned shares. 'Both sexes, all age groups, all occupational groups, and all parts of the country swung heavily to the Labour Party' that May; and though it swung less among groups, and in places, where Labour was already strong, 'even among them, the swings recorded were of an almost unprecedented scale...The change in the country's mood', Anthony King would later write, 'showed itself everywhere and in all sections of society.'[3]

A watershed election?

So for many commentators 1997 joined the other three great realignment elections of the twentieth century. It joined the 1906 Liberal landslide that opened the way to Lloyd George's people's budget, with its early attempts at state-provided pensions and unemployment benefit. It joined the 1945 Attlee landslide that brought the UK its large public sector and its extensive welfare state. And it joined Margaret Thatcher's 1979 counter-revolution that rolled back the public provision of economic services and created internal markets in the public welfare systems that remained. All these had been watershed elections, marking a shift, not just of the party in power, but in the dominant ideas, programmes and supporting cast of social forces that the party in power could mobilize. They had marked a moment at which an electoral bloc was put together around a transformative idea and set of policies that were then delivered in government. Watershed elections always move the entire political furniture: in the language of the New Left, they are always moments of hegemonic realignment. But when the electoral dust finally settled in 1997, it was not clear that Labour's electoral achievement, though impressive, was genuinely of that kind. For there were dimensions of fragility in both the electoral performance and the policy promise of New Labour as it came to power in 1997 that the immediate euphoria of victory could only temporarily hide: dimensions of fragility that would have powerful consequences later.

In electoral and parliamentary terms, New Labour's performance was made to look more impressive on the night than in reality it actually was by the vagaries of the UK's first-past-the-post voting system. The party won a quite remarkable 65.2% of the parliamentary seats, but it did so on the basis of capturing a quite moderate 43.2% of the popular vote. That 43.2%, though impressive by recent party standards, still did not match the 48.8% of the popular vote that Attlee's party had captured while actually *losing* the general election of 1951; or even the 47.9% of the vote that Harold Wilson's Labour Party had captured in 1966 before it too lost power a mere four years later.

Moreover, much of the party's victory in 1997 was less a product of electoral enthusiasm for Labour than of voter alienation from its Conservative opponents. Voting participation was low by UK standards that year – at 71.4%, a clear eight percentage points down on 1992 – a fall caused by the decision of more than 2 million Conservative voters quite simply not to vote at all. The election result in May 1997 was not the product of a long, carefully thought-through and deeply rooted electoral realignment in favour of the centre-left. It certainly made that more permanent realignment possible again, but in and of itself, it was a much more shallow affair than that: a matter of votes won, but hearts not. How could it be judged otherwise when, during the campaign that preceded it, NOP discovered that nearly half of all the people it polled agreed with the statement that 'I'm not enthusiastic about them [Labour] but they can't be worse than the Tories.'[4] As the television pictures on the election night confirmed beyond doubt, Labour Party activists were ecstatic as the results poured in, but across the electorate as a whole the mood was more far subdued, and in terms of support, far more provisional and conditional than the raw numbers of votes cast initially suggested.

New Labour won in 1997 on the scale that it did because the Conservatives had become excessively unpopular in government, and the reasons for that unpopularity carried warnings for Labour too as it settled into office. The Major government lost power in such a dramatic fashion because, between 1992 and 1997, it had managed things so poorly that the Conservatives had 'lost their reputations for economic competence...for strong leadership, for unity, and for probity'.[5] The government's competence in the managing of the economy had been critical here: between sterling's ignominious ejection from the Exchange Rate Mechanism in 1992 and the election of 1997, 'there was no month in which Labour did not lead the Conservatives' in opinion polling on this issue.[6] Equally critically, as the Major government staggered on through the 1990s, the issues preoccupying the electorate had shifted, to Labour's advantage. Over time, the quality of public services – health and education primarily – had increasingly preoccupied voters; with opinion polls consistently recording their increasing *dis*satisfaction with these services and with the government responsible for delivering them. Only 18% of the electorate had named the quality of health care as the most pressing public issue in the UK in December 1992, but by April 1997, 41% of the electorate was of that view.[7] New Labour was the electoral beneficiary of that dissatisfaction in 1997, but people were clearly voting for better services and not simply for the pleasure of seeing new faces in power. In that sense, the voting realignment that carried Tony Blair to Number 10 was both pragmatic and instrumental in nature, and votes won in that way could, of course, be lost just as easily, and indeed in similar fashion and with equal speed.

Moreover, in terms of party programme and potential government policy, 1997 was less of a watershed moment than all the talk of 'newness' implied. For the electoral realignment of that year was genuinely voter-led, not party-dictated. It was not that Labour had formulated a new and telling platform that drew the electorate to some qualitatively distinct and novel position on some ideological map. The rise of New Labour to power in 1997 was much more the product of Labour *chasing* an electorate that was shaped by ideological forces other than that of Labour itself. New Labour won more through the quality of its market research than through the sharpness of its break with previous political orthodoxies. For in truth, the UK electorate in 1997 was less alienated from Thatcherism as a set of political axioms than it was from the Conservative Party as the vehicle for delivering those axioms; and that should not surprise us, for Margaret Thatcher had left a very deep shadow on the entirety of UK public life, a deep shadow that her personal departure from power had not rubbed away.

Margaret Thatcher had been one of the few genuinely 'hegemonic' UK politicians of the post-war period. She had understood, as few of her predecessors had, the vital role of ideas in political life, and in consequence had effected what Stuart Hall once called 'the great moving right show': draining the standard language of UK politics of its centre-left content and filling it with her own brand of neo-liberal conservatism.[8] Like a true hegemonic politician, she had grasped the importance of embedding her values and operating principles into the full range of public institutions and policy areas, so that those values and operating principles could become the very stuff of normal life – could become quite literally the natural way that things were, and needed to be. The Thatcher initiative had never been quite that successful. Strong residual commitments to the public provision of health and education, free at the point of use, remained a feature of the UK's electoral landscape in 1997, a feature that the Thatcherites had never managed to eradicate in total. But so too did the legacy of their drive to push the market into the state sector through privatization where they could, and through internal commercialization where they could not. New Labour inherited an electorate which had lived through the Thatcherite Revolution, and it inherited a set of public institutions that were infused with market processes. Though Margaret Thatcher had long gone from the centre of the political stage, if not yet from its wings, the institutional and ideational changes that she had triggered most certainly had not.

In consequence, in its electoral nervousness prior to 1997, New Labour did not propose a fundamental rupture with the bulk of those institutional changes. For all the talk of newness, and of the qualitative difference between Labour values and Conservative ones, the relationship between the incoming Labour government and that of John Major's Conservatives was not unlike that between Winston Churchill's incoming Conservatives and its Attlee predecessor in 1951: rhetorically distinct across the entirety of their platforms, but programmatically similar in many areas of their policy. As Will Hutton observed at the time:

> The Tories won in 1951 promising to govern as nicer social democrats than the outgoing Labour Government, and they left in place the entire [45–51] settlement. Mr. Blair is going to leave in place the economic and social settlement struck by Major and by Thatcher. There will be no re-nationalization. Privatization will stand. Almost the entire panoply of labour and trade union reforms that took place in the Thatcher and Major years will stand. The attitude to public expenditure will stand.... So in a sense...Blair is in both economic and social policies governing in the shadow of his Conservative predecessors, even while he re-configures the political map of the country, so that the Tories are out of office. The Tories are kind of governing through their surrogates, New Labour.[9]

New Labour was, in that sense, less hegemonically innovative in 1997 than Margaret Thatcher had been in 1979, or Clement Attlee in 1945. Paradoxically New Labour actually entered office to the right of the bulk of its core electorate, and on its initial spending programme to the right of the electorate as a whole.[10] For New Labour did not seek primarily to accommodate its core Labour constituency; nor did it flirt with that significant section of the electorate, steeped in social democratic values, which was willing to trade tax rises for public services. Instead it chased the disaffected Thatcherite vote, and in the process was less ideologically creative, less potentially hegemonic in impact, than its parliamentary numbers might suggest. In seeking office, New Labour positioned itself closer to the programme of the party it was dislodging from power than its core supporters wanted. It made what Polly Toynbee and David Walker later called 'a historic capitulation...to fiscal conservatism for the sake of winning power in post-Thatcher Britain',[11] and it did so because its leaders held to the view that general elections were won and lost not on the solid votes of established supporters, but on the more fickle votes of new supporters in marginal seats. It was the scale of that marginality that shook everyone in 1997, and made it clear, in retrospect, that New Labour could possibly have been more traditionally radical and still won, had it chosen to do so. But hindsight is a great thing in politics as in life. As New Labour shaped its manifesto in the Major years, it had the disappointment of the 1992 result as its governing cautionary tale; and because it had, it stayed close to what, in the Major years, the Tories had established as the governing conventional wisdoms of the day.

New Labour because Britain deserves better

Nevertheless, New Labour entered office with a clear set of understandings of its task, and with a definite range of policy commitments against which it asked to be judged. 'What way forward does the Third Way offer?,' Tony Blair asked rhetorically in 1998:

> Not a shopping list of fail-safe policy prescriptions; still less an attempt to reinvent the wheel where existing policy and institutions are broadly successful. Its concern, rather, is to meet four broad policy objectives:
>
> 1. A dynamic knowledge-based economy founded on individual empowerment and opportunity, where governments enable, not command, and the power of the market is harnessed to serve the public interest

2. A strong civil society enshrining rights and responsibilities, where the government is a partner to strong communities
3. A modern government based on partnership and decentralization, where democracy is deepened to suit the modern age
4. And a foreign policy based on international co-operation.[12]

As we have seen, even before taking office the New Labour leadership put down very clear markers for the *economic role* of the state, one that gave both space and legitimacy to the central role of market forces. 'Where there is no over-riding reason for preferring the public provision of goods and services – particularly where those services operate in a competitive market –,' Tony Blair told the economic community in the immediate run-up to the election, 'then the presumption should be that economic activity is best left to the private sector with market forces being fully encouraged to operate.'[13] As David Miliband put it: 'the case being made here' was 'that to debate the balance between market and state is to misconstrue the issue: the real question is what sort of markets we want to create and what sort of state we want to develop, not how much we have of each'.[14] Or, in Tony Wright's formulation, it was New Labour's intention 'to get into new territory in thinking about how you regulate markets, how you organize the state', asking: 'given the fact that we on the Centre-Left have said we believe in certain things, how can those things be advanced by using the state and using the market in different ways?'[15]

By the time the 1997 election had come and gone, all that rethinking had been joined to three other themes as well. The first was action on *social exclusion and community*: the building of 'a new social order in Britain...based on merit, commitment and inclusion'. New Labour came to power committed to building 'social order and stability through strong values, socially shared, inculcated through individuals and families'. It talked the language of shared rights and responsibilities in a new concept of citizenship: one, as Tony Blair put it as early as 1993, that 'gives rights but demands obligations, shows respect but wants it back, grants opportunity but insists on responsibility'.[16] New Labour linked this new sense of citizenship to the role of the state in at least three ways: through Home Office policies designed to enhance law and order at community level; through education and training policies designed to equip individuals to improve themselves and simultaneously to enhance the quality of the overall stock of social capital; and through welfare policies targeted to move people from welfare to work while still supporting those who, for individual or social reasons, could not use their position in labour markets for self-improvement.

From the outset, all this was also accompanied by an extensive set of proposals for *democratizing the structures of the existing state*: devolving power to newly elected assemblies in Wales and Scotland, reforming the House of Lords, introducing a Freedom of Information Act, signing up to the European Convention on Human Rights, and even exploring the possibility of replacing the first-past-the-post electoral system at Westminster with one based on proportional representation. For behind the New Labour unease with what Tony Blair called 'the era of big centralized government'[17] was a widespread desire within the Labour Party in opposition to break from the habitual secrecy, centralization and patronage of the UK state.

Alongside this, from the outset, New Labour tried to carve out a new role for the UK *globally*. Intriguingly, in the light of what was subsequently to happen in Iraq, the 1997 manifesto committed New Labour to work actively towards multilateral rather than unilateral solutions to international problems, and to develop a more principled foreign policy that would 'restore Britain's pride and influence as a leading force for good in the world'. The protection of human rights was to become a central focus of foreign policy, as was the creation of a new international court for the prosecution of war crimes (including genocide), and policy on the easing of global poverty. Adamant that New Labour could both centre itself in Europe and maintain the UK's special relationship with the United States, New Labour entered office convinced that the space (and the need) existed for a Third Way foreign policy in a world that was increasingly globalized: that the space and need was there for a UK role leading the call for reform in Europe, restricting the sale of arms, and pressing the case internationally for the easing of debt burdens in the Third World.

In 1997 New Labour offered the UK electorate what Tony Blair, in the introduction to the party's manifesto, called 'our contract with the people'. The contract was long and detailed, organized within the manifesto under a series of headings that, by their wording and order, told us much about the priorities and thinking of this New Labour Party. Sequentially, those headings committed a future Labour government to 'make education our number one priority', 'promote personal prosperity for all', 'create successful and profitable businesses', 'get the unemployed from welfare to work', 'save the NHS', 'be tough on crime and tough on the causes of crime', 'strengthen family life', 'help you get more out of life' (by a green agenda and better transport), 'clean up politics' and 'give

Britain leadership in Europe'. It then distilled those various commitments into ten key promises:

Over the five years of a Labour Government

1. Education will be our number one priority, and we will increase the share of national income spent on education as we decrease it on the bills of economic and social failure
2. There will be no increase in the basic or top rates of income tax
3. We will provide stable economic growth with low inflation, and promote dynamic and competitive business and industry at home and abroad
4. We will get 250,000 young unemployed off benefit and into work
5. We will rebuild the NHS, reducing spending on administration and increasing spending on patient care
6. We will be tough on crime and tough on the causes of crime, and halve the time it takes persistent juvenile offenders to come to court
7. We will build strong families and strong communities, and lay the foundations of a modern welfare state in pensions and community care
8. We will safeguard our environment, and develop an integrated transport policy to fight congestion and pollution
9. We will clean up politics, decentralize political power throughout the United Kingdom and put the funding of political parties on a proper and accountable basis
10. We will give Britain the leadership in Europe which Britain and Europe need.

Old questions and new

These then were the benchmarks against which, after 1997, New Labour asked to be judged. The question the Party had settled in 1997 was the question of the wasted years. Could Labour ever be elected to office again? Clearly it could. But another and older question remained: the question of the Wilson years. Could Labour, once elected, win re-election for a full term again? No previous Labour government had ever done that, and in that sense all the previous Labour rebirths, though exciting when they happened, had ultimately been stillborn. 1997 saw the birth of yet another Labour government, and in so doing, raised the intriguing question of how long this particular Labour progeny would survive.

Part 2
The Performance

4
The Pursuit of Economic Dynamism

From the outset, the New Labour government put economic growth at the centre of its concerns, and rightly so. For leading ministers knew well enough that the sustained growth of the economy as a whole, and the enhanced international competitiveness of its leading companies, were vital prerequisites to the successful implementation of the full sweep of the party's manifesto commitments. Certainly they were well aware as they entered office that, without sustained economic growth, they would be unable to put clear water between themselves and the Conservatives. They would be unable to 'switch spending from economic failure to investment',[1] as they liked to put it. They knew too that they would not be able to increase the volume of social expenditure, while freezing personal tax rates as they had promised, unless they could somehow trigger a rising tide of economic output. They were presumably also aware that, down the line, they would not even be able to guarantee New Labour's own re-election unless they had by then produced an economic 'feel-good factor' in the party's voting base, of the kind that had so cruelly eluded John Major. Since that re-election was indeed a dominant policy concern of the New Labour leadership from the outset, it was no surprise that once in office, the Chancellor, Gordon Brown, regularly described 'the Government's central objectives' as the achievement of 'high and stable levels of growth and employment, and sustainable public services, built from a platform of long-term stability'.[2] For in truth those were the central economic objectives of key figures in the New Labour pantheon, and they had been ever since the New Labour leadership first took control of the party in 1994.

To the journalists and party activists who first turned their attention to Tony Blair in that year, the commitment of the potential party leader to the creation of a dynamic and competitive private economy was made crystal clear. They met a politician of the centre-left who spoke first and foremost about the health of the *private* sector, and not – as with Labour leaders in the past – about the *public* provision of basic goods and services. Welfare reform was in Blair's sights too, but it took second place there to the recognition that 'the British economy is not strong enough'. As he asserted in his leadership election statement, 'its wealth creating base [is] not large enough, its levels of investment and skills [are] insufficient to succeed in an era of massive industrial change in a new global market'.[3] The UK, Gordon Brown was equally insistent, was 'plagued by low levels of investment in industry, skills and infrastructure...low levels of investment which had led to an ever dwindling economic base, without the capacity to sustain anything other than slow levels of economic growth without inflation'.[4] 'I want Britain to be one of the really dynamic economies of the 21st century', the New Labour leader told a meeting of Asian business leaders in Singapore in 1996.

> It is sobering to think that just over a century ago we were top of the league of prosperous nations, thirteenth in 1979 and today eighteenth. Yet our people, by their intelligence, grit and creativity, are still a people unrivalled anywhere in the world. We must develop our ability and so make ourselves world leaders again.[5]

The question, of course, was how, and from the outset this New Labour leadership was clear that economic progress would be the product of policies designed to create 'a dynamic market economy': helping 'industry and employees to modernize and equip themselves to change'.[6] It would not be the product of initiatives crafted to protect industry from change or to pick industrial winners. So confident were they indeed of their capacity to deliver that dynamism that the New Labour leadership explicitly committed the party in its 1997 election manifesto '*to raise the trend rate of growth by strengthening our wealth-creating base*',[7] and to do so simply by building 'on the British qualities of inventiveness, creativity and adaptability', combining a skilled and educated workforce with investment in the latest technological innovations, as the route to 'educational and employment opportunities for all'.[8] As Gordon Brown explained later:

We set as one central objective on coming into government – raising our growth rate – raising our long-term growth rate. Some people argue that governments cannot affect the trend growth rate of the British economy. I reject this pessimistic view. Our task as a government is to raise the sustainable trend rate of growth of our economy from the low level we inherited. This is our ambition, and in the next decade we will achieve it in new ways.[9]

The party's strategic vision, as its leaders entered office in 1997, was clear both on what these new ways were and what they were not. New Labour rejected what it presented as the Conservatives' predilection for a low wage economy. It also rejected what it termed the failed policies of the past. 'Many of the fundamentals of the British economy', it told its potential voters, 'are still weak' and mutually reinforcing. 'Low pay and low skills go together; insecurity is the consequence of economic instability; the absence of quality jobs is the product of the weakness of our industrial base.' 'We suffer', the party claimed in 1997, 'from both high unemployment and skills shortages. There is no future for Britain as a low wage economy; we cannot compete on wages with countries paying a tenth or a hundredth of British wages.'[10] There had been 'too much economic instability...too little investment in education and skills, and in the application of new technologies...too few opportunities to find jobs, start new businesses or become self-employed, too narrow an industrial base, and too little sense of common purpose in the workplace': overall indeed 'a fundamental failure to tackle the underlying causes of inflation, of low growth and of unemployment'.[11] The only way forward, Blair told a London audience in 1994, was 'a hard-headed analysis of how to build a high wage, high skill, high investment and high employment economy; and then total determination in the bid to achieve it'.[12]

'The challenge for business', he said, was 'to look beyond "downsizing" towards innovation as the key to the competitive future'. The challenge for an incoming Labour government was to create an economic climate in which businesses had the confidence to do just that, while simultaneously operating within the 'fair standards at work' that 'most employers accept without prompting'.[13] These were some challenges!

To meet them, the New Labour leadership offered its own 'hard-headed' checklist of things that once in office it was determined to do. These included giving priority to the pursuit of 'stable low-inflation conditions for long-term growth', and the adoption of 'strict rules for public spending and borrowing: the "golden rule" of public spending – over the economic cycle only borrowing to invest and not to fund current expenditure'[14] – and the acceptance for Labour's first two years in office of the Conservatives' already announced public spending limits. Labour's 1997 checklist also included policies to 'nurture investment in industry, skills, infrastructure and new technologies': policies that included tougher competition law, more private finance initiatives (PFIs), help for small businesses, the establish of Regional Development Agencies, aid to businesses on R&D, the retention of most of the Thatcherite labour laws, a new welfare-to-work programme, the adoption of the European Social Chapter, and the establishment of what the manifesto termed 'a sensible set national minimum wage'. New Labour, its electorate was informed, 'believes in a flexible labour market that serves employers and employees alike': but it does not believe in flexibility alone. New Labour went to the country in 1997 committed to the delivery of what it termed 'flexibility plus':[15] labour market flexibility plus policies on re-skilling, on economic stability, on investment in R&D, on closer links with the EU, on national minimum standards of pay and conditions, and on welfare-to-work. It went to the country insisting, as Gordon Brown put it later, that

> there are four conditions which must all be met – and met together – if we are to deliver in our generation the objectives of 1944. First: stability – a proactive monetary policy and prudent fiscal policy to deliver the necessary platform of stability. Second: employability – a strengthening of the programme to move the unemployed from welfare to work. Third: productivity – a commitment to high quality long-term investment in science and innovation, new technology and skills. Fourth: responsibility – avoiding short-termism in pay and wage bargaining across the private and public sectors, and building a shared sense of national purpose....The first condition, stability, is needed to ensure a sustainable high demand for labour. The second, employability, promotes a sustainable high supply of labour. The third, raising productivity, provides a sustainable basis for rising living standards. And the fourth, responsibility in bargaining, ensures a sustainable basis for combining full employment with low inflation.[16]

All power to the Treasury

Given so wide an agenda, it is not surprising to find that its implementation in power quickly involved policy initiatives by a whole string of ministries; but though many government departments were (and still are) heavily involved, it is also clear that from the outset the Treasury has been the key driving force in this whole endeavour. So long as Tony Blair retained the premiership, New Labour's attempt to create a dynamic economy was Gordon Brown's show; and it was so from the very beginning of the government. John Prescott may have been Deputy Prime Minister in name during Labour's first two terms in office, but the real power over domestic economic (and by implication much of social) policy resided not with him but with the Treasury, under the commanding presence of its Chancellor.

Over time indeed, a genuine division of labour seems to have built up between Number 10 and Number 11 Downing Street, a division that was simultaneously unusual and uneasy. It was unusual in that prime ministers rarely surrender control over their domestic agenda to the degree that Tony Blair appears increasingly to have done to Gordon Brown. It was uneasy in that the relationship between the two main architects of the New Labour project was soured from the outset by differences of ambition and world view – to the point indeed that we now possess an enormous journalistic literature on what is generally recognized to be an ongoing Blair–Brown feud.[17] However much the existence of such a feud is periodically denied by its main participants, disagreements between the two have clearly shaped the trajectory of New Labour in power, and may shape it further yet. In fact it is probably now impossible to describe the daily detail of political life in and around Westminster without giving the feud centrality, so entrenched and hostile are the two 'camps'. But what the feud does not appear to have done is to have altered qualitatively the development and implementation of the main lines of New Labour's economic and social agenda. They were set in 1997 and have held firm, and that firmness would appear to have been rooted less in the vision and determination of Tony Blair than in the vision and determination of his main rival and Chancellor.

Gordon Brown is a fascinating and elusive political figure in the New Labour pantheon. He is undoubtedly one of the key drivers behind the Labour Party's post-1992 resetting of policy, and in that sense as much an architect of what is 'new' in New Labour as Tony Blair himself. But there are also shades of Old Labour in the politics and vision of Gordon Brown that leave him more ambiguously associated in the public mind with their joint creation than might otherwise be the case, and this is an ambiguity that the Brown camp often exploit to reinforce his claim to the post-Blair leadership of the party and the government. Yet intriguingly, when speculation about a possible Blair resignation was at its peak in the wake of the Iraq war, few commentators anticipated significant resettings of policy by a government led by Gordon Brown. They commented instead on the seriousness of his New Labour credentials, his commitment to the reinforcement of the work ethic,[18] and his relative ease with American rather than European modes of economic organization and productivity growth. And so they should: for it has been Brown, as much as Blair, who has taken to himself the task of educating the party and its electorate in the new realities of a globalized economy, realities that to his mind require again that we harness what, in his very first New Labour budget statement, he labelled '18th and 19th century qualities...creativity... adaptability...belief in hard work and self-improvement'.[19] Margaret Thatcher could not have put it better herself.

Certainly Gordon Brown presented himself from the very start of the New Labour project as a reformer within the party, keen to dispel the old tax, spend, borrow, devalue caricature of Labour. He also presented himself as a serious, intellectually-informed politician with an eye for the long term. The vocabulary that quickly established the public persona of New Labour's Chancellor was built on words like 'work', 'toughness', 'stability', 'credibility' and overridingly 'prudence'. This was not the chosen vocabulary of a 'tax and spend' social democrat. It was rather the chosen vocabulary of a Scottish Presbyterian 'Iron Chancellor'; and that indeed is the role that he came to play. An Iron Chancellor, but also a thinking and an innovative one. Virtually alone among the major figures in the various Blair Cabinets, he has been prepared to explore in public the complex relationship between the state and the market in the modern economy, and to defend the role and importance of universally available publicly provided services.[20] Yet he has also been, and remains, a powerful advocate of business deregulation and of private–public partnerships, and in particular of the various private finance initiatives so disliked by more traditionally left-wing elements in the Labour coalition. To them and to others, Brown regularly deploys the image of a journey with stages: insisting that Labour's first term was about getting certain basic frameworks into place, frameworks from which a sustained assault on continuing economic underperformance and social inequality could and should then be launched. Indeed that was his prime way of defending his policies during Labour's first term: that because of them the economy was 'now robust enough to ride out any squalls in the global economy, giving him the room to concentrate on long-term deficiencies – inadequate public services, poor productivity and pockets of ingrained unemployment'.[21]

Yet at the same time this is clearly a Chancellor who is committed to greater social equality, both at home and abroad. His much-cited disagreement with Roy Hattersley at the start of New Labour's period in office was about the relative importance of 'equality of opportunity' and 'equality of outcomes'.[22] It was not about the importance of equality, fairness and social justice: to all of which the Chancellor is clearly actively committed. This is a Chancellor, after all, who has played an important role on the world stage, seeking to alleviate the burden of debt on the most oppressed and underdeveloped of Third World countries.[23] It is also a Chancellor who, with his prime minister, has publicly committed this government to the halving of child poverty in one decade and to its removal in two.[24] It is less the radicalism of his aims than the moderate nature of his chosen means that has raised, and continues to raise, questions on where Gordon Brown sits on any conventional left–right spectrum of British politics. He is hard to place there because his answer on how best to alleviate poverty and social exclusion at home does rely heavily on the movement of welfare recipients into the world of paid work, and has been pursued with a remarkable tolerance of high levels of income inequality and business deregulation. The social radicalism of Gordon Brown, that is, seems to sit alongside an economic liberalism with which, in other hands, it is normally a very uneasy bedfellow. 'The challenge for Labour', Brown told Larry Elliott in 1999, is to make the UK 'competitive and efficient, but also fair as a society'.[25] This is a challenge that Gordon Brown clearly believes it is possible to meet. It is also one that he seems to think Britain is uniquely equipped to meet, because of what he sometimes refers to as 'enduring British values, our enterprise, our adaptability, our commitment to fair play and internationalism'.[26]

Such British values notwithstanding, and even before coming into office, Gordon Brown appears to have realized, however, that his squaring of the vital circle of economic growth and social justice would require more than political will. It would also require institutional underpinning. Visibly heading for the Chancellorship as soon as the deal on the party leadership had been struck with Tony Blair, a strengthened and expanded Treasury became a major Brown goal. In the political world conceived by Gordon Brown in the last years of opposition, there was to be no repeat of the 1964–70 tension between an unreformed Treasury and a newly-created Department of Economic Affairs. This time it was the Treasury itself that was to be recast as 'a finance and economic super-ministry concerned with increasing economic growth as well as restraining inflation' and public spending.[27] As he reminded his Institute for Fiscal Studies (IFS) audience in 1999, it had been his stated belief as early as 1996 that 'in the modern world you can[not] have a successful Ministry of Finance unless it plays its proper role in successfully equipping British people and British companies to succeed'.[28]

Initially the Brown plan appears to have been to effect a total culture shift across the Treasury as a whole, rather than to create specialist units within it. In opposition, Brown had hoped to create a Treasury, each and every one of whose officials regularly focused on the impact of their decisions on the 'real' economy – on jobs, investment and growth – and on issues of fairness, openness and accountability. But once in office, Brown appears to have settled for a more moderate Treasury revolution. As we will see, he immediately stripped the Treasury of one of its major functions – the setting of interest rates – but he counter-balanced that reduction in institutional capacity by the creation what became effectively his own internal mini-department of economic affairs. He strengthened a new enterprise and growth unit within the Treasury, charged to evaluate the impact of every aspect of policy on growth and on social inclusion.[29] As one insider later put it:

> ...the Treasury has three functions. It's a ministry of finance. It's a budget and tax ministry, and it has sometimes been an economics ministry – that is, a ministry that wants to get the best use of the country's resources. At different times in the Treasury's history, each of these three functions has come to the fore. It is right to say that in the last few years the economics ministry side of the Treasury has perhaps come to the fore as never before.[30]

The resulting new Treasury has been described as 'part finance ministry, part think tank, part policy-making factory', and certainly in this combination has come to constitute 'a formidable political power base'[31] for economic leadership. It has become what Gordon Brown said he wanted it to be – 'more than a ministry of finance', a department that could 'instead work with other departments as the engine of long-term economic and social renewal'[32] – and as such available for use in New Labour's attempt to achieve the central policy objectives that have so far informed the Brown Chancellorship. In November 1999, Gordon Brown's Treasury team listed these as four:

- our prosperity ambition: that we should be bridging the productivity gap with our competitors, after decades of lagging behind
- the full employment ambition: that we should achieve employment opportunity for all, and that we should have a higher proportion of people actually in jobs than we have ever managed before, and do so on a durable basis

- the education ambition: that for the first time at least half of our school leavers should go on to study for a degree by the end of the decade; and finally
- our anti-poverty ambition: that we should halve the number of children living in poverty by 2010, on the way to the Prime Minister's ambition of eradicating child poverty altogether within 20 years.[33]

A plethora of budgets

By the summer of 2004 Gordon Brown had become the longest serving Chancellor of the Exchequer in modern British history. He (and we) had by then long settled into a regular series of annual budgets, autumn pre-budget statements, and triannual comprehensive spending reviews: each presented to the House of Commons and the country in staccato fashion by a politician better equipped verbally to deliver detailed lists than to fashion flowing oratory. As year followed year, and list followed list, the targets of policy shifted somewhat and the claims for policy grew significantly, but what did not change was the underlying logic of the project as a whole. That, as we have said, was established early, and has remained intact throughout.

It was a logic firmly grounded in a linked set of beliefs defining New Labour's economic analysis: that long-term private investment is best encouraged by the provision of monetary stability; that there is a role for private as well as for public finance in the provision of basic services; that the key to sustained growth lies in the development of a lightly-taxed private business sector; and that the route to full employment and social justice lies through the movement of people from welfare to work, and from low to high skills. All these were evident in Treasury policy in 1997, and have remained so since. As Tony Blair told the CBI at its annual dinner in 2000:

...we start today from a set of simple propositions that I believe are now universal in modern economies. 1. Stability in macroeconomic management is the essential foundation for sustainable long-term growth. 2. Monetary policy run independently of government, and fiscal prudence, are the means of achieving it. 3. The primary role of government is not industrial ownership or intervention but investment in education and infrastructure. 4. Enterprise should be encouraged through a good climate for business and a tax system which rewards success; and an active welfare state that moves people off benefit into work. 5. Apart from that, an economy should have as much competition and access to technology as possible. 6. With stability, over time, has come real improvements in productivity and investment from business itself.[34]

Commitment to these propositions gave a standard shape to budget speech after budget speech. There was always an opening peroration on the global economy and on the UK's position within it: weak initially because of the Conservative legacy, stronger year on year because of Labour's policies. There was always a discussion of the need for, and sources of, monetary stability. There was always a pitch for greater productivity and an associated set of policies on education and on business, and there was always an argument for welfare reform and a string of associated changes to the 'New Deal', to tax codes and on occasion to the minimum wage.

Commitment to these propositions also gave a diminishing weight to innovation in the budget process over time. The key budgets were the early ones: the ones that set out the route. The later ones could only tinker with the detail of the line set out before, and micro-manage the message with ever finer shades of meaning. For the Brown budgets that were so central to New Labour's domestic policy agenda in its first two parliaments were not only coherent in objective and consistent in presentational shape. They were also complex and finely grained. Whatever a Brown budget was, it was never simple. For this Chancellor set himself the task of massaging the UK economy onto a new and better growth path, and of nudging UK society onto a fairer and harder-working base: and that massaging, from a Brown perspective, required both a continual tinkering with tax codes and labour regulations and a constant revision of targets for public spending and performance.

Stability and public spending

The key first policy moves were designed to establish long-term confidence in New Labour's capacity to generate monetary and fiscal stability. Within a week of taking office, and without any initial warning, Gordon Brown passed responsibility for the setting of interest rates from the Treasury to the Bank of England. A new Monetary Policy Committee of the Bank found itself charged to set rates designed to effect an inflation rate laid down by the government, and 'to support the government's economic policy, including its objectives for growth and employment'.[35] Within six weeks of taking office, that initiative on monetary policy was then reinforced by the Chancellor's public announcement of an equally rigorous fiscal regime: a 'first rule – *the golden rule* – that over the economic cycle the Government will borrow only to invest and that current spending will be met from taxation'; and a second rule – *the sustainable investment rule* – 'that, as a proportion of national income, public debt will be held at a prudent and stable level over the economic cycle'.[36] These rules had been foreshadowed in New Labour's election manifesto, so came as no surprise. The surrendering of interest rate policy to the Bank of England, by contrast, caught everyone unawares: including apparently even the Governor of the Bank of England himself. But this was to be a budget strategy predicated on what the Chancellor later called 'the new post-monetarist economics', and in that world stability, credibility and the support of the financial markets were central requirements. As Gordon Brown later put it:

- …because there is no long term trade off between inflation and unemployment, demand management alone cannot deliver high and stable levels of employment
- In an open economy rigid monetary rules that assume a fixed relationship between money and inflation do not produce reliable targets for policy
- The discretion necessary for effective economic policy is possible only within a framework that commands market credibility and public trust
- That credibility depends on clearly defined long-term policy objectives, maximum openness and transparency, and clear and accountable divisions of responsibility.[37]

In line with these understandings, the Treasury under Gordon Brown settled into two early policy stances that had enormous long-term ramifications for this New Labour government.[38] It set its face fully against any early or easy move into a common European currency network – there was to be no repeat of 1992. It also voluntarily adopted for the first two years of its administration the tight public spending limits inherited from its Conservative predecessor, and initiated a five-year programme of public debt reduction. All this was premised on the belief that 'in a global economy, long-term investment will come to those countries [and by implication, only to those countries] that demonstrate stability in their monetary and fiscal policies',[39] and that 'in the new open economy, subject to instantaneous and massive flows of capital, the penalties for failure are ever more heavy and the rewards for success are even greater'.[40] Treasury resistance to the submersion of sterling in first the European Monetary Union (EMU) and later the euro did not then go away, in spite of strong pressures from elsewhere in the labour coalition for a more enthusiastic and complete involvement in the next stages of European union. On the contrary, the Chancellor set five high hurdles for EMU participation in 1997, and six years later was still arguing that, because four of the five tests had not yet been fully met, joining the euro would be premature. The questions of whether, when and how the UK might participate in a common European currency were ones that this government continued to duck through both its first and its second terms, and which in consequence now lie in wait – as the big strategic issues yet unresolved – for any third-term Labour government to come.[41]

Where the Treasury under Gordon Brown did act more decisively was on the issue of public debt, and there, initially at least, it met considerable success: to the degree indeed that during the last year of New Labour's first term, the national debt was reduced by a total (£34 billion) that was actually in excess of the cumulative debt reduction achieved by all UK governments over the previous 50 years. Gordon Brown understandably made much of this achievement, as an indicator of New Labour's fitness to rule. The public accounts were in surplus four years in a row during New Labour's first parliament, reversing a trend of heavy public sector deficits that stretched back to 1992. For all that the Labour Party came into power with a 'tax and spend' reputation, in those four years too, net public expenditure after depreciation actually fell. Capital expenditure by departments was particularly low – some 50% lower indeed in 1999–2000 than in the last year of the Major government – less because Gordon Brown wished it so, more because departments were uncharacteristically slow to mobilize the extra resources with which he was by then supplying them. 'The capital investment programme unveiled in the summer of 1998 was simply not realised',[42] and in consequence, overall public expenditure, which had absorbed 40.8% of GDP in May 1997, took only 38.1% as New Labour returned to the electorate in 2001.[43]

In its second parliament, however, New Labour and its Chancellor were less successful on the debt issue and more successful on the public investment one. 'Black holes' in the public finances had to be filled again by public borrowing; and the amounts projected as necessary to the task progressively rose: for 2004–05 eventually £31 billion, and for 2005–06 £30 billion. Even so, in 2004 Gordon Brown was still able to present his record as one of debt reduction: dropping the national debt from 44% of national income to 34% and debt interest payments from 3.6% of national income in 1997 to just 2%, the lowest it had been since 1915. Taken alongside reduced unemployment (unemployment benefits cost

1% of national income in 1997, but only 0.3% in 2004), debt interest and unemployment benefits by the end of New Labour's second term constituted only 2.3% of national income. In 1997, the two together had absorbed twice that amount of national income: 4.6%. This change around in fortunes left the Chancellor with £26 billion in the public finances in 2004 that he would otherwise not have had, leaving him able, as he put it, 'to allocate substantial extra resources to our front line public services'.[44]

That was as well, because by then New Labour in power had rediscovered the electoral necessity in social democratic Britain of maintaining high levels of public spending on those 'front line' services. By as early as the first triannual Comprehensive Spending Review (CSR) (in July 1998) public expenditure was on the rise again: with explicit commitments to a real increase in public spending of 2.75% a year as soon as the two-year freeze was over. Health and education were the great winners in that first CSR, taking £40 billion of the planned £56 billion increase in public spending over the three-year period as a whole. The 2.5% real increase in public expenditure was extended to the 2001–04 period in the 2000 budget, when Gordon Brown committed New Labour to a net doubling of public investment as a percentage of GDP by 2004 (from 0.9% in 2000 to 1.8%). The provision of publicly-funded services was extended further in the third CRS (for the years to 2006) when the Chancellor expanded spending by government departments by a staggering 25% over a four-year period: from £240 billion in 2002 to £301 billion in 2006. Education and the NHS were among the winners again: the health service taking 41% of all the extra money, education an extra 23%. That meant for the NHS a 43% increase in spending over five years, at 7.4% per year; for education a 7.6% annual rise. Transport was another winner in 2002, with expenditure up 12.1% per year on its much smaller budget. Only with the fourth Comprehensive Spending Review did the rate of growth of public provision begin to slow, but even then total public spending was forecast to increase by 2.8% in real terms in 2005–06 and again in 2007–08. With debt payment reductions factored in, Gordon Brown was able to claim a 4.2% increase in average departmental spending through to 2008. He defended his record in this way:

> So over the whole ten year period to 2008...overall expenditure on education will have risen in real terms by an average of 5.2% a year, transport by 5% a year and health by 6.5% a year – a decade of rising investment which is giving us: more staff – teachers and assistants – in our classrooms than ever before; more doctors and nurses in our

hospitals than ever before; and more police and support officers in our communities than ever before. But because of low unemployment, low debt and low administrative costs, we have been able, at the same time, to fund the best defence settlement for 20 years, and in this spending review a 4% annual average increase in housing, a 5.8% annual real terms rise in science, and 10% a year average real term rises in security spending. A Britain that can succeed because of stability, hard choices and rising investment.[45]

Whatever Gordon Brown's weaknesses might have mean, slowness in claiming success for his policies was clearly not among them.

The public–private interface

Nor, it would seem, was a propensity to raise income tax. This continuing largesse in public provision was not financed by New Labour, during either its first or its second parliaments, by any increase in rates of direct taxation. This was not the New Labour way. Both the Chancellor and his Prime Minister were adamant on that, and repeatedly so. In fact, Labour entered power in 1997 with a no-tax commitment embedded in its manifesto: that 'to encourage work and effort, we are pledged not to raise the basic and top rates of income tax throughout the next parliament'.[46] And they didn't. On the contrary, in his third budget Gordon Brown actually *reduced* the standard rate of income tax from 23p to 22p, and brought in a new lower 10p rate for the first £1500 of taxable income. In fact, not until 2002 did Gordon Brown reverse this downward trend in the burden of direct taxation; and even then, because of manifesto commitments, the basic rates of income tax did not rise. National Insurance contributions did, in a budget that also froze personal tax allowances and national insurance thresholds: the cumulative effect of which was to take directly from people's pay cheques the equivalent of at least a 1p increase in the basic rate of income tax. The Opposition cried 'foul' of course, as well they might. New Labour denied it was a 'tax and spend' party, and yet tax and spend it did: to the point indeed of triggering in 2000 a major strike against taxation on petrol that was so intense as to threaten public order. But what it did not do was to rely on taxation alone to fund its programmes. It used two other sources for its funding, in ways that previous Labour governments had not – one public and one private – both of which were immensely controversial in their different ways.

The public one was a serious, sustained and intensifying drive to increase productivity in the public sector. It began, in Gordon Brown's second budget, with the announcement of public service agreements which set, for all departments, clear targets for improved performance. It culminated in the 2004 CSR cull of 104,000 civil service jobs. Reducing absenteeism by civil servants was an early concern of the Treasury under New Labour. Targets were set in 1998 for departments to reduce absence rates by 20% by 2001 and 30% by 2003. With civil servants fully at work, their relocation and reduction in number then took over as a Treasury concern, so that by 2004 departments found themselves charged with the achievement of a 5% reduction in their administrative costs by 2008.[47] For by then more than 5 million people worked for the state in the UK – one worker in every five – almost twice as many as worked in the UK's shrinking manufacturing base. Hardly surprising then that the Chancellor felt impelled to tell the House of Commons in November 1998 that 'the productivity challenge is one that must be met by the public sector and not just the private sector'[48] and that the huge public expenditure rises of the second CSR were explicitly made conditional on departments meeting the 200 public service agreements they had signed. 'All have promised better performance in return for their extra money',[49] Brown said. Indeed this became the standard practice in each CSR and each budget-announced increase in public spending. As the Chancellor put it to the House when introducing the results of the third CSR in July 2002:

> ...the government is today publishing new public service agreements setting out agreed outcome targets and reforms for each department. With independent audit and statutory inspection, departments and agencies will be fully accountable for performance against targets: so in addition to the new police standards unit, we are creating the new health and social care inspectorates and a reformed criminal justice system inspection regime and a single housing inspectorate. While public service providers who perform well will be given more resources, in this review departments have set as a condition for more resources that failing institutions will be dealt with early and decisively.[50]

Laying off civil servants did not do much for Gordon Brown's popularity in 2004 with the trade unions representing those actually/potentially laid off – on the contrary, it triggered in November 2004 the biggest one-day strike by civil servants since 1993 – and in any case the union movement as a whole had by then long made its unease clear about the other source of revenue to which the Chancellor regularly turned to solve New Labour's self-imposed conundrum of high public spending and low direct taxation: the Tory-created private finance initiative. Never easy politically for a party of the centre-left, this policy line began slowly and *sotto voce*. It initially included a modest amount of new full/partial privatizations, and a steady if small stream of PFI initiatives in the areas of transport, education, the prison service and the NHS. But progressively over New Labour's first parliament, PFI moved centre-stage and became inexorably linked to both Blair and Brown personally: as the Treasury blocked alternative solutions to the refinancing of the London Underground, and as Blair looked to private sources of investment to renovate a broad swathe of UK hospitals and schools. PFI was thus a permanent if subordinate element of New Labour's economic strategy in its first parliament. In its second parliament, however, it was not. By then it was on offer as one of New Labour's main answers to the problem of how best to expand capital expenditure on the UK's public services without increasing direct taxation or breaking the Chancellor's 'golden rules' of fiscal probity.

In its first Comprehensive Spending Review New Labour did its own bit of discrete privatization: raising more than £1 billion a year for the first three years of its time in office by selling off assets such as Ministry of Defence land and motorway service stations. The fourth CSR contained a similar round of asset sales by departments, targeted to bring in £30 billion to the Treasury by 2010. New Labour also began discretely to bring private money into the public sector: initially just the national air traffic control system, the Tote, the Royal Mint and the Commonwealth Development Corporation. This too was 'privatization by another name', according to its critics;[51] but if it was, it did not stop the Chancellor from relying on it more and more heavily over time: financing large-scale capital projects through the PFIs that were later subsumed under the more general title of public–private partnerships (PPPs). Indeed as early as November 1998 he was

> pleased to announce that following the modernization of the private finance initiative there will be new investment in our infrastructure – in over 1,000 schools, in over 25 hospitals and in dozens of public transport projects – over the coming three years an additional £11 billion. And I can also confirm that over the next three years from next April, public investment will double.[52]

In fact even at the peak of the political row over PFI in 2002 – when the party conference defeated the platform on the issue, only the second time that had happened since 1997 – even then, PFI was in fact at best only 'a marginal factor in the government's drive to renew the public sector', accounting 'for just 9% of total public investment'[53] and at a time when the scale of public spending and borrowing was nowhere near the limits prescribed by Gordon Brown's fiscal rules. The commitment to PFI was politically anchored, not financially dictated, and the ramifications of that commitment were extensive: by 2002 'all except 10 of the 100 new and refurbished hospitals built under Labour [were] PFI projects, as [were] 500 of the 550 new and cleaned up schools'.[54] By New Labour's second term, that is, the Chancellor as well as the Prime Minister was using PFI as a tool to modernize public sector management and to restrict government debt. 'If we retreat from PFI', Gordon Brown told the *Guardian* ahead of his defence of it to a sceptical Labour Party conference, 'and still say that schools and hospitals still have to be built, we will end up with the old quick fixes and retreat into unsustainable borrowing.'[55] That was clearly a prospect for which he did not care, but there were many in the labour movement who felt that those options were in truth mis-specified, and that the danger to values and outcomes dear to the centre-left lay in more PFI, not in less.

Investment and productivity

Yet however public services are financed – either from private funds or from the taxation of private individuals and institutions – their provision without inflation does require an expanding and competitive private sector. This New Labour government recognized that even more clearly than had Labour governments in the past, and certainly this Chancellor of the Exchequer was at one with his Prime Minister on the centrality of a healthy and dynamic private sector to the achievement of all New Labour's social goals. Yet unfortunately for Gordon Brown, and indeed for the rest of us, when New Labour came to power, the UK's investment record, relative to that of its major competitors, had slipped significantly over a two-decade period. 'Since 1980,' Gordon Brown told the House in his first budget speech, echoing data which we encountered in Chapter 1, 'the UK has invested a lower share of GDP than most other industrialized countries, and GDP per worker has been lower too. For every £100 invested per worker in the UK, Germany has invested over £140, the US and France around £150, and Japan over £160 per worker.' This was some legacy.

To rectify it, the Chancellor moved swiftly on a series of linked fronts. He moved swiftly to strengthen *enterprise*. Over time, he reinforced that by initiatives designed to strengthen *innovation*. Throughout he was keen to stiffen *competition*, and he consistently used the education system to reinforce and develop *skills* in the UK labour force. We will come to competition policy and the re-skilling initiatives later. We need first to grasp the nature of the Brown strategy on enterprise and innovation.

Policy here operated on at least three fronts. Packaged as policy to stimulate 'enterprise', the Chancellor moved swiftly to ease the tax burden on UK-based private companies, large and small. In 1997 he lowered rates of corporation taxation on large and small businesses, doubled first-year tax credits on investments in plant and machinery, and reset the tax code to remove incentives to distribute profits rather than invest them. Similar measures followed in later budgets. The capital gains tax on business assets was a particular target of a number of his budgets, reduced in a series of steps from 40% to 10% over a four-year period. In fact business taxation was cut in each of Gordon Brown's budgets in Labour's first term: enabling him legitimately to claim by the year 2000 that he had reduced the tax take from the small business sector by £1 billion since 1997, and that by then the UK possessed 'the lowest small business corporation taxes in the industrialized world…the lowest ever corporation tax rate for business and the lowest ever capital gains tax for long-term investors'.[56] This trend was only broken in 2002, with the increase in employers' National Insurance contributions. That was a significant tax hike, much against the trend: but even that was softened by a plethora of other tax changes on business designed to stimulate R&D spending and corporate restructuring in the large firm sector, and to encourage the creation of yet more small businesses.

The Chancellor also moved quickly to strengthen the UK's small business sector, to which he looked in particular for innovation and job growth. Small business development took centre-stage in many of Gordon Brown's budgets, particularly his third in 1999, when he introduced what he called 'seven major reforms for a new enterprise economy'. These included yet more cuts in corporation tax for small businesses, tax credits for R&D, an extension and consolidation of capital allowances, and the creation of a new small business agency to ease the burden of tax and red tape. They also included a re-examination of ways to ease the adverse effect on productivity and job creation of complex planning regulations and building controls, and of weak links between banks and the small business sector. Later initiatives included the creation of regional venture capital firms, extensions of employee share-ownership schemes, and the strengthening of regulatory agencies implementing competition standards. 'Our policy', Brown told the House in 1998, 'is pro-small business, pro-share ownership, pro-tax simplification, and pro-competition. Our policy is also pro-skills and pro-science.'[57] John Major's Conservatives could hardly have put it better.

If small business development was the second leg of the Brown industrial strategy after 1997, support of innovation was the third. This sensitivity to the importance of government aid to science and to R&D for growth and competitiveness was initially slow to appear, but became increasingly central to policy. This increasing centrality should not surprise us, because New Labour, at least in its first term, bought heavily into the argument that we now lived in *the age of the new economy*, the one Tony Blair described as

> ...radically different. Services, knowledge, skills and small enterprises are its cornerstones. Most of its output cannot be weighed, touched or measured. Its most valuable assets are knowledge and creativity. The successful economies of the future will excel at generating and disseminating knowledge, and commercially exploiting it....The main source of value and competitive advantage in [such an] economy is human and intellectual capital.[58]

Similar sentiments inspired the 2004 Comprehensive Spending Review that, among other things, launched a ten-year framework for science and innovation: one designed to increase the supply of skilled scientists and engineers, and to enhance their access to appropriately structured supplies of vital research funds. 'Innovation is a key catalyst for productivity growth', an earlier review announced:

> New ideas can act to open up new markets and opportunities for firms, through the creation of new and improved products and services. New technologies and the development of new processes also allow efficiency gains, enabling businesses to reduce their cost base and provide a better deal for consumers.[59]

In New Labour's eyes, both the universities' scientific communities and innovative firms with active R&D capacities were vital components of the UK's science base, which the government wished to expand and whose output the government wished to see commercially applied. Both needed funding support and publicly-designed incentives for growth, which was why, alongside the 2004 CSR, the Treasury launched its ten-year investment framework. Under it and by 2008, New Labour is planning to spend double the amount supporting scientific research that it did in 1997; alongside flows of private funds (through the Wellcome Trust) to match the government's own. All designed, as the Chancellor put it, 'to raise overall spending in Britain on private and public R&D from 1.9% of national income – among the lowest of our competitors – to, by 2014, 2.5% of GDP, among the best of our competitors':[60] all part of a very clear strategy to bring UK levels of productivity up to the world's best. Gordon Brown spoke about that strategy to the IFS in May 1999:

> I do not believe that any of us can wish away the productivity challenge that Britain faces. While 30 years ago governments responded to the productivity challenge with top-down plans, and tax incentives and grants primarily for physical investment, today it is more complex: involving the modernization of capital and product markets, the encouragement of innovation and an enterprise culture open to all, and the building of a modern skills base. *Enterprise, Investment and Risk Takers*. We moved decisively in our first two budgets to encourage new businesses with a cut in the small companies' tax from 23p to 20p. To encourage start ups we have introduced a new 10p rate of corporation tax for small companies and a new 10p rate of income tax which will help the self-employed. And to encourage growth we have provided 40% investment incentives...provided additional support for venture capital and reformed the capital gains tax system....We are putting in place measures to encourage investment in early stage, high technology companies...and next year will introduce a new Enterprise Management Incentive measure to provide help where it is most needed to smaller companies with potential for rapid growth. *Innovation*...we do need to do more to turn scientific inventions in Britain into jobs in Britain by honouring the spirit of invention, facilitating the exploitation of invention, and encouraging the commercialization of invention.... The seedbed is basic science, so we are investing an extra £1.4 billion in basic scientific research, and we are putting in place a new R&D tax credit to encourage small business investment in R&D work....To those who say the Government's approach to productivity is piecemeal I would respond that no one is claiming there are simple solutions, silver bullets....It is a long-term challenge for...all of us working together.[61]

Labour and welfare

Finally, in this cocktail of initiatives designed to trigger economic growth, New Labour and its Chancellor turned their sights on the relationship between labour and welfare. For this was a government determined, as it put it in its manifesto, 'not to continue down the road of a permanent have-not class, unemployed and disaffected from society'. On the contrary, it was a government whose long-term objective was 'high and stable levels of employment' and which believed that 'the best way to tackle poverty is to help people into jobs – real jobs'.[62] It was also a government whose Chancellor, as we have seen, believed passionately in the value of paid work, and who was determined that everyone seeking work should have the opportunity to work. And a Chancellor who believed that work must pay, and that everyone bettering themselves through education and training should genuinely benefit from their efforts at self-improvement. The 'newness' of New Labour stretched beyond its view of the 'new' economy. It stretched to its associated sense of the need for a 'new' relationship between welfare and work.

Gordon Brown had many opportunities after 1997 to explain that new thinking in detail, opportunities that he invariably took. Below are examples from two of those statements: the first explaining why, in his view, entry into paid work holds the key to the reduction of poverty; the second explaining why he believed that active retraining programmes hold the key to that re-entry. First, poverty and work: the Chancellor to the IFS in 1999:

> Our approach is to build a new and modernized welfare state around principles that, in addition to its traditional and necessary function of giving security to those who cannot work, for those who can work the welfare state should promote work, make work pay and give people the skills they need to get better jobs....We face a problem of structural unemployment – large sections of the population excluded from work – as never before:...worklessness...is now the primary cause of poverty in Britain. While 20 years ago, it was pensioners who made up the largest section of those in poverty, today it is those living in workless, working-age households; and two thirds of working-age households on persistently low incomes have nobody in work, with 8 out of 10 having no full-time work. *The best form of welfare for these groups is work.* Simply compensating them for their poverty through benefits is not enough. The task must be to deal with the causes of poverty. We must give people the chance to work, if they can.

On an active labour market policy, this is the Chancellor explaining his 'new deal' to the *Financial Times* in 1997:

For 50 years we have assumed that the unemployed need only wait, doing nothing, passive recipients of benefit, until higher demand in our economies took them back to work. Now we need a new approach to welfare, one that recognizes that unemployment can be structural and technological, that welfare policy must be active rather than passive, and that often the unemployed will need to acquire new skills. The new approach offers the unemployed – especially the young – new opportunities for work and training in return for an obligation to take them up. In my view no young person should be left for months – and no long-term unemployed adult left for years – without the offer of work, training or work experience, and without governments setting targets for action.[63]

In consequence, a 'New Deal' to move people from welfare to work was the centrepiece of Gordon Brown's first budget. Under one of its central proposals, the government offered employers a £75 a week subsidy to employ adult men and women who had been unemployed for two years or more. Under its core proposal, all 18–25-year-olds who were unemployed for more than six months were given four kinds of subsidized work options, all leading to qualifications of some sort: work with an employer, a voluntary organization, an environmental task force or, if the young workers lacked basic qualifications, full education and training. That focus on the young unemployed then progressively eased. In 1998 the New Deal job subsidy was made available to the long- term unemployed aged 25–49. A year later still, the jobseeking advice system was opened to the 'partners' of unemployed men, and the entire New Deal was extended to unemployed workers over the age of 50. By then, under what the government called its 'single gateway' programme, all new benefit recipients of working age were allocated a personal advisor, given a 'work-focused' interview, and encouraged and advised back into paid work. In 2001 the New Deal was extended to the 'partners' of people on various disability benefits, and the programme received extra funds to target particular unemployment black spots. These were the 15 so-called 'employment zones' which paid contractors to find jobs for the long-term unemployed, and which, as David Blunkett put it, then 'threw the rule book out of the window to help get people into work'.[64] Then in 2002 the programme's focus was completely reset: its original aim of moving people from welfare to work being then replaced with a new one of moving people from low to high skills.

As the scope of the New Deal widened and then as its character changed, so too did the degree of coercion tucked away in the detail of its implementation. The impulse to trade genuine jobseeking for benefits was there for the young from the very beginning. The New Deal began for 18–25-year-old unemployed workers with four much-publicized options. What it also began with was the equally clearly specified removal of a fifth option – that of staying at home on full benefit. 'Benefits will be cut', Brown told the House in 1997, 'if young people refuse to take up these opportunities',[65] and they were: when first proposed, to 40% of their value, but by the time of implementation, to 100% of their value after four weeks of non-co-operation. Equally ominously for what was to follow, the Chancellor also included in the launch of the New Deal a proposal that lone parents with school-age children should be 'invited for job search interviews and offered help in finding work that suits their circumstances'. In spite of the political uproar that followed, the invitation was then quietly remade in 2000, when, without uproar, lone parents with children over the age of five suddenly found themselves 'invited' to 'work focused' interviews – and encouraged to take up new choices of training or part/full-time work.[66] By 2001 that 'invitation' had become a 'requirement', in pursuit of a government goal of 70% employment for lone parents.[67] By 2003, the screw had tightened further. By then, participation in a training programme had become mandatory rather than voluntary for the long-term unemployed as well as for young workers. Older claimants as well as young ones now had to take a subsidized job, training, voluntary work or a place on an environmental task force, or risk losing their entitlement to the Jobseeker's Allowance,[68] and jobseekers out of work for more than 13 weeks found themselves obliged to look for employment within a 90-minute travel-to-work zone, and not just in the 60-minute zone as before. They also suddenly found themselves having to sign on every week rather than every two weeks, and having to increase their number of job applications or run the risk of losing benefits – and their childless partners too were also suddenly obliged to look for work. As David Blunkett, the Secretary of State for Education and Employment, put it at the time:

Jobs are there for the taking in most parts of the country. We will always give people the support that they need to get back to work, but we expect something in return. As we have consistently said, our welfare policies are about rights and responsibility – the right to help and to benefit, and in return the responsibility to look for work and train for work when needed. The something-for-something approach has struck a chord with young people on the New Deal. And that is why we have decided to make the New Deal compulsory...for those aged between 25 and 50. We want to ensure that everyone has the opportunity to develop new skills, but we also want them to accept the responsibilities they have towards society. Those who genuinely want to work will receive all the support and practical help they need from us – those who are taking tax payers for a ride will soon find that there is no hiding place.[69]

All this was reinforced by a serious attempt to crack down on an 'informal or hidden economy' that, according to the Chancellor in the House in November 1999, was 'now draining billions of pounds in fraudulent benefit claims and unpaid taxes'. 'I say to the unemployed who can work,' he went on, 'we will meet our responsibilities to ensure there are job opportunities and the chance to learn new skills. You must now meet your responsibility – to earn a wage. And we are ensuring that work pays more than benefits.'[70] Policy was all 'carrot' when New Labour dealt with the business sector, but it was not all carrot when it dealt with the unemployed. There was the 'carrot' there too of subsidized training and initial employment, but increasingly the carrot came with the 'stick' of reduced benefits for those unwilling to be so encouraged. In the language of New Labour, this was a key area in which 'rights and responsibilities must go hand in hand, without a fifth option of life on full benefit'.[71] Or as the Chancellor had it, 'because in future work will pay, those with an offer of work can have no excuse for staying at home on benefits'.[72]

The attack on poverty

It would be quite wrong, however, to create the impression that the Treasury strategy under Gordon Brown's leadership was purely an economic one. It was not. It was also, and from the outset, a social one: concerned to undermine the sources and incidence of poverty in the UK that New Labour had inherited. To an unprecedented degree, Gordon Brown has been a Chancellor sensitive to the problems of combining child care and paid work, and to those of raising children on low and inadequate pay. Even before he married and became a father, this was a Chancellor with a particular sensibility to the problems faced by working women in a society that was still deeply patriarchal in its private divisions of labour. He was also a Chancellor who, as he made clear to the 2003 Labour Party conference, was particularly offended by the injustice of child poverty.

> The greatest unfairness in our society [is] the unfairness to a child born into poverty. Because that child's deprivation is a daily erosion of life

chances, that poverty is a reproach to the whole of Britain....Let us be clear: the only Britain that can genuinely be considered fair for all is a Britain where we have once and for all lifted the shame of child poverty from future generations....It is not the job of government to bring up children. But government must help parents by removing the barriers that stand in their way. Our commitment as a party is social justice from the cradle to the grave...our anti-poverty commitment is based on a progressive principle that all decent minded people can and should support: more for every child, even more help for those who need it most and at the time they need it most.[73]

To ease the difficulties of combining paid work and child care, Gordon Brown launched in 1997 what he labelled a 'national childcare strategy'. The first phase of the New Deal specifically encouraged the training of child care assistants and gave lone parents tax relief on the cost of using their services. 'Helping lone parents into work is the most effective long term way to tackle their family poverty', Brown told the House in November 1997, while the job of government was to facilitate that: partly 'by providing skills for work, making work pay, and creating new job opportunities', and partly by ensuring that adequate and affordable child care existed to bridge the gap between the school timetable and that of industry and commerce. Which was why, as early as his first pre-budget statement in November 1997, the Chancellor committed £300 million of public money over a five-year period – 'the biggest ever investment in child-care', he called it – to set up a network of out-of-school child care clubs with nearly a million places. It was also why, in his second pre-budget statement a year later, he extended the eligibility for child care tax credit to working parents with older children still at school. Within 18 months of New Labour being in office, indeed, the state was paying 70% of the costs of child care for working families on low wages, and two-thirds of all families in the UK were eligible for some form of state aid.[74] The Chancellor was still at it as late as 2004, this time helping all working families and not just those on low pay. In his eighth budget he allowed employers to pay their employees – so long as it was an offer made to all employees – £50 a week for approved child care, free of income tax and National Insurance contributions, and funded a programme to create 1,000 children's centres over a five-year period.

To tackle the problem of raising families on low and inadequate pay, the Chancellor was ever inventive and genuinely radical. Twice he totally reset the tax system to lift low-paid full-time working families with children out of poverty. He did so first through a significant increase in

Child Allowances and the introduction of a new Working Families' Tax Credit, which from October 1999 guaranteed to any family in which at least one person was working full time a minimum income of £180 a week and a freedom from income tax until that income reached £220 a week. Later additional chunks of largesse from the Treasury took that minimum figure to £190 before the scheme began, to £214 in 2000 and to £225 in 2001. Then in 2002, Gordon Brown extended the Working Families' Tax Credit to take in childless couples on low pay, and announced plans to introduce a new unified Child Tax Credit from April 2003, to be paid on top of universal Child Benefit, to integrate all means-tested income-related support for children into one payment: and as such, as he put it, into 'a single, seamless system of income-related support for families with children'.[75]

Gordon Brown used each of his budgets to gently soften the unequal distribution of income inherited from the Conservative years. This was a central priority for him, one that often brought him into conflict with ministers wanting more money for schools and hospitals. He was determined to use public funds to ease the lot of the working poor, and he did. A process of modest 'redistribution by stealth' that used a mixture of new tools and enhanced old ones – universal Child Benefit, a new Child Tax Credit that replaced the married person's allowance, Working Families' Tax Credits and enhanced maternity grants – made the first New Labour government the most redistributive since the 1960s. The third Brown budget in 1999 was a classic example of this Treasury-led 'redistribution by stealth'. That year a new flat-rate Child Tax Credit worth £416 off the tax bill was flagged for introduction in April 2001, using money saved by abolishing the married couple's tax allowance for adults of working age. Given to everyone, alongside a flat-rate increase in Child Allowance, it shifted earning power to families with children, and through the impact of tax thresholds, benefited the poorer families and not the rich. Five million families stood to benefit directly from these 1999 changes, which earned the Chancellor much praise from key figures in the anti-poverty lobby.[76]

Throughout New Labour's first two parliaments, Gordon Brown consistently tweaked these tax instruments, improving them steadily faster than inflation, and micro-managing them always in a way supportive of families wanting to work and of children on the edge of poverty. In the 2000 budget, for example, recognizing the extra costs that families meet when a child is born, and the loss of income associated with the woman's absence from paid work, he increased the maternity grant from £200 to £300, and raised the Child Tax Credit from £416 a year to £442. Individually, none of these changes were earth-shattering in their impact, but incrementally they were cumulatively significant: not least because they were followed a year later by yet more increases in maternity pay, longer maternity leave, a new paternity leave, more help with child care costs for lower-paid families, and even a cut in VAT on child car seats. Again the individual changes were small. Instead of offering 70% of child care costs up to £100 for one child and £150 for two, the new thresholds rose to £135 and £200. The statutory obligation to maternity pay was extended from 18 to 26 weeks, and maternity pay increased from £60 to £75 in stages. All these changes, hard to follow as they were, and even now bewildering when listed, were in truth all steps in the right direction, individually and collectively representing steady progress to a powerful New Labour goal, to 'halve child poverty by 2010 and eradicate it in a generation'.[77] If this was an Iron Chancellor, as Tony Blair labelled him at the 1998 party conference, it was clearly one with a progressive heart.

5
Seeking the Balance between Fairness and Efficiency

Immediately after the Labour Party's general election victory in 2001, the *Guardian* ran an article on what it called 'a government drive to bring about a US-style productivity revolution during Labour's second term'. Alongside the article, the paper ran a photograph of Gordon Brown launching that drive at a breakfast meeting in a London hotel. Alongside him at that photo shoot, looking suitably sleepy and not yet quite fully awake, sat Patricia Hewitt and Estelle Morris, then respectively the Secretaries of State for Industry and Education.[1] The picture served to remind us that the implementation of the Brown strategy for economic modernization involved departments other than the Treasury, and that the target of the strategy was wider than those departments of state whose spending the Treasury so carefully controlled. Implementation of the Brown strategy required initiatives from other parts of the government machine: not least from the Department of Trade and Industry and from a department of education whose precise title and remit changed with the election. Prior to 2001 it was the Department for Education and Employment; then (when its employment functions had been repositioned in an independent Department for Work and Pensions) it became the Department for Education and Skills. Either way, the DfEE/DfES was, and remains, one of the Treasury's key handmaidens in the delivery of the New Labour project, and the DTI was and remains the other.

That the DfEE became the DfES suggests that it did have functions to gather and to shed. The unchanging title of the DTI suggests otherwise, and in truth under New Labour the DTI remained the enigmatic phenomenon in UK politics that it has always been. In its 25-year history it has had 25

Secretaries of State, for many of whom it has proved to be the 'graveyard job'. Will Hutton once called the DTI 'the department of self-loathing...in search of a mission'.[2] It was certainly one that was thought of during the Thatcher years as a unit without purpose or future (hence Nicholas Ridley's famous remark on arriving at the DTI: 'What is this place for?'). Yet in the 1990s the department made a remarkable recovery, bouncing back under Michael Heseltine's leadership to become a powerful force in John Major's government, and triggering a shift in Conservative policy towards what are now central New Labour concerns with investment in education and in R&D. In fact, the continuities between the Heseltine DTI and the New Labour department are striking, both in policy and in the DTI's vulnerability to the political strength of its Secretary of State.[3] Both before and after 1997, the great task of the department, as Peter Mandelson told the TUC, was 'to use all the tools at our disposal to strengthen industry, enhance business performance, and create an environment in which enterprise flourishes'.[4] The department waxed strong under Heseltine, Patricia Hewitt, and (briefly) under Mandelson, but lost political leverage under both Margaret Beckett and Stephen Byers, and came under heavy criticism from the business lobby as it did so.[5] Yet weak or strong, the DTI, like the Department for Education, operated within the parameters set for it by New Labour commitments on labour market reform, investment in human capital, and the strengthening of the UK's industrial and commercial base. The Treasury may have set the general parameters and provided the funds, but much of the real action operated at the departmental level, and did so with remarkable consistency and coherence over time.

A 'lightly regulated' labour market

High on the DTI's list of priorities when Margaret Beckett became its first New Labour President of the Board of Trade in 1997 was the introduction by the department of a new set of rights for workers and their representatives. That new set had been foreshadowed in the manifesto, which had made two specific and two general commitments in the area of labour law. The Labour Party entered office committed to the introduction of a minimum wage, and to legislation granting trade union recognition whenever 50% of the relevant workforce balloted for it. It also entered office committed to the creation of what it called 'a sensible balance in industrial relations law', not least by the retention of 'the key elements of the trade union legislation of the 1980s – on ballots, picketing and industrial action'.[6] The national trade union leadership had long pressed for the repeal of the Thatcherite labour laws, but they now pressed in vain. Tony Blair was not a fan of strong collective rights for trade unions *per se*. Indeed part of what he claimed New Labour had rethought was 'the whole of our philosophy in relation to the labour market', where, as he put it in 1996, 'for the employee today, their best guarantee of long-term security [comes from] promoting the health of the enterprise and their own employability'.[7] Labour's policy paper on labour law in their last days of opposition, *Building Prosperity – Flexibility, Efficiency and Fairness at Work*, did contain the union recognition commitment, but it was otherwise largely concerned with strengthening *individual*, not collective, rights at work. It committed Labour to legislation or inquiries – it was actually heavy on 'inquiries' – on how best to protect workers against such things as unfair dismissal, zero-hour contracts, inadequate maternity rights, lack of training, and excessively low pay. And its very title signalled a New Labour take on this traditional area of party policy: 'fairness' only after 'efficiency' and in the context of a 'flexible labour market'. New Labour entered office committed to the guarantee of 'minimum standards for the individual at work'[8] but not to the reconstitution of the industrial and political power of trade unions as bargaining institutions.

In power, New Labour had both to design its own labour law and to relate to initiatives on worker rights that came to it from the European Union. New Labour had made much, in opposition, of its willingness to sign up to the European Social Chapter, from which John Major's Conservatives had negotiated an opt-out. New Labour's willingness to forgo that opt-out was used to signal both its pro-European credentials and its commitment to a more equalitarian distribution of power and authority at work. Not surprisingly, therefore, the new government did immediately adopt the Social Chapter, amid a considerable fanfare of publicity, and subsequently signed up to other pieces of labour market regulation emerging from Brussels: directives on works councils, on the rights of part-time workers, on worker consultation, even the European Working Time Directive. But the New Labour government did so always with immense reluctance, and always only after prolonged negotiations in which, in a manner similar to its Conservative predecessor, it strove to minimize the impact of European-wide regulations on the management of UK-based businesses, particularly small ones, and it sought to exploit to the full the Tory-won principle of 'subsidiarity' in the national application of European-wide rulings.[9] The relevant ministers within the DTI then always officially 'welcomed' these changes and hailed them as significant and socially progressive. But in reality New Labour's enthusiasm for them was invariably low and their implementation of them was at best parsimonious.[10]

This parsimony was entirely in line with the message that both Tony Blair and Gordon Brown regularly took to Europe from their very first days in office – that job creation within the European Union required an easing of labour laws, not their reinforcement.[11] New Labour came to power convinced that the EU faced a fundamental choice of direction: between, as Tony Blair put it later, 'the old social model that has an attitude to legislation and welfare that is often rooted in the sixties and seventies' and one that recognizes 'that the new economy requires a redirection of European economic policy for the future'.[12] 'Our aim must be to tackle the obstacles to job creation and labour market flexibility,' he told his first meeting of European Socialists as prime minister, 'cutting unnecessary bureaucracy for the small firms that are likely to be the main job creators.'[13] What the Prime Minister said abroad, the Foreign Secretary then said at home. 'We will insist', Jack Straw told the CBI in 2004, 'that any new treaty – among other things – keeps the national veto for tax and social policy; and that the charter of fundamental rights creates no new rights under national law, so as not to upset the balance of Britain's industrial relations policy'.[14] Margaret Thatcher could hardly have put it better herself. She, of course, had set her face against what the Conservatives had thought of as the introduction of 'backdoor socialism' from Brussels, and understandably so, given the gap between their free market sensibilities and the EU's willingness to institutionalize the rights of all the social partners, including those of organized labour. But the very institutionalization of worker rights that previous Labour leaderships had welcomed, the New Labour leadership did not. It had been the original intention of the EU Council in 1999 that its proposed European Charter of Fundamental Rights should be binding on all member states, but because the Charter included a set of legal rights to union membership, strike action and industrial consultation, of the kind legislated away in the UK in the 1980s, it was the New Labour government that led the charge in Europe against their mandatory imposition, gathering bizarre and right-wing allies in the process.[15]

The DTI's own White Paper on labour law reform, *Fairness at Work*, was not published until the middle of 1998. It took that long to appear because its agenda was so contested by the relevant 'social partners', and because in consequence the terms of its new industrial relations framework were so hard to settle between 'old' and 'new' Labour elements in Tony Blair's first Cabinet. It took that long to appear too, because its publication followed on, and indeed was the culmination of, an extensive period of consultation and bargaining, both with and between the major employers' organizations and the TUC. In *Fairness at Work*, the DTI put flesh on Labour's manifesto commitment to the unions: that their legal right of recognition should be restored to them whenever their level of support in the workplace exceeded certain specified thresholds.[16] The DTI also used *Fairness at Work* to signal the government's commitment to the strengthening of the rights of individual workers in their place of employment: proposing, for example, that such workers should have a right to be accompanied by a fellow employee or trade union representative of their choice during grievance and disciplinary procedures; proposing that the length of time someone had to work before they could claim unfair dismissal should be cut from two years to one; and proposing that the dismissal of workers for union membership or participation in legal union actions should be made illegal. The government also used the White Paper to signal its intention to give parents up to 12 weeks of unpaid leave while their children were young, in line with European guidelines, and to extend the current right to a 14-week maternity leave to 18 weeks. The DTI put its case this way:

> For those in work, the Government has two key objectives for the labour market: efficiency and fairness. We want to see efficiency because we want people to work well enough and hard enough to generate prosperity for the country as a whole. And we want to see fairness because people at work deserve to be treated decently – and they perform better when they are. Efficiency and fairness are wholly compatible. It is perfectly possible to have a modern, flexible and efficient labour market which is both a vital engine for economic growth and business output and a means for people to find well-paid and satisfying jobs.[17]

In endorsing these changes in the Foreword to *Fairness at Work*, Tony Blair claimed that they 'steer[ed] a way between the absence of minimum standards of protection at the workplace, and a return to the laws of the past'. It wasn't just, he argued, to deny individual workers 'basic canons of fairness – rights to claim unfair dismissal, rights against discrimination for making a free choice of being a union member, rights to unpaid parental leave – that are a matter of course elsewhere'. But those rights had to be 'matched by responsibilities…the days of strikes without ballots, mass picketing, closed shops and secondary action are over'. What was needed instead, what the government sought by these changes to engender, was 'a culture of fairness and opportunity at work'. New Labour, the Prime

Minister insisted, was trying 'to change the culture of relations in and at work, and to reflect a new relationship between work and family life'. 'Even after the changes we propose,' he wrote in the introduction to the White Paper, 'Britain will [still] have the most lightly regulated labour market of any leading economy in the world.'[18] And so indeed it did.

Even so, the government was determined to minimize the impact of even these modest changes on the viability of the business community, avoiding 'bureaucracy and unnecessary burdens on business' as it put it. So in the White Paper it invited consultation on 'how change can be implemented without imposing such burdens, as well as to points in the proposals themselves'.[19] That willingness spoke volumes about the priority New Labour gave to entrepreneurship and profit-taking in the private sector, over any resetting of power relationships there. If there was to be partnership, it was partnership within the existing structures of authority and reward, in the manner of its Conservative predecessors.[20] Periodically, it is true, government ministers spoke out about the excesses of executive pay, but they did nothing effective about it. Periodically also, particularly of late, government ministers have spoken out about the culture of long hours and low pay that this most lightly regulated of labour markets has sustained, and as we will see later, there are plans afoot to do a little at least about that.[21] But in general, ever since 1997 and in truth even before, New Labour has tacked with the business wind. Its ministers have softened regulations and legislative proposals under business pressure. They did so even in the gap between the publication of *Fairness at Work* and its implementation in the 1998 Employment Relations Bill.

By then, two more Secretaries of State at the DTI had come and gone, with the 'soft left' Margaret Beckett having been succeeded in quick order by two ultra-Blairite MPs: first Peter Mandelson, and then Stephen Byers. All three had come under sustained pressure from business leaders to moderate the key proposals in *Fairness at Work*: after all, employers' organizations were no longer used to legislation that actually strengthened the collective and individual rights of workers. That had not been Margaret Thatcher's way, and the Institute of Directors in particular proved to be extraordinarily strident in its condemnation of a White Paper scored by the *Financial Times* as 'Unions 6, Employers, 2.'[22] But there was no need for stridency here; for the business lobby was pushing at an open door. John Prescott and Margaret Beckett might indeed have favoured the TUC position and the strengthening of worker rights; but to a significant degree the Prime Minister did not. Tony Blair was reportedly more concerned about 'the impact the new regulations could have on competitiveness and the government's business-friendly image':[23] so concerned, in fact, that at his key meeting with the TUC General Secretary, John Monks, when the controversy was at its peak, he apparently 'spent most of the 45 minutes promoting the CBI case to Monks'.[24]

The CBI could not win from Tony Blair a reversal of the party's commitment to restore to the trade unions their legal right to recognition in the face of employer resistance. That was too entrenched and supported a position; but the CBI could, and did, win concessions on the thresholds of support required before recognition was granted, and on the size of company that could be excluded from the recognition procedures. Indeed it is a measure of the degree of trade union support inside Tony Blair's Cabinet that what John Monks called the CBI's 'wrecking amendments'[25] did not carry all before them. But in the detail of the subsequent Bill, as against that of the initial White Paper, the business lobby was able to report significant progress. Indeed, 'all the major differences between the proposals that were laid out in the White Paper and the [Bill's] provisions reflect[ed] the employers' preferences'.[26] In the Bill the recognition process for trade unions was more complex and time-consuming than originally proposed; the automatic right to recognition with a membership of '50 percent plus one' was hedged about with employer 'escape' clauses; 5 million workers in small firms were excluded altogether; new restrictions limited the right of individual workers to be accompanied into disciplinary meetings by a trade union official of their choice; and employers were even able to dismiss workers involved in lawful disputes after eight weeks, if they could show they had 'taken all reasonable steps to resolve the dispute'. The Labour Party's 'business manifesto', issued ahead of the general election in 1997, had foreshadowed this, saying:

> It is a complete nonsense to suggest that it is our policy to prevent employers dismissing those who are on strike....The law will remain as it is now. And an employer cannot be compelled to reinstate those who successfully claim unfair dismissal....We propose merely that, whereas at present employees who are selectively dismissed when on lawful strike can claim compensation from an industrial tribunal for unfair dismissal, this should apply also to the situation where all those on lawful strike are dismissed. This reflects an entirely fair balance between the rights and responsibilities of employers and employees at the workplace.[27]

So John Monks was right: the new law 'would tilt the balance towards fairness in the workplace for the first time in a generation'.[28] But Bill Morris of the TGWU was also right: the Bill was at best 'a first step, not the last word, on workers' rights'.[29] It was, however, the last word on the subject that the unions in the UK were to hear from this New Labour government in its first term. Margaret Thatcher might have overseen a string of Industrial Relations Acts. Tony Blair intended to oversee just one.[30]

A national minimum wage

That is not to say, however, that New Labour was entirely Thatcherite in these matters. It was not. A clear pink line existed between the industrial relations policy of the New Labour government and that of its Conservative predecessors. It was a very thin line – that must be said – but it was there nonetheless. After all, the Conservatives had done their utmost to dismantle the Wage Councils that, from the 1920s, had protected the lowest paid in the UK economy; and New Labour had inherited, as we have seen, a low-wage economy against whose perpetuation it had publicly set its face. So here, if what the New Labour leadership said was to be believed, was a definite difference between the parties. There was 'the Tory way – inequality, insecurity and low wages for the many, very high rewards for the few', which Tony Blair publicly dismissed as 'not the answer'; and there was New Labour's way: 'different...a government committed to fairness at work',[31] a government committed to the installation of what it called 'a sensible set national minimum wage': to the establishment in the UK, as in 'every modern industrial country...including the US and Japan,...a statutory level below which pay should not fall'.[32]

The ministerial team at the DTI which supervised the implementation of this commitment consistently presented it as part of the wider anti-poverty programme built around the welfare-to-work initiative and Gordon Brown's tax and benefit changes. They insisted that the introduction of a national minimum wage would end 'the scandal of poverty pay'[33] and lift the earnings of significant numbers of workers. Ian McCartney, the minister in charge, occasionally mentioned a figure of 2 million such workers,[34] and he regularly coupled this claim with another: that a national minimum wage was actually of assistance to the business community, even to its small business sector. For by blocking off 'cowboy competition', a national minimum wage would protect high-quality producers from unfair competition based on low wages, and help to generate for modern businesses a highly-motivated and committed workforce. 'A minimum wage', he said, 'will establish a level playing field so that firms can compete on the basis of efficiency and on the quality of the goods and services they provide, and not solely on rock-bottom costs.'[35]

Yet these claims could do little to obscure the fact that New Labour was actually in retreat here from the policy commitments of its own immediate past. The government came to power promising a national minimum wage, but not one of either a specified amount or one linked in any specified way to the general level of either wages or earnings. Labour's manifesto in 1997 promised only that the level of its national minimum wage would be fixed 'not on the basis of a rigid formula but according to the economic circumstances of the time and with the advice of an independent low pay commission, whose membership would include representatives of employers, including small businesses, and employees'.[36] The decision to involve employers in the determination of its level represented a sharp break from the party's policy in the past, when the figure had been settled in dialogue only with the national trade union leadership. New Labour broke from its past in other ways too: by declining to link its proposal to earnings (the party had promised a national minimum wage in 1987 that would start at 50% of men's median earnings, to be upgraded gradually to two-thirds of that figure), and by failing to specify an exact value for its national minimum wage (the party in 1992 had promised £3.40 an hour).

Instead it left the settlement of that figure to its newly-created Low Pay Commission; but it gave that Commission explicit terms of reference that required it both to consult widely and,

> in making their recommendations...to have regard to the wider economic and social implications; the likely effect on the level of employment and inflation; the impact on the competitiveness of business, particularly the small firms sector; and the potential impact on the costs to the Exchequer.

Those tight terms of reference were the product of at least two political forces beyond the control of either the Commission or the DTI. One was Gordon Brown's Treasury, which was concerned that too high a minimum wage could disturb the arithmetic of the 'New Deal' and fuel wage inflation. The Commission came under heavy pressure from that source to set a lower rate for workers aged under 25, in spite of strong trade union opposition to such a recommendation. Even more significantly, the

Commission came under pressure from circles close to the Prime Minister, who believed that too high a national minimum wage would undermine the competitiveness and job-creating capacity of the small business sector. Peter Mandelson in particular waged an extensively reported behind-the-scenes campaign for a variegated national minimum wage: one sensitive to the differing needs of firms of different size, region and sector. Military pay apart, however, that specific fight on behalf of the business community was lost. Even Tony Blair eventually distanced himself from it, and the DTI won its fight for a uniform rate country-wide. But the general sensitivity of the Commission (and of the DTI itself) to the needs of the business community did not go away with Mandelson's defeat. On the contrary, the Commission's chairman remained determined that the Commission should only 'make recommendations which business could afford'. 'No one', he said, 'wants a wage that cannot be paid.'[37] As a result the minimum wage that was to be initially paid was fixed at an extremely modest level. The Commission proposed £3.60 an hour for older workers. The government took that proposal, and tweaked it the Treasury way. It set a minimum wage of only £3.20 an hour for workers aged 18–21: to be introduced only in stages, and extended neither to 16–17-year-olds nor to young workers on formal apprenticeship schemes. These initial levels were way below the £4.26 an hour adopted as a policy goal by unions gathered at the 1996 TUC, and were accordingly deeply disappointing to them.

Union dues

In fact, the fight over the national minimum wage was just the first of many such fights over pay and policy between this New Labour government and the industrial wing of the organized labour movement. Of course, the national trade union leadership welcomed the creation of a minimum wage. How could they not? But they simply did not believe, as Rodney Bickerstaffe put it, that '£3.60 for an hour of anybody's life at the end of the 20th century in one of the richest countries on earth' was 'something to be proud of'.[38] Not surprisingly, they contrasted government resolve to hold down wage levels for the poor and powerless with its lack of any equivalent resolve when facing the incomes of the rich and the powerful. John Edmonds in particular, as President of the TUC in 1998, launched a scathing attack on boardroom greed and on ministerial indifference to it, and contrasted that tolerance of corporate largesse with the government's willingness to hold down public sector pay below the rate of inflation year upon year. The 1998 TUC then adopted a £4.60 target for the national minimum wage for all workers over the age of 18. The 2000 TUC raised that target to £5. But all to no avail: the national minimum wage initially withered on the vine. The government did eventually raise it, in October 2000, but only by the paltry sum of 10p; and only after huge union lobbying did it finally agree in the run-up to the 2001 election to move the minimum wage up to £4.10 and to tie its subsequent movement to that of average earnings. It had crept up to £4.85 per hour for adults by October 2004, and to £4.10 for 18–21-year-old workers. By then a new £3.00 an hour rate had been introduced for 16–17-year-olds, and the coverage of the national minimum wage had been extended to homeworkers.

This partial dialogue of the deaf on the national minimum wage was, and remains, part of a bigger story within this whole New Labour saga. It was and is part of the complex dynamic of union–party relations that has always stood at the heart of New Labour politics. New Labour defined itself as *not* a party of the unions. The days when union bosses openly negotiated with Labour politicians were the days of 'Old' Labour, and were not to be repeated. Indeed in opposition, certain New Labour figures had even floated the idea of a formal separation of the party from the unions that had created it, and though that did not occur, the internal 'modernization' of the Labour Party prior to 1997 had been largely a matter of curtailing the role of trade unions in the formulation of party policy. And yet New Labour had not split from the unions. The party still needed union funds and the organizational capacity of the unions at election time. Indeed on occasions, even a New Labour Prime Minister needed Old Labour style backroom deals and union bloc votes to avoid embarrassing defeats at conference: Tony Blair certainly did to avoid defeat on the Iraq issue in 2004. Moreover, the party's activists remained disproportionately trade union members, and in government, ministers did open the portals of power to the union leadership again, and did use the unions as a conduit through which to finance some of its re-skilling initiatives. There was accordingly genuine pleasure and real hope for change in union circles when Labour came to office,[39] and after 1997 the TUC joined Labour ministers in pressing for productivity gains and in advocating the economic advantage of a genuine partnership, in industry and commerce, between capital and labour. The unions, that is, came on board the New Labour project in a big way in 1997. After all, they were in their own way as 'new' and 'modernized' as the party, and as keen as Blair himself on seeing companies succeed and the economy grow.[40] However, what they found was that, although they were on board, they were not in the top cabin. Their voice was heard, but only intermittently – and over time, unevenly so.

'Fairness, not favours' was what the union movement was offered by New Labour: 'influence' in return for 'responsibility'. As Peter Mandelson told them in 1998, it was New Labour's view that 'unions have an important role that extends beyond the workplace...in setting workplace minimum standards; in ensuring adequate health and safety; in promoting training and skills; and in pressing for proper provision of pensions and other benefits'.[41] But the extent to which they would have 'a voice that carries influence and respect' on even that modest range of issues would depend, he insisted, 'on the credibility and persuasiveness that unions themselves command'. Mandelson was clearly offering them a trade-off, one that was qualitatively different from Old Labour's open door, full-agenda exchange between the unions and the party. New Labour would listen to the unions on that narrow band of issues, the Secretary of State made clear, if, and only if, the unions remained loyal and uncritical of a wider set of policy initiatives: 'co-operating', as he put it, 'in the modernization of public services...working with us in forging other reforms, in the welfare system, in the schools and higher education, in de-centralizing government'. It wasn't a subtle message that Peter Mandelson took to the TUC that September, but at least it was clear!

Clarity and truth are not however necessarily the same thing. The problem with the Mandelson specification of how 'new' unionism and New Labour would interact was that the unions continued to have difficulty in cashing in their 'influence and respect' even on the narrow range of issues that he singled out for them as legitimate agenda items. They continued to discover that, as an internal TUC paper put it in 2001, 'the government has been listening too much to business interests and has not given equal weight to the concerns of working people'.[42] Union leaders remained, almost without exception, profoundly disappointed with the government's lack of enthusiasm for European labour law, not least (in New Labour's second term) in relation in the protection that European directives provided to temporary workers. On this directive, as on so many others, New Labour led the right-wing charge to moderate its terms. John Monks called this policy stance 'bloody stupid',[43] and he had a point. It didn't seem right, to the TUC at least, for UK workers to have fewer social rights than their European counterparts, or for the government to resist European standardization in order to defend a uniquely flexible UK labour market whose creation by the Conservatives the Labour Party had once so heavily condemned.

Those same union leaders also remained dissatisfied with the limited resetting by the New Labour government of the national labour laws it inherited. It didn't seem to them right that secondary action should still be illegal, or that employers could legitimately sack workers after only a brief period on official strike.[44] They didn't like the way the DTI, under CBI pressure, legislated in 2001 to deny workers penalty-free access to industrial tribunals until they had fully exhausted their employer's own grievance procedures, and they were particularly incensed earlier in Labour's period of office by Tony Blair's refusal to honour John Smith's 1992 promise to extend protection from unfair dismissal to workers from the very first day of their employment. They clashed bitterly with Gordon Brown over his continued refusal to link state pensions to average earnings. In fact, over time, the TUC became increasingly concerned with, among other things, what it called the 'threat of pensioner poverty': one brought about by Gordon Brown's own tax changes on pension funds and by a generalized employer retreat from the provision of final salary pensions that did not seem to stretch to the boardroom's own 'golden parachutes'. By the middle of Labour's second term, indeed, many unions had formulated their own wish-lists of policy goals not yet achieved, and those lists were both long and broadly consistent. Better pension protection and stronger employment rights for all workers occupied central places on those lists.[45]

The union movement had two other enormous areas of concern with this New Labour government over time. One was a concern over pay for public sector workers, of whom there were nearly 5.5 million in 2003. Pay settlements in the public sector were extremely tight in the first two years of the New Labour government because of the adoption by the Chancellor of the Conservatives' spending limits – the 1998 pay settlements were actually given in stages, the first of which was set at less than the rate of inflation – but things eased as Gordon Brown then exploited the accumulated reserves built up by that process to give above-inflation awards in the run-up to the 2001 general election. Heavy public deficits after 2001 brought wage retrenchment again – public sector wage settlements averaged between 2% and 4% in 2003, and the Chancellor budgeted just 2% for public sector wage rises in 2004, with another 1.5% pencilled in to finance regrading – and this time his tightness triggered a wave of strikes by low-paid workers. These workers were tired of waiting for a promised relief that continued not to come, and they were resentful of government-led attempts to intensify their work processes and erode their working conditions. The longest and bitterest of those disputes was with the firefighters' union,[46] but the firefighters were not alone in striking against tight pay settlements negotiated within Treasury-imposed spending limits and under Treasury-inspired productivity targets. London teachers took strike action in 2002 over the inadequacy of their London cost-of-living allowance. Workers on the rail and Tube networks also took industrial action; as did 85,000 civil servants and nearly 1 million low-paid council workers. The firefighters apart, these strikes were short, yet still they took the strike figures up to levels not seen in almost two decades. In 2002 alone, 1.323 million days were 'lost' to strike action, a 13-year high. In 1997 that figure had been a mere 235,000.

If that was not enough, there was also the issue of PFI. The unions opposed the public finance initiative consistently from its inception. They opposed it when it was first introduced by the Conservatives before 1997, and they resisted it after 1997 as its role in the New Labour policy mix grew over time. It was an opposition predicated partly on a disagreement about claims. Many union officials and members, not to mention the public at large, simply did not believe the government's assertion that PFI represented a saving on the public finances.[47] It looked to them more like a mechanism that shifted the burden between generations, to leave future ones paying an inflated price for an earlier generation's public investment. It was also an opposition predicated on fear: fear that behind the rhetoric of PFI lay an intensification of the labour process and an undermining of working conditions across the public sector as a whole. More and more trade unionists came to believe over time that PFI only worked by creating a two-tier labour force: that private companies were able to underbid existing public sector-based providers of basic services only by paying even less adequate wages and benefits than those originally in place. They came to believe, as Seumas Milne observed at the time, that the very term 'modernization' had been subverted; that what had 'started as a catch-all mantra to justify the party's acceptance of the main social and economic changes driven through in the Tory years had become a code-word in public services for privatization, closures, job cuts, longer working hours and flexibility on the employers' terms'.[48] The unions, that is, feared PFI would ratchet down the returns paid to workers across the public sector as a whole; and they fought it accordingly.

On all three fronts, their pressure was never totally unsuccessful. Rather, their moments of success ebbed and flowed. They flowed normally in the run-up to general elections, where the votes of trade unionists and the funds of the unions figured again in policy-making. But they ebbed, and often ebbed quite quickly, once those elections were out of the way. 2001 was a case in point. Prior to the election and in the wake of the trauma of the 2000 fuel-tax strikes in which union support for the government had been critical, the two wings of the labour movement moved closer together. In the run-up to the election, Labour ministers promised to link the national minimum wage to average earnings – the manifesto talked of raising it to £4.20 – and Tony Blair committed the government in its second term to extensive spending on the public services. In fact Labour ran on a 'cash and reform' programme in 2001, highlighting significant budget increases for health, education and welfare while also committing itself to the 'fundamental reform' of the public sector. 'There should be no barriers, no dogma, no vested interest that stands in the way of delivering the best services for our people', was how the Prime Minister put it when launching Labour's election campaign.[49] With the election safely behind him, however, the tone changed, the Prime Minister then launched a blistering attack on those who opposed reform in the public services as 'wreckers'.[50] He didn't single out the trade unions *per se*. In fact, when immediately and publicly challenged by the TUC on the Thatcherite tone of his remarks, Number 10 denied that the unions were his target, but that was hard to believe, given that the major opposition to continued privatization moves in the public sector continued to come primarily from the 'awkward squad' of left-wing leaders elected into office across the entirety of the union movement: in Unison, Amicus, the GMB, the TGWU, the CWU, the RMT and the FBU.[51] It was even rumoured, in the wake of that speech, that the Prime Minister had abandoned his commitment to end the two-tier workforce in the public services created by the outsourcing of particular functions to private firms,[52] but in the event, that proved to be a rumour too far. For under intense union pressure, Tony Blair was forced to confirm in 2003 that new contractors providing services for local authorities would be obliged to offer new workers terms and conditions that were 'no less favourable' than those enjoyed by colleagues already switched from the local council to the contractor. This was an important if limited concession,[53] but it was not enough to prevent regular Commons rebellions and union and party conference defeats on PFI-type issues throughout New Labour's second term in office.

Not surprisingly therefore, the disaffiliation of unions from the party, once a New Labour predilection, now became an 'Old' Labour one. Where New Labour once contemplated separating the party from the unions, many of New Labour's more strident union-based critics now contemplated separating the unions from the party. Not surprisingly too, the very fear of that separation, with its immense financial and electoral consequences for the party and the government, then triggered a major charm offensive by key New Labour figures. In fact this was the DTI's time again: on this occasion, to cry *mea culpa*. This was Patricia Hewitt, New Labour's fourth Secretary of State for Trade and Industry, speaking to the 2003 TUC:

> We are at a very significant moment in the relationship between a Labour Government and the trade union movement. I am not thinking, actually, about the headlines and the rhetoric that have dominated the last few days. I am thinking about the fact that we are half-way through our second term. We are looking ahead to try and win a third term, and there has never been a Labour Government in that position before. I know very well that a lot of you here think that we have got far too close to big business and we have somehow cold-shouldered or elbowed out the unions. I do not happen to think that is the reality but I am very worried that that is such a widespread perception, and we have to change that. We have to make our relationship and our partnership work better.

Indeed both sides are now trying. The unions have a 56-point action plan, agreed at the Labour Party national policy forum at Warwick in 2004, which is now the template against which they judge the receptivity of this New Labour government to their concerns. The government, for its part, is promising to legislate on at least some parts of that action plan during its third term, should that occur: tiny but important parts like the protection of Bank Holiday pay, and longer maternity pay. But when Tony Blair spoke to the TUC at Brighton in the wake of the Warwick agreement, his speech (and indeed his attempts at humour and self-deprecation) was met with *total* silence, suggesting that, at the very least, the relationship between the unions and the party is once more extraordinarily strained. The Fire Brigades Union has already disaffiliated. The RMT has also gone (expelled for allowing branches to support the Scottish Socialist Party); and the GMB, the TGWU and the CWU have all withheld much-needed campaign contributions because of rank-and-file opposition to the financing of a party so unresponsive in government to union calls to slow privatization in the public sector, give full protection against unfair dismissal, and to protect the pensions of workers in private firms. In the relationship between New Labour and new unionism, we are definitely in new and troubling times: still perhaps for the moment in a stage of domestic violence, but apparently moving ever closer either to murder or to divorce.[54]

A 'New Deal' for workers

If New Labour in power was insufficiently proactive for the unions' tastes in the provision of collective and individual *rights* for workers at their point of employment, it was far more proactive as a government in relation to the ability of those workers to *arrive* at that point and in relation to their *capacities* to flourish there. We have seen already the seriousness and centrality of the Chancellor's pursuit of a 'New Deal' for the unemployed; and we have noted already his determination to ease the pressures on families trying to combine work and child rearing, by redirecting public funds into the greater provision and utilization of child care facilities and after-school clubs. What we have commented on less, but must examine now, is New Labour's continuing and serious attempt to equip those workers, once in employment, with the skills to perform better there and to progress up their own particular occupational and professional ladders. New Labour came to power, we must remember, committed not simply to adding to the *quantity* of the workforce by its employment initiatives and family-friendly tax changes, though that was certainly high on its list of things to do. New Labour also came to power committed to improving the *quality* of that workforce, by investing in human capital.

Indeed, in its 1997 manifesto, education was listed as its 'number one priority'; and justified as being so, not simply because 'it is good for the individual' but also because 'it is an economic necessity for the nation'. 'We will compete successfully on the basis of quality,' the party said, 'or not at all. And quality comes from developing the potential of all our people.' As Tony Blair later put it:

> Learning is the key to individuals succeeding in the new economy: at school, in further education, throughout their working lives. The key capacity for people to survive and thrive in the new economy is their capacity to learn, and then to apply that learning.[55]

It was New Labour's view in 1997 that the realization of educational potential required action on a series of fronts: at a pre-school level, by expanding access; at a school level, by extra funding and a 'zero tolerance of underperformance'; and at a post-school level, by the development of systems of lifelong learning. All this, it knew, would cost money; and money was exactly what it promised to provide. 'Over the course of a five year Parliament,' it said, 'as we cut the costs of economic and social failure we will raise the proportion of national income spent on education.'[56] We will do that. We will raise standards; and we will re-skill the labour force.

In this area, as in many others, New Labour in power was true to the form of its word. It certainly spent more, year on year, on education: in absolute terms, in terms adjusted for inflation, and eventually, if not initially, as a percentage of national income. It opened access to pre-school education in ways and on a scale without precedent in the UK, and it also systematically pursued higher and higher standards of performance by the children so admitted. On the schools front, New Labour in power was very proactive. On the re-skilling side of the equation, however, activity was more patchy and the results slower to emerge. Certainly by early in its second parliament, New Labour had created a new national system for the training and retraining of adult workers, but the effectiveness of that new system still by then remained largely untested. Where New Labour operated through its own employees, as in the school system, things changed quickly. Where New Labour ministers had to persuade and cajole independent actors, the pace of change was significantly slower.

But cajole they did: for those ministers knew well enough the importance, to the economic and social goals they had set, of the skills revolution they now attempted to trigger. Indeed if exhortation was a guaranteed pedagogic tool, the average skill level of the British worker would have soared, so often and with such enthusiasm was that revolution proclaimed. 'We are making', Gordon Brown told the TUC in 2000, 'the biggest investment in education and skills in our country's history',[57] and they were doing so because

...it is crucial that instead of matching our economic activity to the current skills of the nation, we reverse that process and develop a labour force which can cope with the challenge of the new technology, with the cutting edge of competition in the 21st century, and with the changes facing us today. If we are to create a pool of employable labour which can help us to sustain growth without the dangers of inflation, then we have to concentrate on learning and skills.[58]

There was much concentration, particularly by the DfEE, and particularly in its traditional area of responsibility: the school system of England and Wales. There, from the outset, David Blunkett made clear his determination, not simply to meet election promises on class size and pre-school provision, but also to drive up standards. The DfEE set about that raising of the bar through what quickly became a characteristic mixture of 'stick' and 'carrot'. The 'carrots' came regularly in the form of small but significant increases in funding, both for the school system as a whole and for specific target areas. So for example, the DfEE used extra money released in the 1998 budget to set up 25 Education Action Zones (in areas of significant educational disadvantage). It found an extra £143 million to widen participation in further education, and later in 1998 found £500,000 to ease the backlog in the repair of school buildings. Each year indeed saw initiatives of this kind. Alongside that focused funding (and the general increase in funding to the education sector released in each year's budget) the DfEE's ministers also issued regular exhortations to intensified effort, regular chastisements of educational 'actors' who were underperforming (including, it should be said, on occasions the parents themselves) and regular sets of standards and goals. So for example in April 1998 David Blunkett issued the first set of guidelines to parents on the amount of homework their children should do, and backed those up with lottery-funded homework clubs. Later the department mandated all primary schools to teach one hour of basic literacy and numeracy each day. It set mathematics tests for nine-year-olds. It gave failing schools only two years to turn their performance round, and so on.

We will come back to these key aspects of DfEE policy in the next chapter. Here we need to focus instead on the linked policy area of adult education and training, responsibility for which the DfEE shared with the DTI. This too was deemed a vital part of the overall policy mix, and accordingly given its own minister within the DfEE. The minister then delivered in a characteristically New Labour way. He (and it was initially 'he', Kim Howell) began by reviewing and revamping his inheritance from his Conservative predecessors, and by setting up a task force to report on both the skills shortage and on how best to alleviate it.[59] What remained of the system of industrial training boards was surveyed, given new targets, expanded and retitled: initially as a system of 73 National Training Organizations (NTOs), then from 2002 as a set of Sector Skills Councils.[60] The cornerstone of the Conservatives' vocational training initiative – the system of locally based Training and Enterprise Councils whose steering committees were dominated by members of the relevant local business community – were surveyed, given new targets, and reset as a set of 47 local Learning and Skills Councils: with their national body (the Training and Standards Council) renamed and given new powers in 2001 as the National Learning and Skills Council (LSC). Those new powers included responsibility for the planning and funding of post-16 education and training, which meant, among other things, LSC control of the funds Local Education Authorities received to finance sixth-form education. And the old system of craft apprenticeships and union education schemes, long in decline under the Conservatives, was reviewed and revived. They were suitably modernized, with government money going for the first time directly to the unions themselves, who from May 1998 made bids to a Union Learning Fund, to aid in what the government called 'the creation of a learning society'. The LSC, for its part, was given as its mission statement nothing less than the raising of skill levels in the UK workforce to that of the world's best by 2010!

Alongside all this, New Labour after 1997 poured money and speeches into newly created Centres of Excellence designed to enhance training in, and access to, the new information technology. 'We have to make sure', the Prime Minister told a conference in London in 2000, 'that the new economy is not just for a privileged few...for the relatively tightly-drawn social grouping which tends to use the internet today.' 'We have to democratize the new economy. We must ensure that it is open to all.' Which was why his government, among other things, leased refurbished computers to poor families, linked schools and libraries to the internet, and in 2000 set itself a new goal: 'the remaining barriers to e-commerce removed...fast and cheap access to the internet...the goal of Britain being the best place for e-commerce by 2002' and 'a new goal [of] universal access to the internet by 2005'.[61]

The New Labour government also poured money and speeches into the revival of a national system of adult learning, one focused on the development of basic literacy and numeracy skills in 500,000 disadvantaged adults. Ministers were concerned that in the UK,

> ...too many firms today are trapped in a 'low skills equilibrium' where they are competing on price in a low-value added product sector and demanding low skilled, low cost labour....[Ministers believed this to be] a very poor strategy for most British companies [at a time when] globalization means that we cannot compete against countries like China, which have a tenth of our labour costs...[and when] major advances in science and technology, and the outstanding science base we have in this country, provide industry with plenty of opportunities for moving into high-tech areas.[62]

In 2000, David Blunkett went so far as to set up an Adult Basic Skills Strategy Unit within the DfEE to work alongside the Standards and Effectiveness Unit that he had created in 1997. That latter unit's job had been to raise standards of literacy and numeracy among schoolchildren. The new unit had the same remit for the reportedly 7 million UK adults who, at the end of the twentieth century, still had serious reading difficulties.[63] Ministers became increasingly aware over time of what a barrier to employment poor basic skills actually were, and in consequence increasingly pushed extra resources into the various New Deal programmes in order to improve basic skills training for those still trapped in unemployment. As the head of the DfEE, David Blunkett often presented himself as 'a living example of how lifelong learning can bring about success whatever the background of the individual',[64] and because he did, lifelong learning remained high on the department's priority list throughout New Labour's first term. That priority then carried through into its second term, funded there to the tune of £1.5 billion over three years as part of the biggest-ever national drive of its kind. Whatever else New Labour in government was or was not, it was deadly serious about raising basic literacy standards among the UK's working poor.[65]

Moreover, once in power, New Labour did more than revamp what was already there; even though that revamping came to be the core of what it actually did in the area of adult retraining. It also brought to the feast two flagship initiatives of its own. It brought its own lifelong learning agenda of 'individual learning accounts' and the 'University of Industry': both trailed in opposition, both floated in the Green Paper *The Learning Age*, both launched as 'the heart of [New Labour's] new approach',[66] and both given the big sell. For example, Gordon Brown said this to the 2000 TUC:

> This Government will work with you as you bargain for skills – the right to one million individual learning accounts at £150 each, and another 750,000 able to benefit from adult literacy courses by 2004, and the new University for Industry. And let me tell you the scale of our ambitions – what, from the 1970s the Open University achieved for thousands in second chances in higher education through TV and distance learning, we are now ready to achieve for millions in lifelong learning through the University for Industry – recurrent, permanent educational opportunity through cable, satellite and interactive media, and learning direct in workplaces and homes....Our aim is any course of study – at any age, at any grade.[67]

Here however, claim and reality really have diverged. The Individual Learning Accounts were indeed initiated in September 1998, with the first million people opening them guaranteed a reduction in the cost of their chosen course of up to £150. In fact so attractive indeed did this seem to the workforces at which the scheme was directed that by October 2001 over 2.5 million people had applied to open an account.

This blew the budget, of course, and left the government subsidizing some extremely problematic programmes and some extremely dubious claims: so problematic and dubious in fact that Estelle Morris, then Education and Skills Secretary, actually shut the department's own flagship programme down in 2001.

The University for Industry was not closed, however. It simply took much longer than anticipated to launch, and when it came, was quite different an undertaking to the planned collaborative venture with the Open University on which it had initially been modelled. The University for Industry emerged in 2000 as 'Ufi Ltd': a learning system delivered over the internet and through a series of centres in factories, libraries and community centres. By 2004 it was offering more than 800 courses, 80% of them online, and had more than 500,000 learners enrolled through its more than 2000 learndirect centres. Ufi Ltd was given four initial teaching priorities by the DfEE: to trigger improvements in basic literacy and numeracy; to offer training in information and communication technologies in the workplace; to meet the skill needs of small and medium-size businesses; and to offer training to workers in four particular sectors (motor components, multimedia, environmental technology and services, and retail/distribution). Each of those priorities came, in proper New Labour fashion, with targets of numbers of students to be serviced under each heading by particular dates. Ufi is therefore clearly a project that is still in the making, and the priorities set for it make it simply one of the many initiatives launched to meet David Blunkett's professed aim for New Labour policy on human capital in 1998: 'to have a working population whose skill and education levels are the envy of the world'.[68] Thus far, however, it would seem that there has been more policy than envy; and certainly whatever else Ufi Ltd is, it is in no sense a *university* for industry as that term is conventionally understood in the wider world.

Productivity and the holy grail

These various attempts to raise the skill level of the UK workforce were of course part of a wider drive, by senior New Labour figures in all the key economic ministries, to raise the quantity and quality of the goods and services generated by both capital and labour across the UK economy as a whole. Productivity growth, understood in that general sense, was the key requirement of the entire Brown project; for without it there could be no quantum leap in the UK's trend rate of growth, no significant sustainable improvement in the UK economy's overall international competitiveness, and no long-term guarantee of either generalized job security or the large tax base required to sustain an expanding welfare state. Gordon Brown knew this. He knew that 'only with rising productivity can we meet people's long-term expectations for rising standards of living without causing inflation or unemployment'.[69] He made that requirement clear all the time; and because he did, the pursuit of productivity growth – New Labour's economic holy grail – was central to every major initiative that emerged from both the Treasury and the DTI from the very first moment that New Labour took charge of both these key ministries in 1997.

There was general agreement between all the social partners – the TUC and the CBI, as well as the government itself – about the general causes of the UK's poor productivity performance, and hence about the legitimate targets of government action. Indeed it was a feature of the period that both the government and the peak organizations of capital and labour regularly produced reports on the UK's productivity gap and how best to get rid of it.[70] On the Treasury's own analysis, the problem was clear if intractable: that 'the UK's productivity gap can be accounted for by its deficit in physical and human capital, and its lower rate of innovation compared to other major economies'.[71] It was also a feature of the period that New Labour regularly relaunched its productivity initiatives, amid great fanfare from the Treasury as well as from the DTI, and that when it did so, there was generally broad agreement and clarity on the long-term goal of the entire exercise: a productivity performance level that matched the world's best – not 'millions of people feeling that they have to work harder and harder and longer and longer just to stay still', but instead 'businesses and organizations...producing better products, better services, better goods because there is more investment, higher skills and higher wages'.[72]

There was broad agreement too, within the policy-making circles that surrounded this New Labour government, of what in consequence governments should do and what they should not. It was widely agreed there that, in the public sector, ministers should seek greater productivity by direct initiatives of their own, but in relation to the private sector there was no longer an influential policy constituency for the 'top down plans, and grant aid for physical equipment'[73] so characteristic of industrial policy in the 1970s. In fact, as we noted earlier, by 1997 the tide had turned entirely the other way. As Gordon Brown put it, the general view now prevalent in policy-making circles was that 'because productivity growth will come principally by managers and workforces addressing the obstacles to growth, the best thing the Government can do in many areas is get out of the way'. The government's job was not to steer but to *lubricate* the economy: working with the private sector (and with co-operative unions)

> to address obstacles to productivity that we may overcome together but sometimes each of us cannot solve on our own: the shortfall in skills; improving the quality as well as quantity of investment; speeding up the use and spread of technology and, of course, examining how Britain can more effectively adopt best practice and innovative techniques.[74]

Thinking of that kind then gave New Labour its productivity agenda, one rehearsed in public in the papers accompanying every budget, pre-budget and Comprehensive Spending Review that emerged from the Brown Treasury. The 2002 statement was typical:

> The Government's strategy for closing the productivity gap has two broad strands: maintaining macroeconomic stability to help businesses and individuals plan for the future, and implementing microeconomic reforms to remove the barriers that prevent markets from functioning efficiently. These microeconomic reforms address historic weaknesses in the five key drivers of productivity performance.
>
> - Strengthening competition to encourage firms to innovate, minimize costs and provide better quality goods and services to the consumer
> - Promoting enterprise and innovation to unlock the potential of new technologies and working practices, supporting entrepreneurship, risk taking and management across the country
> - Encouraging investment to improve the UK's stock of physical capital in every sector and industry
> - Improving the skills base to maximize the contribution of human capital to growth; and
> - Improving the productivity of public services.[75]

Not surprisingly therefore, New Labour in power moved quickly to emphasize the importance of competition as vital to both consumer protection and business efficiency, to move the government's Competitiveness Unit back into the DTI from the Cabinet Office to which it had migrated with Michael Heseltine; and to amend the UK's competition laws in order to strengthen the DTI's capacity to block the emergence of market monopoly power. It also moved quickly to reassure an initially nervous business community that it was set on building 'a real partnership' with it: on the basis of what Margaret Beckett, in an immediate letter widely distributed across the entirety of UK industry, called the 'three pillars...of strong markets, modern companies, and encouraging enterprise'.[76] Likewise a later Secretary of State for Industry, newly in office, moved quickly to reassure the City that, for this New Labour government at least, 'wealth creation was more important than wealth distribution', and that in consequence 'the approach is clear: competition wherever possible, regulation only when absolutely necessary'.[77] Which was why the new powers the government took to itself to regulate mergers were by no means as substantial as the party had proposed in the period of opposition immediately before Tony Blair became leader: party policy had become significantly more tolerant of big business since then. Old Labour had wanted a public interest test for corporate mergers. New Labour did not, but nonetheless once in power the DTI legislated. It legislated twice, first in 1998, then again in 2001. On the first occasion, and only after consulting widely across the business community and equipping itself with an extensive audit of existing levels of competitiveness, the New Labour government replaced the Monopolies and Mergers Commission with a stronger Competition Commission and a reinforced Office of Fair Trading (OFT), able to block anti-competitive agreements and prohibit the abuse of dominant market position. Three years later New Labour strengthened the OFT still further, even going so far on that occasion as to float the idea of jail terms for the directors of price-fixing companies.

Between these dates, and on a regular basis, Secretaries of State for Industry cleared most proposed mergers and blocked others, and created new regulatory systems for industries as diverse as the City on the one side and the private providers of basic utilities on the other. This was classic DTI stuff, with ministers attempting to square the contradictory roles of the department as both business advocate and business regulator: persistently claiming that competitive companies were the main thing that consumers required, while in practice generally lightening the burden of regulation on the business community behind a camouflage of fancy words. And in truth, while remaining deliberately 'business friendly' throughout, New Labour did slightly reposition the DTI from its first term to its second: to accentuate the department's role as the protector of UK citizens as 'consumers'. Indeed, even in Stephen Byers' time as Secretary of State, consumer protection against overcharging in the retail, motor and electricity sectors was a particular feature of the policy regime of his DTI: one part indeed of his more general concern to monitor the implementation of the 75 policy commitments by then contained in the DTI White Paper *Our Competitive Future: Building the Knowledge Driven Society* issued by his predecessor in 1998.

For the second distinctive feature of New Labour's attempt to bridge the productivity gap was the regular production of highly publicized White Papers laying out targets and specifying policies for their attainment. *Our Competitive Future* was produced when Peter Mandelson was Secretary of State for Industry, and it reflected his enthusiasm for the new knowledge-based 'dot.com' economy. Indeed it was accompanied by a 32-page background paper on the role of knowledge in the stimulation of economic growth, a background paper replete with 'new growth theory' thinking. The whole thrust of that background paper was that modern changes in information technology, in the rate of technological advance, in global competition and in sophisticated demand patterns had all combined to increase the importance of innovation and entrepreneurship, and to make vital new sources of investment that were sensitive to the potential embodied in the knowledge of the workforce. The Mandelson DTI set out to stimulate that innovation and enterprise, to back those knowledge-based companies, and to bring them into close working relationships with similar companies, university-based scientists and enterprising venture capitalists. 'Capabilities', 'collaboration' and 'competition' were the watchwords of the day, and 'clusters', 'research triangles' and 'Silicon Valleys' very much the flavour of the month. The White Paper, for example, set out plans to create ten industrial forums in key growth sectors, to promote collaboration between firms; and promised extra funding to Regional Development Agencies to facilitate regional link-ups. It also carried the clear message that henceforth DTI backing would be concentrated on industries that were unequivocally knowledge-intensive in their production processes and product design; that in future the DTI would focus its energies, not on industries in decline, but on businesses keen to develop their capabilities (and the skills of their employees) as players in the new knowledge-based global marketplace.[78]

Mandelson presented the DTI as having a key role to play in auditing the economy's progress towards competitiveness in world markets – to engage in 'benchmarking' the UK economy in various ways, and he understood his own role as primarily a 'proselytizing' one: that of encouraging best practice and setting out ways to 'modernize the micro-economy'.[79] For like Lord Young in an earlier Thatcherite DTI with whom Mandelson shared an enthusiasm for privatization and the liberalization of the business community, New Labour's second Secretary of State for Trade and Industry saw his job primarily as one of effecting cultural change: in the words of the White Paper, of creating 'a broadly-based entrepreneurial culture in which more people of all ages start their own business'. And in truth he was not alone here. His successor was equally evangelical on this topic: that 'our first and major task has to be to lead a crusade for greater enterprise in this country'.[80] 'There is a clear role for government', the White Paper insisted, 'in acting as a catalyst, investor and regulator to strengthen the supply side of the economy...addressing market failures to promote science and technology, foster enterprise and innovation, develop education and skills, facilitate collaboration and promote modern competitive markets'.[81] Which was why, among other things, in the wake of the White Paper, the DTI unveiled a new enterprise fund to provide venture capital for high-tech-based small businesses. That fund did not contain a lot of money – just £150 million over three years – but it did contain enough to signal the government's enthusiasm for what it thought of as the industries of the future, and that was its primary purpose.

Our Competitive Future set the pattern for the White Papers that followed. The DTI and DfEE combined early in 2001 to produce a second White Paper: this time, one on *Enterprise, Skills and Innovation* under the banner title *Opportunity for All in a World of Change*. The thrust of this second general statement of New Labour's industrial policy was very much in line with that of its predecessor, though on this occasion the argument was slightly more focused on regional underdevelopment and the skills gap than Mandelson's had been. The 2001 White Paper proposed the creation of new university–business partnerships at the regional level – 'university innovation centres', it called them – and the setting up of two new technology institutes in each region. 'The university innovation centres and technology institutes will', the White Paper said, 'form a major new network based in each region, to boost the level of research and development, innovation and technology transfer and to provide regions with the skills in ICT and technology they need.' The aim was nothing less than 'a step-change in the capacity of regions and communities to grow new dynamic businesses and hi-tech employment'. 'Raising the trend rate of growth by 0.5% for the worst performing regions would increase GDP in 10 years by £20 billion', the White Paper announced, and to that end the government committed itself to creating for the businesses in those regions what it called a 'world class ICT infrastructure' on which they could then successfully innovate and compete.

By this point, one thing at least had changed. The DTI's 1998 enthusiasm for knowledge-based industries above all others had given way to a more broadly-based concern with the health of UK manufacturing in general.

Indeed Patricia Hewitt admitted as much when launching her White Paper on the government's *Manufacturing Strategy* in 2002, saying that

> in our first term we quite inadvertently gave the impression that British manufacturing did not matter to us. We never set out to downgrade manufacturing, but in part because of all the dot.com hype, we gave the impression that manufacturing was not a priority.[82]

Well, by 2002, it certainly was. Michael Porter, the management guru, was brought in to advise on the problems of UK management.[83] James Dyson, the successful entrepreneur inventor – he of the novel vacuum cleaner – was brought in to advise on how best to compete with low-cost producers. The DTI continued to monitor the competitiveness of the UK economy, both nationally and regionally – it issued 'productivity and competitiveness' indicators on an annual basis from 1999 – and on occasion even accompanied those with a sharp wake-up call to UK-based businesses. 'We are poor on innovation,' Stephen Byers told them in 1999, 'have poor basic skills, don't have a culture of enterprise, there are not enough spin-offs from universities, and we don't have strong and confident consumers.'[84] In an attempt to rectify that, a later DTI then organized its own innovation summits and productivity seminars. It set up its own internal Manufacturing Policy Team, and as we have just seen, it issued its own *Manufacturing Strategy* in 2002.[85] But by then, of course, the pattern of policy was set, and there was little new to either say or do. There was a new goal and role: 'assisting companies to move up the value-added chain to more knowledge-intensive, high-skilled manufacturing'. There was that much at least of a genuflection back to Mandelson's 1998 White Paper. But the policies to achieve this were as before: policies to aid investment, to raise skills and education levels, to spread best practice, to modernize the transport network, to strengthen the science base and to reinforce competition.

Consistently since 1997, government resources, tax changes and institutional initiatives combined to encourage scientific research, to increase the supply of scientists and engineers, and to promote new technologies, technology transfer, and the access of small businesses to the latest available research data.[86] Consistently through the whole set of White Papers, policy systematically encouraged small businesses to begin, to invest and to grow.[87] Increasingly over time, policy has also systematically attempted to spread economic growth between and across regions – in 1999 the government created eight Regional Development Agencies specifically for that purpose – and to ease the burden of regulation, bureaucracy and red tape on the business community. Policy has even continued, if only in a limited way, to extend direct financial assistance to firms and industries in trouble. In fact, direct financial aid of that kind to parts of the UK's troubled manufacturing base occasionally made all the headlines – both when given, as with Rolls-Royce and BMW, and when not, as at Corus and Motorola – but in truth, under New Labour, direct financial assistance to ailing industries was low by general EU standards.[88] This was a government that funded the new and the innovative, in both companies and in people, rather than the old and the tried. 'The only way for Britain to be at the forefront of the new knowledge-based economies', Brown told the House in November 1998, 'is by modern policies for education, employee participation, small business development, and science and innovation.'[89]

> Knowledge and skills, creativity and innovation, adaptability and entrepreneurship are the ways the winners will win in the new economy. We all have a responsibility to ensure that we are all equipped to succeed in it. That way we can all prosper. All our people. And all our businesses. For the benefit of Britain.[90]

When push came to shove, this was indeed a 'new growth theory' government of a kind that the UK had not seen before, and nowhere was this 'newness' more obvious than in the instruments, priorities and targets of its industrial policy.

6
Campaigning in Poetry, Governing in Prose[1]

The final ingredient in New Labour's strategy to narrow the UK's productivity gap was its commitment, as we noted in the last chapter, to 'improve productivity in public services'. Though that commitment invariably came last in any listing of the strategy's component elements, it was never a minor or a residual one. On the contrary, the condition, delivery and expansion of public services in the UK since 1997 has been, and remains, absolutely central to the New Labour project, and critical to its potential for regular re-election. Public sector productivity preoccupied the Treasury under Gordon Brown as part of his campaign to raise living standards without raising direct taxation, and it preoccupied Number 10, as one of the defining elements of what is 'new' in New Labour. The Chancellor has invariably approached the issue of productivity in the services that his budgets finance in primarily cost terms: the cost to the taxpayer, and the cost to UK business and its competitiveness if government departments do not play their 'part in meeting the productivity challenge'.[2] The Prime Minister has shared those concerns and on occasions that vocabulary, but more normally Tony Blair has presented the 'modernization' of the UK's welfare state as the only way of protecting old Labour values in an increasingly competitive and globalized world. 'We have reached the limits of the public's willingness to fund an unreformed welfare system through ever higher taxes and spending',[3] he told the House of Commons in his first debate on the Queen's Speech as Prime Minister; and because we have, sweeping reforms of welfare provision became, and indeed remain, a central part of what New Labour in power actually does.

Not, of course, that New Labour began with a clean sheet here. Far from it: it began with at least two very complex inheritances, between whose contradictory imperatives it had gingerly to pick its way.

It began with an *electoral inheritance* that was more nuanced than the Prime Minister's bald assertion implied. It was true that there was a lack of enthusiasm for taxation, but that position on taxation cohabited with broad popular support for extensive state provision of schooling, and for health care free at the point of use. In fact lack of enthusiasm for tax rises in general actually went along with a growth in expectations about the quantity and quality of those free public services – a rising bar of minimum acceptable standards set by larger and larger sections of the population – and did not preclude repeated examples over time of a professed willingness, by significant majorities within the electorate, to pay *more* direct taxation, so long as that funding could be targeted on particularly-valued welfare services in order to ensure their enhanced availability and quality.

New Labour began too with a set of *structural problems* that seem to be endemic to the large-scale public provision of welfare services. Those services are necessarily very labour-intensive to provide: so they come with large labour forces, many of whom are low paid, lots of whom are highly skilled, and most of whom are highly unionized. (In the case of health care provision, they also come with drug costs set by multinational suppliers, over which ministers exercise no direct control.) Welfare services also attract to themselves a large client base: a client base built up partly of people dependent on welfare cheques for their income, and partly of people who either regularly or intermittently make use of welfare services. New Labour, in consequence, faced in 1997 a complex public sector workforce that stretched from soldiers and civil servants to teachers and nurses. It faced a variegated client group that included pensioners, people on various kinds of disability allowance, and the unemployed; and it faced a wide-ranging consumer group that included parents, NHS patients and even the motoring public who 'consume' publicly provided roads. One thing that could therefore be absolutely guaranteed was that New Labour could do very little 'modernizing' of the welfare state, and certainly very little 'meeting [by public sector workers of] the productivity challenge', without at the same time disturbing the existing balance of interests, resources and ambitions of a significant majority of its potential and actual electorate. Telling business to get its act together was one thing. Sorting its own house into a new order was likely to be quite another.

If that was not enough, there was also the inheritance of failed attempts at modernization in the past. New Labour came to power insisting on the viability of its 'third way', of course, trying desperately to keep clear pink water between itself and both Old Labour and Thatcherism. Yet it could not break completely with the Old Labour tradition of universally available welfare services, and indeed its leading figures did not want to do so. Even Margaret Thatcher, who arguably did, could not do that: so deep was, and indeed still is, popular support in the UK for the *public* provision of schooling, health care and pensions. But nor did its leading figures wish to break entirely from the Thatcherite willingness to use market forces to trigger efficiencies in the provision of those services. New Labour, unlike Old Labour, was not in principle opposed to the use of privatization and internal markets as tools of policy, or to the strengthening of the consumer voice among the stakeholders in UK welfare provision. New Labour ministers, in ways that their Conservative predecessors were not, were willing to concede the complexity of measuring 'productivity' and 'efficiency' in the welfare arena. They were also willing to block the Tory practice of simply replacing public sector monopolies with private ones. But they too, like their predecessors in power, insisted that efficiently provided public services were a vital ingredient in any strategy designed, over the long term, to increase living standards in a modern industrial society.

Gordon Brown, more than any other New Labour leader, has on occasion pondered these dilemmas out loud and at length, and arguably his 2003 address to the Social Market Foundation represents the greatest moment of clarity yet achieved by New Labour ministers as they struggle to deal with the complexity and detail of their various 'modernization' initiatives. His address was partly a defence of the use of market forces wherever New Labour deemed them appropriate, and of strengthening markets as one strand in the struggle for international competitiveness, economic growth, individual job security and generalized social justice. It was actually an address that was partly a dialogue with the Labour Left. But the address was also a defence of the public provision of services that were not appropriately delivered by market means, and a reflection on the difficulty of protecting consumer interests in services so provided: and that part of it was as much a dialogue with his opponents across the floor of the House of Commons as it was a dialogue with his internal party critics. He put his understanding of the central issue facing New Labour in relation to the provision of services in this way:

In almost every area of current controversy...the question is, at root, what is the best relationship between individuals, markets and governments to advance the public interest and whether it is possible to set aside, and indeed move beyond, the old sterile and debilitating conflicts of the past....In each area the questions are, at root, whether the public interest – that is, opportunity and security for all – and the equity, efficiency and diversity necessary to achieve it, is best advanced by more or less reliance on markets or through substituting a degree of public control or ownership for the market and whether, even where there is public sector provision, there can be contestability.

After a lengthy defence of the use of markets in New Labour policy, he had this to say on their limits:

...there are limits to markets – not only where, as a matter of morality, we have always accepted they have no place; but also in those areas as a matter of practicality where they do not and cannot be made to work, and hence where we should support public provision as the more equitable, efficient and responsive solution....Our clear and robust defence of markets must be combined with a clear and robust recognition of their limits.

Taking health care as his example, he insisted that there at least, 'price signals do not work, the consumer is not sovereign, there is potential abuse of monopoly power, it is hard to write and enforce contracts, it is difficult to let a hospital go bust; [and] we risk supplier-induced demand'. But by the same token, he did not accept that therefore it automatically followed 'that the future lies in a wholly centralized service, that we rule out contestability or a role for the private sector in the future, and that we need devalue or ignore the important issue of greater consumer choice'. That was not so, for Gordon Brown at least,

...because we also know that public services can fail too. The experience of telephones, gas, electricity and water was of public sector monopolies created to guarantee supply of service but which had become, over time, not an empowerment for the consumer but a restriction of their choices.

Which was why it was absolutely vital, in his view, to

...avoid the trap of simply replacing market failure with state failure; and...[to] achieve equity, efficiency and diversity by reforming and modernizing the public realm for decades ahead, in particular through devolution, transparency and accountability....Even in a world where health care is not organized on market principles with consumers paying for their care, it is in the public interest to have devolution from the centre and to champion decentralized means of delivery.

'Even when a market is inappropriate,' he told his audience, 'old command and control systems of management are not the way forward.' Instead, 'we are seeking and should seek – in the NHS and other public services – a decentralized...means of delivery compatible with equity and efficiency'.[4] It is this search for a new way of running a welfare state that has so far underpinned all that New Labour has done in the area of welfare provision.

Modernizing the welfare state

Both at the beginning of New Labour's period in office and later, Tony Blair's commitment to what he once termed 'our core mission: to improve our public services' was made crystal clear on many occasions. Before party audiences at more than one conference he defended public services as 'the power of community in action', as 'social justice made real',[5] and there seems no reason to doubt the sincerity of the private conviction that underpinned the public rhetoric here. But what that conviction delivered in policy terms changed in focus and level of specificity over time. On the brink of New Labour in power, the language was grand and the target general. 'We claim to be the party that can modernize the welfare state', Blair told the journalists covering the 1997 election campaign. 'We accept it needs modernization, but we believe it has to be done on the basis of the principles of fairness and opportunity for everyone.... You can either have the two-tier Britain under the Conservatives, two-tier schools, two-tier health service, too-tier pensions, a two-tier society, or we can build this country as one-nation under New Labour.'[6] Five years of power later, the same ostensible commitment was still there: to fairness and to opportunity for all. 'I will tell you why I am passionate about reform...':

...because poor public services and welfare are usually for the poorest. The better-off can buy a better education or move to a better area or know a better doctor, or find a better job. Those great governments of 1906 and 1945 did great things. They inherited a situation where the majority were have-nots and made them haves. But prosperity never reached all the way down. We went from being a 30–70 country to being a 70–30 one. Today it's not enough. Not morally. Not economically.

But now it was all specifics, and reform was aimed less at Conservative legacies than at Old Labour ones.

> In *education*, we need to move to the post-comprehensive era, where schools keep the comprehensive principle of equality of opportunity but where we open up the system to new and different ways of education, built around the needs of the individual child. We need an *NHS* true to the principle of care on the basis of need, not ability to pay, but personalized, built around the individual patient. Both require an end to the 'one size fits all' mass production public service. The purpose of the 20th century welfare state was to treat citizens as equals. The purpose of our 21st century reforms must be to treat them as individuals as well.[7]

Things shifted in the New Labour lexicon between the government's first term and its second. 'Welfare reform' in the first term was very much a matter of resetting the rights and responsibilities of welfare claimants. It was a 'New Deal' reform based on the principle of 'work for those who can, security for those who cannot'.[8] We have seen some of its details in previous chapters, and we will see more in the chapters to come. In that first term, 'reforming' the provision of public services took second place. The lines of reform that would become so evident after the 2001 election were there before 2001, but only in embryonic form. For New Labour in its first term had things to prove to its electorate about its capacity to sustain the *quantity* of education and health care provision, in the wake of its 1997 decision to restrict public spending in its first two years in office to the levels set by its Conservative predecessor. After 2001 the New Labour government chose in addition to prove things about the *quality and character* of that provision. It chose, in Blair's words, to 'accelerate the pace of change in our public services,[9] and accordingly, instead of just 'flogging the system harder' as Blair put it to the 2002 party conference, set in process reforms designed to improve the output of public service provision and to make that provision more consumer-friendly.

> This is the historic mission of this Government: it is to take the welfare state, the public services, the great 1945 settlement, and completely revolutionize it for today's world....we are engaged not on a set of discrete reforms, area by area, but a fundamental shift from a twentieth-

century welfare state with services largely collective, uniform and passive, founded on low skills for the majority, to a twenty-first century opportunity society with services [that] are personal, diverse and active, founded on high skills.[10]

This shift in focus and priority was signalled by the Prime Minister in a major policy address in July 2001, one justified in his view by the 2001 election result itself. Tony Blair chose to interpret that result as a mandate for welfare expenditure and reform. He said repeatedly in the immediate aftermath of the election, that it was 'a watershed, because for the first time is [his] adult political lifetime, in the battle of tax cuts versus public services, the public services won'.[11] But he took the result to be a mandate for reform, not for complacency. 'My argument is this,' he said, 'if we who believe in public services don't change them for the better, there is an alternative political party and position that will seize on our weakness and use it to dismantle the very notion of public services as we know them. It is reform or bust.'

Why then did the public services have to change to survive? This was his answer:

First expectations have risen enormously yet public services designed for a previous age find it difficult to respond. Unlike 1945, people don't put up with the basics. In a consumer age, they expect quality, choice and standards and too often don't experience them. *Secondly*, the demands on the system have risen: more people live longer, more diseases are treatable, more go to nursery and to university, more people use public transport. *Thirdly*, there has been chronic under-investment that has run down the essential infrastructure, buildings, equipment, track and trains in transport. *Fourth*, staff recruitment is so much harder with employment at record levels and the spectrum of private sector jobs, many with higher pay, is so much greater; and where in many key public service jobs there is real and growing stress.[12]

Given that third reason, one leg of the resulting policy initiative was indeed greater *investment* in the public services. 'Without investment, reform will get you very little further – as the Tories found in the eighties. There is no point', Blair told an audience at the London School of Econmics in 2001,

...designing new structures for the health service if you don't tackle the fundamental problem of inadequate capacity....So the country is faced with a choice. Either we continue investing. Or we cut back. We aim to continue investing. Under this Labour government there will be no blank cheques – but nor do we expect public services to run on empty.[13]

The other leg of the policy of public service regeneration was, however, *reform*: and root and branch reform at that. Tony Blair again, this time in 2002: 'We are never going to get the public services we want, which give genuine equality of opportunity and access to people, unless we change the way they are run.'[14]

> Without investment Britain will never get the modern public services it needs. But investment is not enough. Public services need reform if they are to deliver the uniformly high standards and consumer focus that people expect in the 21st century. The best people to make that reform are those who believe in the values, the ethos, and the potential embodied in our public services. This government wants to work in partnership with public servants on the frontline to make the often difficult changes that will deliver more opportunity and more security to the vast majority of people who rely on our education, health, police and public transport systems.[15]

This commitment to investment and reform was then followed up by a new Fabian pamphlet and a glossy government brochure, both bearing the Prime Minister's name and laying out the benchmarks for the new reforms. There were to be four. The first was '*national standards driving equality*': a determination to establish them as floors below which public service provision was not to fall, and a commitment to raising them over time. The second was what Tony Blair called '*devolution to the front line*': a commitment to decentralize decision-making within the various public services, and to establish a system of 'earned autonomy'; a 'right for the successful who are achieving good standards to manage their own affairs and innovate with greater freedom from central oversight'. The third carried the anaesthetizing label of '*reform of the professions*': the promise of better pay and conditions for public sector workers in return for greater 'flexibility' in working practices; and the fourth was '*choice*' – the creation of more options 'not only between public service providers but also within each public service'.[16] Tony Blair told the Local Government and Women's Conference in Cardiff in 2002:

We want public services, built around 4 key principles of reform. National standards, backed by proper systems of inspection and accountability....Devolution to the front line so that doctors and nurses, heads and teachers, police officers, get real power over resources, and freedom to innovate. More flexible terms, conditions and working practices so that their time is spent doing what they do best – helping the users of public services. More choice for the consumer, being prepared to use alternative providers, including where it makes sense and gives value for money and with guarantees that staff are properly treated, using the voluntary and private sector.[17]

In fact, if 'welfare-to-work' was the dominant concern in the area of welfare reform in the first term, and 'reform of the public services' the dominant one of the second, New Labour looks set to make the 'choice' issue – the issue of 'consumer sensitivity' – its big concern should it be re-elected again. The capacity to generate 'tailor-made services' or 'personalized public services' have now joined the list of New Labour ambitions for the public sector, since as Gordon Brown said in his Social Market Foundation address, echoing his leader's 'reform or bust' thesis,

...it is only by developing decentralized non-market models for public provision that respond to people's needs, extend choice, and are equitable and efficient, that we will show to those who assert that whatever the market failure the state failure will always be greater, that a publicly funded and provided service can deliver efficiency, equity and be responsive to the consumer.[18]

The big danger, of course, is that with 'personalized public services' will come new forms of inequality, as universalism is surrendered in the name of choice, and the poor and socially-marginalized are squeezed out of the system in order to maintain broad middle-class support for public over private forms of provision. But the Prime Minister remains adamant that New Labour's reform of the public services can avoid that fate and produce 'services personal to each and fair to all'. 'Choice isn't an end in itself', he has recently claimed. It 'is one important mechanism to ensure that citizens can indeed secure good schools and health services in their communities'. It 'puts the levers in the hands of parents and patients so that as citizens and consumers they can become the driving force for improvement'. It is, in fact, 'an entirely different dynamic...to drive the public services: one where the service will be driven not by the government or by the managers but by the user'.[19]

Public targets, private money

Though the creation of a special office within Number 10 to oversee all this – the Office of Public Service Reform – only followed the general election in 2001, the first moves in this process of modernization came earlier, and they came in two different forms. They came as a set of public service agreements, and they came as private finance initiatives (PFIs).

As we saw in Chapter 4, public service agreements (PSAs) first saw the light of day in Gordon Brown's initial Comprehensive Spending Review in 1998 – the one that took the brakes off the limits on public spending voluntarily inherited by New Labour from its Conservative predecessor – and 'by linking funding to the delivery of service improvements, key reforms and modernization', such agreements quickly became 'central to the Government's strategy for improving public services'.[20] The brakes were taken off public spending in 1998, but they were taken off only at a price. They were taken off in a trade-off between funds given and performance targets adopted and met. The philosophy was clear, even if the initial mechanisms of implementation were not. Gordon Brown in 1998:

> ...so today we begin not, as all spending announcements for the last 30 years have done, with annual allocations, but by setting out: the new three-year objectives and targets for each service and therefore the results we are demanding; the new standards of efficiency which will have to be met to ensure every penny is spent well; the procedures for scrutiny and audit that will now be set in place; and the reforms we have agreed. *First*, each department has reached a public service agreement with the Treasury, effectively a contract for the renewal of public services. It is a contract that in each service area requires reform in return for investment. So the new contract sets down the new departmental objectives and targets that have to be met, the stages by which they will be met, how departments intend to allocate resources to achieve these targets, and the process that will monitor results....*Second* the contract will stipulate new three-year efficiency targets for the delivery of services – targets that range between 3% and 10%. The terms of these will be made public. The purpose of these efficiency targets is to ensure that more resources go direct to front-line services...so that by securing greater value for money, we secure more money for what we value.[21]

By the time of the second Comprehensive Spending Review in 2000, the procedures surrounding this trade-off had tightened. Many of the original targets – some 600 in total – had been rejected as vague and contradictory, and by 2000 had been whittled down to some 200. By then, Treasury reviews had included issues that cut across lines of departmental responsibility, so that the 2000 public service agreements often came with pooled budgets and more than one departmental signature. By 2002 the whole system had its own monitoring, training and advocacy unit within the Cabinet office, and its own public bible: *Reforming Our Public Services: Principles into Practice,* published by the Office of Public Service Reform in March 2002. By 2002 a full system of independent and statutory inspection and audit was in place across the entire public sector, and the PSAs to be audited had been tightened still further, with departments wanting more resources now having to demonstrate that 'failing institutions will be dealt with early and decisively', as the Chancellor put it.[22] Moreover, by 2002, a public system of league tables was also in place: school performance tables, hospital rankings, and measures of local council efficiency and effectiveness. By 2002, that is, and for the first time, public service providers operated in a culture of formal performance agreements, incrementally increased targets, ever tighter monitoring of performance against agreements, and extensive codified publicity on successes and failures.

This monitoring was always driven by twin motives: better public services for social reasons, measured in terms of higher levels of performance, of course, but also better public services for economic reasons, measured in terms of units of resource. 'Not only [are] public services...a key determinant of society's welfare', as a Treasury discussion document put it in 2003, but 'high quality public services [also] provide the conditions that enable private businesses to grow'.[23] For by then the Comprehensive Spending Reviews (and their associated public service agreements) had gathered to themselves another purpose: not simply the traditional one of 'dividing up the national wealth...concentrating on who gets what' but also now a deeper concern with 'how we can expand that national wealth...how every department from transport to home affairs, from education to industry, [can] play...its part in meeting the productivity challenge'.[24] The government remained well aware of the difficulties of measuring productivity and performance in the public sector: indeed it readily and regularly conceded as much. But that did not stop it streamlining the PSA system over time: reducing the number of targets set, devolving implementation down to successful local providers, and ratcheting up the level of performance required. The 2004 PSA exercise – the one in play as this volume is drafted – has committed the public sector as a whole to efficiency gains of 2.5% a year over a three-year period, and also, controversially as we have seen, to a gross reduction in civil service posts of 84,150 and of net relocations by 2010 of a further 20,028 posts. The 2004 exercise set 110 PSA targets across government as a whole: targets which included, among others, 14 typically detailed and ambitious ones for the DfES. Here are numbers 4, 5 and 6:

> 4. Halt the year-on-year rise in obesity among children under 11 by 2010 in the context of a broader strategy to tackle obesity in the population as a whole.
>
> 5. Narrow the gap in educational achievement between looked-after children and that of their peers, and improve the educational support and the stability of their lives so that by 2008, 80% of children under 16 who have been looked after for 2.5 years or more years will have been living in the same placement for at least 2 years, or placed for adoption.
>
> 6. Raise standards in English and maths: so that by 2006, 85% of 11 year olds achieve level 4 or above, with this level of performance sustained to 2008; and by 2008, the proportion of schools in which fewer than 65% of pupils achieve level 4 or above is reduced by 40%.

But it was not all targets and auditing with this government in relation to public services. There was also funding to help public service providers meet the targets agreed with them, and that funding came from this New Labour government in two forms. It came as public money, to all services and in considerable volume, and it came as private money, to some services and on a limited scale. The flow of public money did not cause serious political difficulties or attract much public censure of New Labour in power, but the flow of private money definitely did.

As we saw earlier, the idea of bringing private firms into partnership with government in the provision of public services had come into vogue in the early 1990s, as the then Conservative government began to run out of publicly-owned industries to privatize. In the last years of Tory rule, the Treasury signed a string of PFIs, primarily to help finance transport developments and prison expansion: in total value, just over £7.5 billion by 1997. New Labour signalled in its 1997 election manifesto that it intended to continue the practice, promising to speed up the process and manage it better, as one way of responding to what it then called a 'dangerously run down infrastructure'.[25] And once in power, if initially more slowly than its manifesto suggested, the government did begin to do exactly that. In its first year, over 80 new PFI projects were commissioned to the value of £10.5 billion, 60% of them by John Prescott's new monster Department of Environment, Transport and the Regions. The fast rail link to the Channel Tunnel was responsible for £3 billion of that total on its own, but there were also flagship deals struck to build hospitals and to modernize schools. Once underway, the process quickened; to the point indeed that by 2003, on the government's own figures, the PFI programme had expanded to 617 projects with a total value of £56 billion (some 11% of total investment in public services), and 'PFI investment [had] delivered over 600 operational new public facilities, including 34 hospitals and 239 new and refurbished schools'.[26] By then, 90% of all hospital building and school refurbishment was PFI-based, and public finance initiatives had become just part of a much wider set of government–private sector joint ventures, known collectively as public–private partnerships.

In a typical PFI,[27] private firms compete with each other for the right to supply the capital for a particular investment project, to build the facility to meet government-specified requirements, and to maintain and manage it to an agreed code for a specified number of years (typically 15–30); all this in return for a guaranteed annual payment from the public purse. The claims made for those partnerships, first by Conservative ministers and then by New Labour ones, were considerable. They were presented as the conduit for an extra flow of investment resources, one that was in many cases 'off the books', and so not subject to the Chancellor's fiscal rules on public sector borrowing. They were presented as a vehicle for bringing private sector expertise and cost-consciousness into the public sector, and they were presented as great value for money to taxpayers, who received modernized social services without having to stump up the capital sums necessary for their creation. The Treasury put it this way, in its cautious review of the PFIs signed and implemented in Labour's first six years in office:

> Evidence to date suggests PFI is appropriate where there are major and complex capital projects with significant ongoing maintenance requirements. Here the private sector can offer project management skills, more innovative design and risk management expertise that can bring substantial benefits. Where it is effective, PFI helps ensure that desired service standards are maintained, that new services start on time and facilities are completed on budget, and that the assets built are of sufficient quality to remain of high standard throughout their life....However PFI is unlikely to deliver value for money in other

areas, for example where the transaction costs of pursuing PFI are disproportionate compared to the value of the project or where fast-paced technological change makes it difficult to establish requirements in the long term.[28]

The caution in that report was well-founded, because by 2003 the claims made for public–private partnerships were being heavily contested across the labour movement as a whole, and indeed had in 2002 been the cause of a rare defeat for the leadership at their normally impeccably-managed party conference. Critics did not buy any of the claims that were being made, and grew increasingly irritated over time as those claims were continually repeated.[29] They saw PFIs as privatization by another name, the thin end of a commercial wedge that could only, over time, corrode the communal ethos of public service provision by commodifying the services provided.[30] They feared that, for PFI to be worthwhile for the private firms involved, the wages and working conditions of their employees would have to be set lower than those prevailing in the rest of the public sector;[31] and they just didn't buy the 'off the books' and 'value for money' claims that tripped so easily from ministerial lips. Why go off the books, they asked, when the scale of public investment was nowhere near the limits set by Gordon Brown's fiscal rules? And where was the 'value for money' in schemes that avoided laying a tax burden on this generation only at the cost of laying a heavier one on generations to come? Even the normally loyal IPPR, via its chief economist, castigated 'the idea that the government could not afford new schools and hospitals' as 'economically illiterate'. 'It's just wrong.' Peter Robinson said, 'to present the PFI as a free lunch from the City. It is simply an alternative and more expensive financing method.'[32] For 'every penny raised for PFI schools, hospitals and prisons...is paid for by the public purse, plus interest, plus profits'.[33] To its critics therefore, PFI was spending 'on the never-never: future state expenditure...inflated as a result of the PFI boom',[34] and they wanted none of it.

Not surprisingly, ministers moved quickly onto the defensive as the critique of public–private partnerships intensified; though it was a defensiveness that was always balanced in Blairite circles by a near messianic commitment to the use of private funds nonetheless. There were important concessions on detail. The trade unions were allowed 'to vet but not to veto' the early PFIs signed by New Labour,[35] and in 2001 they won from the Prime Minister a guarantee that no deals would be struck that worsened employee terms and conditions of service.[36] Both Stephen Byers and Alan Milburn, when respectively heading the Trade and Health departments, were obliged to balance their enthusiasm for the mobilization of private funds in their respective areas of responsibility by commitments on the abolition of a two-tier labour force; and the Treasury, in reviewing the overall record in 2003, emphasized time and again that private investments were only a tiny fraction of total investment in the public services, and that the public provision of such investment funds was rising, would rise further, and was anyway already at record levels.

Indeed from Gordon Brown by 2003 there were signs of a reluctance to carry public–private partnerships much further. That was very much the force of his Social Market Foundation address, and particularly of its strategically chosen example of 'health care' as an area in which public provision was sacrosanct. It was also very much the message laid out by his closest advisors as internal wrangling over the desirability and future of foundation hospitals peaked later in 2003. But even that address included this strong defence of PFI in its right place and under tight controls. 'It must be right', Gordon Brown said,

> ...that the government seeks to secure, over the long term, the most cost-effective infrastructure for our public services. PFI enables us to do this by binding in the private sector into open and accountable long term relationships with the public sector aimed at securing a proper sharing of risk and access to private service managerial expertise and innovative ideas to secure better public services....So there should be no principled objection against PFI expanding into new areas where the public sector can procure a definite product adequately and at no risk to its integrity, and where the private sector has a core skill the public sector can benefit and learn from.[37]

What the Chancellor defended in qualified terms, his Prime Minister then regularly advocated in even stronger and less qualified ones. 'The notion that', by using private finance in public sector capital projects, 'the government has gone anti-public service is fatuous', Tony Blair announced in his first newspaper interview after his 2001 election victory. 'I believe strongly in the public service ethos: that is why I am trying to reform and deliver better public services, not privatize them.'[38] 'There is a nonsense often written and spoken about the role of the private sector', he said, but

> ...we should never forget the public are not ideologues, they are realists. If you are knocked down in the street and you are taken to a brand new PFI built hospital, rather than a run-down Victorian hospital

built, incidentally, entirely by the private sector, then you are probably relieved rather than angry....A mother who is shown round the new suite of computers at her child's secondary school is not going to berate the headteacher who tells her that it came through an enterprising deal with a computer company....Where it makes sense to use private or voluntary sectors better to deliver public services, we will.[39]

In that spirit, ministers consistently emphasized that the use of private funds was only a part, and a small part at that, of an overall expansion of spending and capital investment on the public services that has occurred on their watch; and for their second parliament at least, there was much substance to this claim. But not for the first: for, as we saw earlier, under New Labour in its first term in office, public spending as a percentage of GDP actually *fell*: from 40.8% of GDP to 38.1%. It was only in the second term that their policies began to inch the share of economic resources moving through the public sector up to a projected new plateau of 42% of GDP for the years from 2004–05 to 2007–08. Of course, given that GDP also continued to rise, the government found itself able to increase public expenditures in real terms at the same time, especially for the two sectors that it most privileged: health and education. Sustained GDP growth also allowed New Labour to reverse the shrinkage in public sector employment that had been such a feature of the Conservative years. More than 7 million people had worked in the public sector in 1979. Less than 5 million had worked there as New Labour came to power. By 2004, however, both private and public sector employment had grown significantly, and had done so at pretty much the same rate. It would be quite wrong to think that New Labour in its first two parliaments markedly altered the balance of employment across the public–private divide. It did not, but within the public sector itself, New Labour policy did shift employment into education and into the health service, and out of other local and central government services. Between 1997 and 2003 an extra 257,000 people found employment in the education sector, and an extra 216,000 found employment with the NHS:[40] the two sectors of public provision on which, along with law and order, the Prime Minister began increasingly to insist that he and his government's record ought properly to be judged.

Going for the foundations

Making that judgement, however, was no easy matter by the middle of Labour's second term. For by then the party itself was sharply divided on the desirability of the chosen line of march. It was divided on the line of march in Iraq.[41] It was divided on the line of march in higher education; and it was divided, from the bottom to the very top of the party, on the desirability of foundation hospitals.

'Foundation hospitals' were the legacy left by New Labour's second Secretary of State for Health to its third, and were the particular *bête noire* of its first. Divisions at the top rarely come more visibly than that. Alan Milburn initiated them.[42] John Reid introduced them, and Frank Dobson denounced them as a threat to the very foundation of the NHS itself. Foundation status was the prize that Alan Milburn wanted to offer to successful hospital trusts, allowing them to own and manage their own assets and retain their surpluses, while being free from detailed control by the Department of Health, free to pay their staff more than nationally-agreed settlements, and free to raise private funds for investment purposes, subject only to the monitoring of an independent regulator. To their advocates, these freedoms were an incentive to local managers to make health provision by their hospitals more efficient, dynamic and responsive to patients, and by 2003 the Department of Health had policy in place to raise all hospitals to foundation status by 2008. But to their critics, the creation of such hospitals marked a dangerous turn of policy: with better hospitals sucking resources away from poorer ones, so opening the door to a two-tier health service which would widen, rather than reduce, existing inequalities in health care provision between geographical regions and social classes. The critics of the 'foundation hospital' idea feared that such 'three-star status' hospitals would become in reality *private* institutions within a public health service, perhaps initially only in their attitudes and practices, but eventually in their standing and funding as well.[43] The critics feared, that is, that, unless things changed, 'the Labour Government's health policies will mean the end of the NHS'.[44]

By the time Frank Dobson launched this critique of foundation hospitals, he had been out of office for over four years. His therefore was a critique from the backbenches, free of the constraints of office. The Chancellor's, by contrast, was not. It was in consequence more muted, and as often focused on the freedom of such hospitals to account for their investment programmes 'off the books' and outside Treasury controls as it was focused on the principle of local institutional autonomy as such, but the critique was potent nonetheless. In an address full of praise for the Secretary of State for Health, the Chancellor still found space to say:

The market for health care is dominated by the combination of, on the one hand, chronically imperfect and asymmetric information, and the potentially catastrophic and irreversible outcome of healthcare decisions based on that information and, on the other, the necessity of local clusters of medical and surgical specialisms. This means that, while in a conventional well-functioning market the price set by the producer is the most efficient, in health not only is the consumer not sovereign but a free market in health will not produce the most efficient price for its services or a fair deal for its consumers....The asymmetry between the consumer as patient...and the producer [leaves] the consumer unable – as in a conventional market – to seek out the best product at the lowest price....[And] market failures do not only exist because of asymmetry of information and the irreversibility of decisions, but because local emergency hospitals are – in large part – clusters of essential medical and surgical specialities and have characteristics that make them akin to natural local monopolies.[45]

Alan Milburn was sufficiently stung to immediately hold a press conference with the new Secretary of State for Education, Charles Clarke, to defend the view that standards in education and health could best be improved by an extension of consumer choice. Less than a week after the Brown Social Market Foundation address, Milburn went on record that

> ...most markets operate on the basis of what is called information asymmetry. If you go and buy a Ford, the company will probably know more about its faults than you do. But it is not true in this more informed and inquiring world, where the internet is redistributing knowledge as never before, that patients do not know things. Patients increasingly do![46]

In the fight between the Treasury and the Department of Health on whether foundation hospitals would be free to borrow and invest in excess of Treasury guidelines, the Treasury eventually won, but on the existence of foundation hospitals *per se*, the victory so far has gone elsewhere. It has gone to the 'modernizers', to those who equate reform with the Blairite agenda of modelling public service provision as closely as possible to the practice of the best of the private sector.

In truth, this outcome is not surprising, for the fight over foundation hospitals, though in the moment intense, was only one stage in a process of commodification and marketization of health care that had been underway since the early 1990s: a process that actually stretched back to, and indeed well before, the Dobson years as Secretary of State for Health. Maybe some Rubicon-moment was crossed by the Milburn proposal on foundation hospitals – Frank Dobson obviously thought so – but others, including Milburn's successor as Secretary of State for Health, John Reid, equally clearly did not. For them, the introduction of foundation hospitals was simply another element in a consistent and broadly-based process of health reform that stretched back to the beginnings of New Labour in power: a pattern of reform that was now geared 'to giving patients real choice to go elsewhere for treatment, paid for by the NHS if they are waiting too long'.[47] It is true that in opposition prior to 1997, the Labour Party had indeed opposed reforms of the NHS based on the introduction of an 'internal market', but once in office that principled opposition, as in other areas, had discreetly and quickly given way to a technocratic resetting of an inherited system. New Labour didn't label the administrative processes it called into being in the NHS in its 1997 White Paper in quite the manner of its Conservative predecessor. The Tories had organized the GPs as individual 'fund holders' working with local health authorities to buy services from hospital trusts. New Labour replaced local health authorities and individual GP fund holders with 'primary care groups' doing much the same thing, while imposing on hospital trusts a statutory duty to improve the quality of health care. But though the incoming government, in line with its manifesto commitments, formally replaced the NHS's 'internal market' by something it called 'integrated care', and offered what it called a 'third way' in health administration that was 'based on partnership and driven by performance', in reality *The New NHS: Modern and Dependable* changed very little. The NHS did come to possess a more complex system for monitoring performance – Frank Dobson's White Paper anticipated the creation of a new performance framework, tracking six indicators that included efficiency, fair access, effective delivery of appropriate healthcare and general health improvement. It also anticipated the creation of a Commission for Health Improvement,[48] a series of National Service Frameworks, and a National Institute for Clinical Excellence: all geared to 'raising quality standards, increasing efficiency and driving performance'.[49] But otherwise New Labour's NHS prior to the 2001 general election differed from the Conservatives only in degree,[50] and it certainly shared with its predecessor more than a similarity of internal procedures. It also shared a generalized shortage of investment and cash.

By 2000, all that was beginning to change. Under clear electoral pressure on the issue of public provision, the New Labour government began to push greater and greater resources into the health system: £65.4 billion in 2002–03, £87.2 billion by 2005–06 and £105.6 billion by 2007–08 – overall an increase in spending on the health service of more than half in cash terms and a third in real terms between 2000 and 2005, to bring the UK up towards the European average on health spending. In doing so, as across the rest of the public sector, the government traded money for reform. The Treasury under Gordon Brown was the key player here and, as elsewhere, Treasury directives set both the line of policy and its limits. There were limits. The Treasury commissioned the Wanless Report in 2001, which came down definitively on the side of a National Health Service financed out of general taxation, and providing health care free at the point of use.[51] There was to be no major privatization of an underfunded NHS. If underfunding was to end, taxation (as in the 2002 budget) would have to rise. But by the same token, there was to be no funding without reform, and the issue over which internal disagreement then grew within and between the government and its parliamentary supporters was the direction and mechanisms of the reforms that New Labour required.

In 2000 the new Secretary of State for Health produced a radical new ten-year plan for the NHS that prefigured those reform terms. The plan was big on vision, and ambitious on targets. The department set the vision. The Treasury negotiated the targets. The NHS was then reset to deliver them. It was partly a matter of funding, but it was also a matter of internal change. The targets were ambitious, and the change commensurately large. So too was the vision.

> A health service fit for the 21st Century: a health service designed around the patient…an NHS where staff are not rushed off their feet and constantly exhausted; where careers are developed, not stagnant; where staff are paid properly for good performance; and where child care is provided in every hospital. Ours is a vision of a renewed public service ethos, a system that values the dedication of staff and believes that trust is still the glue that binds the NHS together.[52]

The targets included significant reductions in waiting time (down to three months for any stage of treatment by 2008), and a commitment to fast access to front line services (within 24 hours to a primary care professional, and 48 hours to a GP, by 2002); all to be delivered by substantial increases in the number of beds, consultants, GPs and other health professionals. They also included commitments on the equality and quality of care, with more cancer screening, cleaner hospitals, more private rooms, and better standards of care for the old. By 2005, the

White Paper said, 'the traditional waiting list will become a thing of the past': waiting lists for hospital appointments and admissions will by then have been replaced by a booking system. By 2005 as well, a new generation of modern hospitals will be under construction, and half of all the hospitals then operating would have new quality controls on the food they provide: with cleanliness and food quality by then subject to annual published independent audits. *The NHS Plan: A Plan for Investment, a Plan for Reform* set extremely high goals for the service and for the government that funded it, and so, of course, set an extremely large number of hostages to fortune.

The government, of course, was determined to be the victim of none of them: so in return for the extra money and the resources it offered to the health service, it insisted upon the hitting of performance targets by the institutionalization of change. 'Reform of the supply side' was how the Department of Health described it in 2002, a strengthening of incentives to better performance within the newly agreed architecture of primary care trusts, national service agreements and the NHS Modernization Agency. There were to be new contracts for consultants and GPs, new roles for nurses, midwives and therapists, and new structures of pay. Primary Care Trusts were to be given the freedom to purchase care from 'the most appropriate provider – be they public, private or voluntary'. Hospitals were to switch their payments systems to one geared to results – hospitals doing more were to get more – and patient choice was explicitly extended. By 2005, the plan was that 'all patients and their GPs [would] be able to book appointments at both a time and a place that is convenient to the patient', and that place could include 'NHS hospitals locally or elsewhere, diagnostic or treatment centres, private hospitals or hospitals overseas'. 'Diversity in supply' was now the aim, foundation hospitals one way of delivering it, in an NHS in which funding was increasingly to be devolved to locally-run Primary Care Trusts. 'Fundamental changes in job design and work organization' was the other aim, for an NHS in which performance was now to be monitored by 'a new tough independent healthcare regulator/inspectorate covering both the [public] and the private sector'. The government, the Department of Health announced in 2002, was 'determined to ensure that additional funding [was] backed by independent oversight of how resources were used',[53] and the Treasury for its part was determined that that oversight would squeeze ever greater efficiencies out of the NHS year on year – to the point, indeed, that the Chancellor set a 38% staff reduction target for the Department of Health in his 2004 budget statement, and an annual 2.5% per year productivity target for the health system.[54]

For the Blairite wing of the party, even this was not quite enough. Reform also had to involve the making of an explicit and public concordat with the private sector, in addition to the creation within the NHS of structures and processes that drew heavily on successful private sector models. Frank Dobson, who was definitely not a Blairite, had quietly issued directions in 1998 that the NHS should draw on spare capacity in the private sector only as a last resort, and only after notifying regional NHS offices, but at Tony Blair's behest, Alan Milburn turned that hostility to the private sector completely around.[55] The 2000 *NHS Plan* laid out the details of a remarkable agreement between the NHS and its private competitor in the field of long term and clinical care, the Independent Hospitals Association: a grandly titled 'concordat' that allowed the NHS and the private sector systematically and on a regular basis to exchange patients, share or lease each other's facilities, and jointly participate in local health planning and data exchange. Milburn saw no danger or surrender of principle in this offer of a share of the NHS 'market' to the private sector.[56] Patients transferred by the NHS to private care would still receive treatment free at the point of delivery, and for him at least, 'the relationship between the NHS and the private sector [was] not a one-night stand. It [was] a long-term relationship in the interest of NHS patients receiving better NHS services.'[57] But his critics remained extremely uneasy about the impact of commodification and decentralization on the NHS's ability to provide equality of treatment for all NHS patients, and to maintain the public service ethos that guaranteed access to health on the basis of need rather than ability to pay. 'The sick can't shop around,' Roy Hattersley said, 'life in the health service isn't like that': but foundation hospitals will certainly be able to 'cherry-pick the most remunerative and glamorous services'. 'The private sector,' he said, 'is being insinuated into the NHS through the back door.'[58] It was a fear of backdoor privatization that was shared by many.

By 2003–04 indeed, that unease ran so wide and deep across the various institutions of the labour movement that the government felt obliged significantly to limit the freedoms that foundation hospitals would enjoy, particularly their freedom to take more private patients and to poach skilled staff by paying more than union-negotiated rates. Those concessions were not enough, however, to prevent defeats for government policy on foundation hospitals at both the TUC and the party conference in 2003, or to avoid defeat in the Lords and near-defeat in the Commons. The government majority on its Health Bill slipped to just 35 in May 2003 and to 17 in November 2003, kept from defeat in November only on the promise of a moratorium on new foundation hospitals pending an independent review. Yet defeats and promises notwithstanding, the department created foundation hospitals anyway: 25 in April 2004, and 32 the following October.

No child left behind

By then, the Government's backbench critics were really crying foul. The 32 new foundation hospitals were launched by John Reid as 'wave 1a' to get round that moratorium promise about no more such hospitals after the first wave! 'How do you sue a government for breach of promise?' Frank Dobson wanted to know, and he was not alone.[59] For by early 2004 this New Labour government was at loggerheads with its backbenchers on more than foundation hospitals. It was at loggerheads with them on Iraq, of course, and it was at loggerheads with them on the funding of higher education. In the education sector as in the health one, by 2003–04 the New Labour drive to 'modernize' the provision of public services was increasingly straining the loyalty of core Labour supporters across the whole of the government's reform agenda. As Frank Dobson put it, speaking for far more people than himself:

> I think we are in very dodgy territory now. I was concerned to bring together as one problem foundation hospitals and a lot of stuff in education....It seemed to me that there was a pattern emerging, and we needed to put some chocks under the wheels.[60]

Because it was, the political scrap about top-up fees early in 2004 was to a significant degree a fight about other things as well. The crucial vote came only a day before the Hutton Report was to be published on the government's involvement in the events leading to the death of Dr David Kelly. There was in consequence a huge 'unease with policy on Iraq' dimension to the closeness of the government's margin on the fees issue – not to mention also a huge element of dissatisfaction with the direction and style of Tony Blair's leadership, and in certain quarters of the Parliamentary Labour Party (PLP) at least, a huge desire to see him replaced by Gordon Brown as Prime Minister.[61] But there was also, in that vote, genuine disagreement with the policy line adopted on what had become by then a long-standing problem area for New Labour's education policy.

In 1997 the government had inherited a university system in which public funding per student had fallen systematically over two decades, as the number of students involved in it had grown. Spending per student in 1995 was only 58% of the level of public support per student in 1976. Yet though the number of students had risen, the class structuring of their entry had not: in 1997 only 10% of children from social classes IV and V went to university, as against 60% of the children born into social classes I and II. Those full-time students still received a means-tested maintenance grant from the government, as part-time and further education students did not: a grant frozen but not abolished by the Conservatives, and one supplemented by low-interest loans that left graduating students in significant amounts of debt. New Labour's first move here was to abolish the maintenance grant entirely, and to replace it with a means-tested flat fee for university education of £1,000 per student per year. Counter-intuitive as that might seem as policy for a party of the centre-left, it was presented by David Blunkett, then Secretary of State for Education – and in the event presented successfully to the 1997 Labour Party conference – as a route to greater equality in access to, and payment for, what he termed the 'privilege of university education'. For New Labour in its first term freed low-income students of the burden of their newly-introduced fee for university education, and made available to all students access to virtually interest-free loans that were repayable only after graduation, and only then by graduates whose salaries reflected the bonus in wages that a degree still brought in most of the UK's labour markets.

By 2001 however, that particular settlement was coming unstuck. It was coming unstuck at the student end, as evidence mounted of the sheer scale of debt accumulated by the vast majority of students in higher education in the UK, and of the amount of part-time or even full-time paid work that they were in consequence obliged to seek alongside their university studies.[62] It was also coming unstuck by divisions within the university community itself, as the most prestigious institutions sought the right to charge top-up fees that reflected the greater market value of their degrees over those of others. New Labour went to the country in 2001 explicitly committed, in its manifesto, *not* to introduce such top-up fees, but by 2003 that was exactly what the government was proposing to do.

Between 2001 and 2003, first Estelle Morris and then Charles Clarke, Blunkett's successors as Secretaries of State for Education, repeatedly chewed over – in private and occasionally in public – the relative strengths and weaknesses of loans, fees, graduate taxes and maintenance grants as ways of meeting New Labour's specific commitments on university entrance targets and its general ones on social inclusion and equality of opportunity. At various stages of that period of internal reflection, they and other ministers discreetly briefed the press on their preferences one way or the other. But by 2003 the course was set. The Prime Minister had come out in favour of top-up fees, payable after graduation only if salary permitted, and supplemented by maintenance grants for the poorest students. So too eventually did his Secretary of State. Significant elements within both the Cabinet and the PLP, by contrast, did not, fearing the re-emergence of the binary system in higher education and a further barrier to university entry by students from low-income families. In the end the vote was as close as any experienced by New Labour in power. Tony Blair and Charles Clarke did prevail, but the victory was a Pyrrhic one. In January 2004, they won their top-up fees by a parliamentary majority of only five.

In truth, it was rather strange that the big fight within the PLP on education policy should have occurred around a higher education issue, because until the middle of New Labour's second term the reform of higher education had been low on the DfEE's priority list. New Labour entered office with educational reform as its stated first priority – as we saw earlier, 'education, education, education' had been the 1997 mantra – but its main goals and concerns were with the school system and the pre-school years, and with issues of standards and performance rather than funding *per se*. It is true that in Labour's second term the focus shifted slightly: from primary to secondary education, and from a single-minded concern with standards to a wider set of issues – those of parental choice and private sector involvement in what the Prime Minister then called a 'post-comprehensive' era – but in both terms New Labour got to the universities late. Like the children whose educational standards they wished to raise, New Labour started with the very young.

The commitment to raising educational standards within the school system was signalled by David Blunkett immediately he became opposition spokesperson on education in 1994. 'Our first and absolute priority', he said in his first interview in that position, 'is to get the message across that standards and achievement are the top of our agenda.' 'I have given priority', he said, to shifting the party's 'profile, so that it is clear we are speaking for pupils and parents in situations...where there has been a failure to meet the potential of young people and where the system has let them down'.[63] New Labour in opposition accordingly and immediately abandoned its hostility to the construction and publication of league tables of school performance, and once in power moved quickly to produce first a White Paper and then an Education Act designed to drive that performance upwards. Teachers were to test children in English and maths when they first entered school, and again when aged nine. An hour a day was to be set aside in each primary school for instruction in literacy and numeracy, and the rest of the curriculum lightened to make that possible. Schools that repeatedly failed to show sufficient progress by their students in these subjects would ultimately be closed and reopened under fresh management. Smaller class sizes for five-, six- and seven-year-olds were phased in, as promised in the manifesto, as were more places for children in pre-school nurseries and kindergartens. Within months of being in office, David Blunkett had made clear his willingness to resign if the target improvements set were not attained: and in the pursuit of that attainment, he had 'named and shamed' a set of failing schools, financed a programme of extra summer school tuition for failing 11-year-olds, lectured parents on the importance of discipline and homework, and issued the first ever set of guidelines on how much homework should be done, and when.

His December 1997 *Schools Standards and Framework* Bill also introduced a pilot set of Education Zones in some of England and Wales' most deprived areas: zones in which extra resources, drawn from the local business community as well as from the local education authority, were sent to a linked set of primary and secondary schools, in order that they might then buy the services of teachers with advanced skills and of 'super heads' with the managerial capacity to run more than one school at any one time. In those zones, schools were allowed to replace the national curriculum with one more focused on the acquisition of basic skills, and their managers were allowed to ignore national agreements on teacher pay, conditions and length of the working week. In those zones too, local authority control of the schools was replaced by a partnership arrangement, with the local authority sharing control with local training and enterprise councils, businesses and community organizations. The first 25 such zones came into being between September 1998 and January 1999, and attracted extra funding from the government of £75 million and from the business community of £19 million.[64] They joined a series of new specialist schools inherited from the Conservatives by New Labour – secondary schools emphasizing technology, language, arts or sport in their curriculum – where again supplementary private funding helped to bring extra resources to a hard-pressed publicly-provided school system. David Blunkett did not close these, any more than he closed the grammar schools that New Labour also inherited. On the contrary, he welcomed and encouraged them. 'Specialist schools', he said,

> ...are at the heart of my vision – and that of the new Government – of an education system where education caters for the individual strengths of children rather than assuming a bland sameness for all. Some people

were surprised that the government wanted to continue the specialist schools programme. They do not understand the philosophy of the new government. We welcomed this great opportunity to further the cause of school improvement and school diversity....Comprehensive education must modernize. It cannot forever be stuck in the past – what some might see as a sixties time warp. High and improving standards, setting by subject ability and the ability to foster specialist talents, must be all part of the way forward....We must have more specialist schools which offer diversity within a single campus. We must allow children to play to their individual strengths and aptitudes – those who want to see sameness for all are betraying our children. We must move from an education system which caters for the producers to one which puts the needs of the consumers – pupils and their parents – at the heart of its approach. [65]

That set the tone. Under New Labour even more than under their predecessors, the DfEE became proactive in the setting and raising of educational standards, by intervening directly to close failing schools and by working with local business leaders to develop and fund schools of excellence. From 1998, the educational targets set were linked to DfEE funding through the Treasury's system of public service agreements, and were increased in level as one Comprehensive Spending Review gave way to the next. From 1998, the Chief Inspector of Schools, Chris Woodhead, and the organization (Ofsted) that he headed, became an ever more visible and powerful presence in the lives of the UK's half a million teachers,[66] and from 1998 too, the door was open to the active participation of the private sector in the fringes of the public school system in which those teachers worked. In fact, public funding for education was slow to grow in New Labour's first term. For all the government's manifesto commitment to make education their first priority, as we saw earlier the percentage of GDP going to education actually *fell* to 4.5% in 1999: a casualty of the decision to stick for two years to the Conservative spending limits, and a level lower than under Margaret Thatcher.[67] Only after 1999, and only at any speed after 2002, did public expenditure on the school system then rise: and when it did, it came with the by-now standard requirement for systemic and systematic change.

In New Labour's second term, the bulk of that pressure for change fell first on the secondary school sector, and then on higher education. 'The boldest reform programme for 50 years', the Prime Minister called it, in characteristic fashion[68] – a programme for a 'post-comprehensive' age. Comprehensives had helped end selection in the 1960s and 1970s, Tony

Blair conceded, but in his view were now failing to meet the needs of children, particularly the brightest. He wanted to see 'every one of the country's secondary schools build their own individual ethos – through schemes such as business-led specialist schools, church schools and private-sector backed City Academies'. We need, he said, 'to change the law to allow external sponsors – from the business and voluntary sectors and from within the education world itself – to play a far greater role in the management of schools'. And not just in the management of failing schools: it was the Prime Minister's view in 2001 that 'if a successful school want[ed] to engage with reputable external sponsors, this should not only be allowed – it should be strongly encouraged'.[69]

The Green Paper, later White Paper and the Education Bill that followed then all applied the lessons learned in New Labour's first term on how to raise standards in primary schools to those same children now in the secondary sector. 'The central task for this parliament,' the Schools Minister said, 'is to start a process of improvement in secondary schools as profound as that kick-started in the last parliament in primary schools.'[70] Ministers were particularly concerned with underperformance by pupils early in their secondary education, as evidenced by the stagnation in test results for 14-year-olds in English and maths. They responded in a characteristically New Labour fashion. That is, they set very demanding targets for each local education authority in turn: so, for example, requiring that 68% of 11-year-olds be at grade level in English by 2002, 72% by 2003, and 76% by 2004. In the policy documents it issued either side of the 2001 general election, the government proposed that testing for children aged 11–14 be brought forward one year, that bright students be encouraged to take their GSCEs a year early, and that a new set of league tables be produced, based on the national results achieved by 14-year-olds and amended to include a value-added measure, one demonstrating the contribution that each school made to their pupils' rising level of performance. The government also proposed the creation of a national academy for talented youth, and changes in the law to allow the wider participation in secondary school government to which the Prime Minister clearly attached such importance. This was all very standard New Labour stuff.

Most significantly of all, in its 2001 education White Paper, *Schools: Achieving Success*, the government proposed the creation of many more of the specialist schools it had inherited from the Conservatives (1,500 by 2006) with new subject specialisms in engineering, science and business, and it proposed to fund the creation of more beacon schools and more City Academies, and to give extra financial help to religious schools. All these categories of school drew on private as well as public funds for their maintenance and growth, and all of them exercised some element of selectivity in their admissions policy. Not surprisingly, therefore, the proposed expansion in their numbers brought down on ministerial heads a widespread accusation that selection was being reintroduced by the back door. 'Watch my lips,' David Blunkett had said to rapturous applause at the Labour Party conference in 1995, 'no selection by examination or interview'; but by 2001 his lips were not in charge of education, and with specialist schools able to apply for extra funding and to choose 10% of their students on the basis of aptitude, selectivity in entry to differentially-resourced secondary schools was definitely on the march again.

It was not a march, however, that went either unnoticed or unchallenged: so challenged in fact that, at the Labour Party conference in 2004, the new Secretary of State for Education, Charles Clarke, had to promise to halt the drift to selection in secondary education.[71] Throughout this entire process of educational reform, ministers found themselves periodically at loggerheads, not simply with the 'usual suspects' on the parliamentary backbenches, but also with the leaders (and occasionally the members) of the various teaching unions. It was the union leadership who regularly voiced the generalized concern about the reintroduction of selectivity. It was the union leadership who tried to slow down the various ministerial attempts to introduce performance-related pay, or to solve shortages in the supply of particular subject teachers (especially maths and science) by awarding salary bonuses, bursaries and the like. And it was the union leadership, joined this time by the bulk of their membership, who challenged the government on the adverse impact on the teaching process of the presence of so many performance indicators, and on the adverse workload consequences for teachers of so much testing, report writing and extra training.

The testing controversy actually sparked a ballot in 2003 by the National Union of Teachers (NUT) on a possible boycott, and though that boycott was avoided,[72] unease with the pedagogic consequences of excessive testing remains widespread in the teaching profession.[73] The workload issue came to a head in 2001–02, when the threat of strike action precipitated first an independent review (which set a 45-hour week target for the average teaching week by 2006) and then a package of measures designed to effect a 20% reduction in the then 53 hours on average actually being worked each week. To a degree, the workload issue was at least temporarily resolved: only the NUT of the teachers' unions has so far declined to sign the new workload agreement. What has not been resolved, however, is the wider sense of unease, evident in various sectors of the education system, about the long-term implications of all this New Labour activism on standards and structures: a sense that too much testing actually distorts the educational process it is meant to enhance, and a fear that the proliferation of types of school, all variously funded, will actually intensify educational inequalities over time. What has not been resolved, that is, is the fear that though the rhetoric is progressive, the policy consequences may not be.

Safe in their hands?

But then that is the underlying issue with New Labour across the entirety of its policy towards the public services. Are they actually safe in New Labour hands? Is the Prime Minister's enthusiasm for extending the role of the private sector within a still predominantly publicly-provided set of services a catalyst for change, as he regularly claims, or is it the harbinger of the replacement of the entire system by one based on market principles and ability to pay, as his critics regularly insist? Tony Blair's view on this is clear, and it is consistent. It is that

> ...to deliver opportunity and security today, public services must be radically recast. Our challenge is to ensure that they are universal – an engine of equality; and personalized – responsive to the rising aspirations of the public. In short, universal services with personalized provision.[74]

But conviction and repetition are no substitute for evidence and truth. Simply because Tony Blair believes it, and repeatedly says it, it doesn't automatically follow that New Labour, by modernizing the public services, is also preserving them. Certainly it is not preserving them in unaltered form, and its salami-slice requirement of regular and permanent change does systematically move the goalposts over time. Specialist schools and the comprehensive system are a case in point. Inherited from the Conservatives, specialist schools were bolstered incrementally during Labour's first term. They were expanded to cover half the country's secondary schools in New Labour's second term, and they are now foreshadowed, in Charles Clarke's 2004 five-year education plan, to completely replace the old comprehensive system by 2010. That five-year plan envisages more and more schools seeking independent foundation status, taking their funding directly from Whitehall and from private sources, and, as they do so, entirely sidelining the old local education authorities that once were the key players in educational provision. This is permanent revolution with a vengeance.

Little wonder then that periodically an issue – such as top-up fees – should suddenly become emblematic of a wider set of concerns. For in relation to the public services, the Labour Party still speaks with two voices. It speaks with a Blairite one, for whom it is 'a defining battle between the forces of conservatism within [the] party who will doom public services to unreformed mediocrity, and the forces of radicalism, led by' the Prime Minister himself. And it speaks with the voice of the rebels, for most of whom 'the struggle is emblematic of exactly the same but with the roles reversed, with them as the doughty defenders of public services from marketization'.[75] The terrain of the battle periodically shifts and its intensity ebbs and flows, but to date at least, the battle itself is as permanent a feature of New Labour in power as is the Prime Minister's desire, in relation to the public services, consistently to 'step up the pace of reform'.[76]

7
The Politics of Social Inclusion

These two faces of the New Labour government – the reforming and the conserving – are not restricted to its education policy. They crop up everywhere, for there seems to be a genuine, and indeed quite legitimate, tension in what New Labour is about. To a far greater degree than in Labour governments in the past, the key figures in this government – and certainly its leader – are in one sense profoundly *conservative*, particularly in social terms. This is not a libertarian government, afraid of order or hostile to traditional institutions like the family. Far from it: this is a government committed to the view that 'families are the core of our society. They should teach right from wrong': one whose initial critique of their predecessors' crime policy was precisely that 'the Conservatives have forgotten the "order" part of "law and order"'.[1] No, this is a government whose leading figures repeatedly insist that, if their policies are new, their values are not, and yet it is also a government that sees itself as engaged in a long-term and wide-ranging programme of fundamental *reform*. It is a government that perennially seeks to conserve the best of the past only by persistently changing many of the key institutions and practices that have come down to it from that past. Being a reforming conservative is never an easy endeavour, and it certainly has not been easy since 1997.

If that was not problem enough, New Labour governments since 1997 have manifested another and related set of tensions as well: those between the devolution of power and the micro-managing of change. The values that New Labour's leading figures have brought to the policy-making process have been progressive ones: values of social justice, democratic accountability, social inclusion, national unity and equality of opportunity if not of outcomes. Those values have indeed been around for a long time on the left in British politics – Tony Blair is quite right to say that – and in the past they regularly underpinned major processes of social engineering. But this time they came packaged in a view of the world that set only a limited role for the state. This after all has been a Labour government committed, at the level of its rhetoric and initial policy stances, to the view that social rights come with individual responsibilities, and that 'the making of one nation is not just a job for government, it is a task for everyone': it is a task that requires governments to tap 'a wider ethic of responsibility'.[2] The whole logic of New Labour's social thinking when in opposition was that power should be devolved, democraticized and spread about, but in office that impulse has weakened over time. New Labour came into power promising constitutional reform, open government and a revitalized civil society. Yet the longer it has been in power, the more that constitutional revolution has slowed, and the more the authoritarianism incipient in its insistence on 'responsibilities' has come incrementally to the fore.

The tension between the democratic and the directional face of the New Labour project was always there, of course: it is simply that its significance was initially buried. When Tony Blair spoke in 1997 of his desire to build a 'compassionate society', he did not hesitate to add that 'it is compassion with a hard edge'. The rhetoric was triumphalist, but the message was tough. The rhetoric: 'the chains of mediocrity have broken, the tired days are behind us, we are free to excel once more. We are free to build that model 21st century nation, to become that beacon to the world.' The message: 'a strong society cannot be built on soft choices. It means fundamental reform of our welfare state, of the deal between citizen and society.' 'Help us,' he asked the party faithful, 'to make Britain that beacon shining throughout the world.'[3] So they did, and yet sadly, over time, it was the hardness rather than the freedom that increasingly caught the sun: a hardness that, in retrospect, was pre-programmed into the problem specification that New Labour adopted in relation to the poor and marginalized in the society it began to govern. For although this was a government that believed that there was a moral as well as an economic case for tackling the Tory legacy of 'an underclass of people cut off from society's mainstream, without any sense of shared purpose',[4] the message that it sent to the members of that underclass was, from the outset, not a conventionally compassionate one. To the very people whose experience of previous social contracts had been so devastating, and who were extraordinarily poor in a society where levels of inequality were extraordinarily high, New Labour did not talk of restitution and recompense. It talked rather of new bargains, new balances of rights and duties, new things that the poor themselves had to do. 'The basis of this modern civic society', the Prime Minister announced, when visiting one such group of the poor in June 1997, 'is an ethic of mutual responsibility or duty. It is something for something. A society where we play by the rules. You only take out what you put in. That's the bargain.'

Oppositions, of course, invariably favour limits on power that governments do not: so the movement here is in no sense unique to this New Labour period of UK politics. What is less common, however, and what has been more disturbing of late, has been the speed and trajectory of that movement. For as New Labour's grip on office weakened after the Iraq war, so too did its hold on progressive positions on things like petty crime, asylum-seeking and immigration. The centre of gravity of policy here shifted significantly over time. Though the 'hardness' was there from the beginning, so too initially was the 'compassion'. After all, the central theme of social policy in New Labour's first term was the targeting of social exclusion; that in its second term was the pursuit of equality of opportunity. These concerns did not go away, but they were eventually replaced in centrality by the pursuit of law and order. The moral – and indeed moralizing – dimension of the New Labour project was focused initially on empowering the excluded, and then on extending opportunities for personal advancement. Not everything that was tried worked, or was unambiguously free of compulsion even when it did – try asking a lone parent 'invited' for a job interview about compulsion in New Labour's welfare-to-work programme – but at least the motivations seemed benign. Not so by 2004, for by then the full weight of New Labour moralizing had been turned against asylum-seekers, illegal immigrants and the anti-social behaviour of the delinquent young. In 1997 New Labour came into power determined to help the poor. By 2004 it was increasingly policing them as well.

Social inclusion

It all started just fine. None of us should doubt either the seriousness of New Labour's commitment in 1997 to the revitalization of social life in the UK, or the quality of the thinking that informed that commitment. On the contrary, the quality is very clear. In social terms, as in economic ones, New Labour came to power armed with a view of what was wrong, and what needed to be done to put it right. What was wrong was social division, and the exclusion of the poor from the benefits of mainstream society. What was needed was a new form of social order. The soon-to-be Prime Minister put it this way in 1996:

For far too long we have defined ourselves as a nation not by what unites us but by what divides us. We have a class-ridden and unequal society; a social fabric which is tattered and torn; and a politics where centralization and secrecy drive out democracy and accountability. The majority of Britains are insecure and unsure of their future. We still have two education systems – one public, one private. We have what amounts to a new 'underclass', cut off and alienated from society. Part of our job is to ensure that the people frozen out of Tory Britain are brought in from the cold, their talents used, their potential developed.... When we talk about strong families, responsibility and duty we are not aping the Tories but recapturing values in which our forebears and supporters believe. Similarly, when we talk about being tough on crime and tough on the causes of crime, it is a message warmly welcomed in housing estates across the land, where people, often trapped by poverty and unemployment, are tormented by criminal behaviour, antisocial or violent neighbours, and drugs. This is not a Tory agenda, but a Labour one....The only way to rebuild social order and stability is through strong values, socially shared, inculcated through individuals, family, government and the institutions of civil society.[5]

New Labour's response to its recognition of the scale and nature of poverty in the UK was the creation of the Social Exclusion Unit within Number 10, charged with nothing less than finding the ideas and the policies that could block the growth of a disaffected underclass and draw them back into the mainstream of society. The 12-strong Unit, trailed in June 1997 and up and running by December, had the Prime Minister's full backing, and indeed initially attracted his endorsement as 'his personal project – the defining difference between his government and the Tories'.[6] Peter Mandelson, who was its first political head, certainly presented it as that important: as a new kind of government institution, able to work through and across departments, to create policies that responded to the multiple causes and consequences of social exclusion. Under New Labour, the term 'social exclusion' came quickly to carry a specific connotation: as 'a shorthand label for what can happen when individuals or areas suffer from a combination of linked problems such as unemployment, poor skills, low incomes, poor housing, high crime environments, bad health and family breakdown'.[7] The government was aware of the cumulative nature of these individual components of the standard 'cycle of deprivation'. It also knew that it had discrete policies addressed to each of them. What it did not have was a unit to link and integrate those policies into a coherent whole. In institutional terms, New

Labour saw the problem of policy ineffectiveness here as primarily the product of poor co-ordination. 'Joined-up government' was the solution, and the Social Exclusion Unit was the key to that joining. As Tony Blair put it as the Unit was launched:

> ...government has to learn to work more coherently. In every poor housing estate you can encounter literally dozens of public agencies – schools, police, probation, youth service....City Challenge Initiatives, English partnerships, careers services – all often doing good work, but all often working at cross-purposes or without adequate communication. This matters because it leads to poor policy and wasted resources – like schools excluding students who then become a huge burden for the police. Our challenge must be to overcome these barriers.

The Prime Minister referred there to the existence of poor housing estates, and certainly in 1997 there were no shortages of those. In fact the Unit initially targeted 1,400 of them, 879 of which were in London alone: seeking to reduce homelessness and school truancy/exclusion among the children living there, and to develop integrated policies on quality of life issues there – mainly crime, drugs, unemployment and community breakdown. The initial pace of investigation and reporting was breathless – the truancy report was in by Easter 1988, the street living report by the same date, the report on quality of life issues on the worst estates by June 1998 – and the follow-up was equally rapid and well publicized: an £800 million 'New Deal for Communities' programme by September 1998 based on 17 estates, funding housing demolition and improvements, improved educational and health facilities, and more job creation and training. It could hardly have been otherwise, given the devastating nature of that first Social Exclusion Unit report, documenting as it did the widening inequalities inherited from Conservative Britain and the associated concentration, in particularly deprived areas, of unemployment, poor housing, high mortality rates, low educational performance, excessive underage pregnancies and high incidence of petty crime. A generation before, the deprived and the privileged had been divided by more than class. They had also been divided by geography; but increasingly in New Labour's new Britain, areas of deprivation and areas of prosperity were often only miles apart. The task of the Social Exclusion Unit was in that sense even more pressing than hitherto. It had to find ways of bringing those deprived estates up to speed, and to do so quickly.

Not, of course, that it was acting alone, for from the outset this integrated approach to the problem of social exclusion sat in a wider set of policies designed to reset the welfare state. New Labour's initial thinking on the nature of that resetting was laid out in a Green Paper in March 1998, *New Ambitions for Our Country: A New Contract for Welfare*. That paper listed eight guiding principles for welfare reform, of which the 'attack social exclusion and help those in poverty' principle was merely number 6. In that paper, the bifurcation in policy that emerged later was clearly foreshadowed: a bifurcation between the 'welfare state' as a set of universally-available public services and 'welfare" – understood in the American fashion – as payments to people unable to sustain themselves by the earning of a paid wage. The commitment to high-quality public services produced the policies discussed in Chapter 6. The reform of welfare centred on moving people from welfare to work, as we saw in Chapter 4. The first of the White Paper's eight principles was of that kind: obliging the government to 'help and encourage people to work where they are capable of doing so', by initiatives of a New Deal kind and by putting more lone parents, and the sick and disabled, 'in touch' with the labour market, as the Green Paper euphemistically put it. In New Labour Britain, rights did indeed come with responsibilities. The government set itself tough new anti-poverty targets, while simultaneously laying on individuals the responsibility 'to work, to support family members, and to save for retirement – unless there are exceptional reasons for not doing so – and not to defraud the taxpayer'.[8]

New Labour began, that is, with a 'stick and carrot' approach to the problem of social exclusion: it began with the 'stick' of reduced benefits if people failed satisfactorily to hunt for work, and the 'carrot' of joined-up policy initiatives to make that hunt easier. Initially, the main policy moves came on the joined-up side, but over time the balance of 'stick' and 'carrot' shifted. For what on the 'carrot' side had started so well eventually lost momentum and political traction. The Prime Minister's agenda filled with other things,[9] and the Social Exclusion Unit settled back into a quieter life. It is true that it continued to produce detailed and extremely high-quality analyses of different aspects of the social exclusion 'problem'. In fact by 2003 there were 29 of these analyses – a veritable library indeed of new research on the mechanisms creating and perpetuating an underclass in the United Kingdom – reports covering such things as the education of children in care, transport and social exclusion, young runaways, and ways of reducing reoffending by ex-prisoners. It is true too that by 2004 the Social Exclusion Unit could – and did – claim significant progress on many of these aspects of the 'problem' because of policy initiatives that either it had triggered or that the Treasury more generally had launched. The main elements of improvement singled out in the 2004 report – in the areas of child poverty, child care provision, reduced unemployment and pensions – were not actually core elements of the exclusion problem as the Unit defined it, but even in relation to the core elements of homelessness, truancy and deprived estates, the Unit was able to report in 2004 some narrowing of the gap on 'rates of employment, educational attainment and teenage contraception'.[10]

But these claims were to a degree disingenuous. For by then the Unit was no longer at the centre of the policy-making process that its reports chronicled. Instead it was obliged to feed its recommendations into the policy-making process through the office of the *Deputy* Prime Minister, and to report its recommendations through a wall of spin. By 2004 there was a visible disjuncture between the way John Prescott's office wrote up the state of progress on social exclusion and the way in which the Social Exclusion Unit itself reported that progress when reflecting on matters alone. To see that, all we have to do is to contrast the list of claims in the 'official' Social Exclusion Unit stocktaking published in December 2004 with the more downbeat estimate of the state of play contained in the Unit's preliminary report published only months before. In the official report, we were told that 'policies are now in place to tackle *all* the main drivers of social exclusion'. In its preliminary report, by contrast, the Unit was clear that only *'some* of the most important drivers of social exclusion [had] been tackled'.[11] 'We have seen some major gains in tackling social exclusion,' the Unit reported in March, 'but there is still a long way to go.' 'Persistent levels of worklessness and concentrations of high unemployment in particular areas' remain; as do persistent and 'significant inequalities in life chances...for a wide range of families – inequalities in employment rates, health, low income and educational attainment...between different social classes, different ethnic groups, and different areas of the country'.[12]

In 2004 the Unit was still calling for renewed and sustained efforts to reach those groups, and characteristically it was focusing that call on the development of better policy and delivery mechanisms – on the generation of better 'joined-up' initiatives. What the Unit was not doing in 2004 was making any public concession to the force of the argument of those who, from the outset, had recognized that its terms of references had been set too narrowly, and that in consequence key drivers of social exclusion were pre-programmed to be missed. For the Social Exclusion Unit was commissioned to solve problems that were embedded in the very core of an unequal society, and yet given only a very limited range of tools with which to tackle them. On the Unit's own evidence, 'the latter part of the twentieth century' had seen 'worsening trends in social exclusion and inequality', social exclusion which then created 'deep and long-lasting problems for individual families' by passing 'from generation to generation'. Yet even so, it was sent into action, as Ruth Lister and others noted at the time, 'with one hand tied behind its back':[13] denied the full range of policy weapons necessary to reach the underlying drivers of poverty in our time. In particular, the New Labour government commissioned the Unit to address the exclusion of the poor while simultaneously ruling out any moves to redistribute income in the society from which the poor were excluded. The poor were supposed to heal themselves, in a society whose central mechanisms of poverty creation were from the outset defined as off-limits to reform. Little wonder then that in the end what the Unit produced was less the diminution of social exclusion than a chronicle of its persistence.

Social opportunity

All this notwithstanding, the fact that the Social Exclusion Unit was able to list a series of improvements in employment rates, child poverty figures and pension provision does speak to an important and consistent element in New Labour's social policy stance since 1997: its commitment to equality of opportunity, and its awareness – certainly an awareness among key New Labour figures – that the ability of individuals to improve their social position does require their acquisition of key assets. In a New Labour understanding of the world, it requires them primarily to acquire the assets of paid work, good schooling and adequate skills. This New Labour government has not been keen on the provision of standardized public services or of ceilings on the ability of people to earn, but it has been keen to break the cycle of deprivation between generations by tackling the sources of child poverty, and it has been keen to encourage the expansion of the middle class by their own meritocratic endeavours.

Tony Blair has been particularly vocal on the superiority and desirability of a meritocratic society, and on the associated need for enhanced social mobility. Indeed, very early in his tenure, he defended his government's then emerging programme on 'poverty and social exclusion' in precisely those terms: saying that 'at the end of it I believe we will have an expanded middle class' since

> ...slowly but surely the old establishment is being replaced by a new, larger, more meritocratic middle class, a middle class characterized by greater tolerance of difference, greater ambition to succeed, greater opportunities to earn a decent living. A middle class that will include

millions of people who traditionally will see themselves as working class, but whose ambitions are far broader than those of their parents and grandparents.[14]

In fact, in the run-ups to both the second and the third general elections of his premiership, Blair made this meritocratic goal a key feature of what New Labour was about. 'As a nation,' he told a North London audience in February 2001, 'we are wasting too much of the talents of too many of the people. The mission of any second term must be this: to break down the barriers that hold people back to create real upward mobility, a society that is open and genuinely based on merit and the equal worth of all.'[15] And when, during that second term, he continued to find that, in spite of his best efforts, 'the truth about the country is that for almost 30 years social mobility has stayed relatively constant', the discovery did not lead to any dilution of this commitment to the creation of a meritocratic alternative to the status quo. On the contrary, it spurred the Prime Minister on. 'I want to see social mobility,' he told the IPPR, 'as it did for decades after the war, rising once again, a dominant feature of British life.'[16]

> Our goal is a Britain in which nobody is left behind; in which people can go as far as they have the talent to go; in which we achieve true equality – equal status and equal opportunity rather than equality of outcome. It must be a Britain in which we continue to redistribute power, wealth and opportunity to the many not the few, to combat poverty and social exclusion, to deliver public services that people can trust and take down the barriers that hold people back.[17]

In this, he was at one with his Chancellor, though Gordon Brown's formulations of so meritocratic a universe were characteristically more economic in focus and more traditionally Labourite in vocabulary. When the Chancellor spoke of replacing 'the old walls of privilege' with 'new paths of opportunity for all', he spoke not of 'meritocracy' but of 'equality of opportunity', and he presented that equality as 'an economic necessity' in the modern world and not just as 'an ethical imperative'. But the basic message was much the same, and the focus on education and skill acquisition was identical. 'We waste too much of the talent of Britain', Gordon Brown told the Bevan Society in 2002, which was why New Labour intended to 'open up the opportunities for education to an extent never before seen in this country, so that every child will have the best possible chance in life'.[18] The result would be a fairer society that was also better placed to compete economically in the world. In the Brown litany, even more than in the Blair one, economic necessity and social justice walked hand-in-hand. We have seen this in Brown speeches before. Here, to reinforce them, is the Chancellor giving the Joseph Rowntree centennial lecture in July 2004.

> ...what has always been right on ethical grounds can now, today, be seen as good for the economy too. In our information-age economy, the most important resource of a firm or a country is not its raw materials, or a favoured geographical location, but the skills and the potential of the whole workforce....In an industrial age, the denial of opportunity offended many people. Today, in an economy where skills are the essential means of production, the denial of opportunity has become an unacceptable inefficiency and brake on prosperity. Full prosperity for a company or a country can only be delivered – and Britain properly equipped for the future – if we get the best out of all people. And that cannot happen without opportunity that taps the widest pool of talent.[19]

As we have seen, in a New Labour understanding of the world, the route out of poverty lies through entry into paid work: hence the New Deal strategy of welfare-to-work that has underpinned New Labour's employment programme since 1997. But getting people to work, for New Labour, has been more than an answer to their poverty. It has also been an answer to the poverty of their children. For to their immense credit, the New Labour leadership announced early their determination to break the cycle of deprivation by designing policies to halve child poverty in a decade and to abolish it in a generation. Their sharpest condemnation of the Thatcher years lay here: in 'the return in the last three decades of the life cycle of poverty...the great and unacceptable concentration of poverty amongst households with young children'. The Chancellor condemned that as 'the greatest indictment of our country in this generation and the greatest challenge for us all',[20] and the Prime Minister led the way with the now widely-cited policy commitment. 'Our historic aim', he said, 'will be for ours to be the first generation to end child poverty. It will take a generation. It is a 20-year mission, but I believe it can be done.'[21] Done to 25% by 2004, to 50% by 2010, and completed by 2020. It was a remarkable commitment.

Policy has followed that commitment in numerous and important ways, as we have seen. There have been tax changes to create a guaranteed minimum income for working families with children. There have been tax changes to make the combination of work and child care easier. Lone parents have been 'eased' back into paid work wherever possible, on the grounds that their children constitute three-quarters of the poor. There are now plans afoot to provide day care for working parents at each end of the school day, and the government has developed a full programme of pre-school initiatives designed to strengthen the skills and learning capacities of children from deprived backgrounds. True, the target has slipped a bit. These days it has been scaled back into ensuring that by 2020 'the child poverty rate in Britain is among the best in Europe',[22] but nonetheless progress has been considerable. Certainly the Institute for Fiscal Studies felt as late as December 2003 that the government was well on its way to reducing the rate of child poverty by 25% by 2004, understanding 'poverty' here as less than 60% of average income, and there was general agreement by 2004 that as many as a million children had been lifted out of poverty since New Labour came to power. Ominously however, by 2004 it was still the case that more than half the children living in poverty had a parent in work, and that for them at least the New Labour claim that 'work is the best route out of poverty' simply had not proved to be valid.[23]

This governmental concern with equality of opportunity certainly stretched to issues of gender and ethnicity. It stretched to new sets of paternity rights and extended maternity ones, as we have seen, and to new rights and resources for carers, the bulk of whom are women. It stretched to a Domestic Violence Bill in 2003. It even stretched to the proposal for a new all-encompassing Commission for Equality and Human Rights in 2004, and to changes in employment law making it illegal to discriminate on the basis of sexual orientation or religious belief, as well as disability, age and gender.[24] But what it did not stretch to was any sustained assault on the existing – and indeed intensifying – inequalities of income and wealth enjoyed by the most privileged strata in New Labour Britain. That, the most potent form of inequality, was decidedly off-limits. There was no increase in direct taxation in either of Labour's first two terms – the leadership were adamant about that – and there was no increase in the higher rates of taxation. He did not come into politics to stop David Beckham earning lots of money, the Prime Minister once famously told Jeremy Paxman, and there were accordingly many David Beckhams whose super earnings flourished under light taxation after 1997. Tax loopholes remained unfilled, and the government was harder on benefit fraud that it was on tax evasion. New Labour, like governments before it, succumbed to the embrace of the rich[25] and articulated their own version of 'trickle down' economics.

On their watch, the salaries and benefit packages, the golden handshakes and the perfumed parachutes that senior executives continued to give each other continued unabated: rising in value on average 17% in 2001 and 28% in 2002 alone. Which is why, for all the talk of a more open and meritocratic UK, New Labour in its first two terms presided over a society in which levels of income and wealth inequality remained high and entrenched. The Gini index on male wage inequality actually rose from .337 to .361 for the UK during New Labour's first five years in office. In 1979 it had read only .246.[26]

Of course, a 60% average income definition of poverty is always a moving target. The level goes up as average incomes rise, and if top earnings continue unchecked, rising faster than average earnings and significantly faster than the wages of the low paid and welfare recipients, then clearly poverty levels, in relative terms, will actually intensify. Moreover, and on the government's own evidence, many means-tested benefits failed to reach the people for whom they were intended, and the gaps in social performance that New Labour inherited – in educational performance, in variations of access to wealth and income by ethnic group, region and gender, even death rates by region – all these proved to be remarkably resistant to the new reform programmes.[27] For as Ruth Lister noted as New Labour's first term approached its end, 'redistribution by stealth [was just] too weak an instrument in the face of the massive redistribution to the rich under the Conservatives', and could never be effective so long as 'taxation continue[d] to be cast as a burden, rather than as an expression of citizenship responsibility on the part of the better off'.[28] The kindest thing that can be said in this regard is that New Labour rode the tiger on poverty and inequality issues after 1997 – talking the talk but not walking the walk – so that it went to its third term with its programmes all up and running, but doing little more than treading water. The more honest thing to say might be that New Labour had set itself an impossible task – of raising the poor without taxing the rich – and that it was the poor themselves who have paid the price of a set of policies that were so basically misconceived.

Social order

In that gap between aspiration and reality, New Labour in power had to confront the issue of order, and it did so with a facility often lacking in Labour governments in the past. For this was a party that came to power behind a leader who had established his own national credentials – and won Labour a slice of the 'law and order vote' that traditionally had been overwhelmingly Conservative – by promising to be simultaneously 'tough on crime' and 'tough on the causes of crime'. The Social Exclusion Unit, and the associated attempts to fast-track people out of poverty, were New Labour's key mechanisms for being 'tough' on the social conditions and individual circumstances triggering criminality, but they always existed, in the New Labour policy lexicon, with initiatives designed not to reform but to dissuade. Young offenders were a particular target of New Labour policy from the outset, not least because one of the party's five election pledges in 1997 – the one indeed it found in practice to be the most difficult to meet – had been to halve the time it takes persistent juvenile offenders to get to court. So from the outset of their time in office, social reform and the enforcement of law went hand-in-hand as Ministers battled to bring progress to areas of high social deprivation; but as that social deprivation persisted in spite of their best intentions, over time the government increasingly switched both its attention – and its public presentation of its priorities – to the maintenance of social order *per se*.

Early on, in both constitutional and social terms, this was a reforming government. On the constitutional front, ministers moved quickly to devolve power to Scotland and Wales, to promise a reform of the House of Lords, to explore the possibility of a new electoral system, and to design a Freedom of Information Act. On the social front, they moved quickly to protect the rights of the gay community, and (much more slowly, in their second term rather than their first) to explore the legalization of certain social drugs.[29] The constitutional agenda then stalled, as the social one initially did not. The Freedom of Information Act proved to be a profound disappointment to the government's more liberal supporters, and New Labour's periodic attempts to reform the House of Lords quickly became a joke – marooned as they were in the no-man's land between the hereditary House they had abolished and the new appointed/elected House on whose construction they could not agree.[30] New Labour's first Home Secretary, Jack Straw, troubled his liberal supporters still further by legislative proposals that would have weakened the jury system, but even so, at the end of the first term, progressive opinion was still divided on this government's attitude to crime, policing, anti-social behaviour and the rights of the citizen. Indeed, there was much shared ground on the UK left about the need to prosecute hardened criminals to the full extent of the law, and to protect the victims of petty crime on the housing estates of the urban poor. Tony Blair had been clear on the latter in 1997, and what he said had resonated well across the entire labour movement:

I back zero tolerance on crime. I back powers to tackle anti-social behaviour, to make parents responsible for their children, to overhaul the youth justice system so youngsters stop thinking they can commit a crime, get a caution and carry on being a criminal. To those who say it's all a threat to our civil liberties, I say the threat to civil liberties is of women afraid to go out, and pensioners afraid to stay at home, because of crime and the fear of crime, and we're going to help them.[31]

Where the plot went wrong on the issue of social order, at least when judged from any conventional progressive viewpoint, was when the New Labour leadership decided to do more than simply help the victims of petty crime on embattled estates. They decided in addition to outflank the Conservatives on their right, for fear of electoral loss. This more authoritarian move, driven by electoral concerns, was very evident in the run-up to the 2001 election, and is even more evident in the run-up to the election of 2005/06. In February 2001 Tony Blair suddenly conceded out of the blue that, with violent crime still rising, New Labour's policies on crime and punishment needed to be strengthened: that the government needed to do more both to contain the 'yob culture' of loutish behaviour and to regulate the rights of those seeking asylum. And it was no accident that he did, given the advice he was by then receiving from his electoral planners that key sections of the electorate still thought of the Labour Party as soft on crime and asylum issues. Indeed in 2004 the Prime Minister even went as far as to condemn what he called 'the 1960s liberal consensus on law and order' that had focused, in his view, too heavily on offenders' rights and on miscarriages of justice, and too little on the need for parental discipline and individual responsibility: this, in a speech timed to coincide with a doubling of the tagging and satellite tracking of low-level offenders and the launch of a five-year law and order campaign by the Home Office.[32]

What the Prime Minister promised, his new Home Secretary then delivered. The 2001 Criminal Justice Bill proposed a system of fixed penalty fines for loutish behaviour, more police powers to close clubs and to impose curfews, tougher penalties for hardened criminals, and new mechanisms for seizing the assets of drug lords and others of their kind. Legislation a year later promised to 'rebalance the system in favour of victims, witnesses and communities' and accordingly tightened the terms of bail, increased the range and powers of magistrates courts, and introduced changes in the rules of evidence to allow the release of the accused's previous convictions. Legislation in 2003 even eroded at the margin the right to jury trial and the protection given to the accused by the 'double jeopardy' principle in English common law. That protection was removed from the accused in 30 major categories of crime. Between 1997 and March 2003, these various legislative initiatives created between them 661 new offences in the UK's criminal code. They were the product of the 31 law and order bills that the government presented to parliament in its first term alone, and were in addition to the many anti-crime initiatives launched by the Home Office – 154, for example, (about one a week), between June 2001 and June 2004.[33] Martin Kettle called this 'legislative incontinence',[34] and given the centrality of law and order issues to the government's election strategy at the end of its second term, it is clear that such incontinence is not yet over.[35]

This flow of new anti-crime measures since 1997 has had three main targets: the hardened criminal class, the anti-social lout and the migrant/ asylum-seeker. On all three, New Labour policies have toughened over time. The main way that New Labour has dealt with persistent criminals is through changes to court procedures and to sentencing policy. The main way that New Labour has dealt with anti-social behaviour has been by the strengthening of police powers and the institutionalization of summary justice. The way New Labour has dealt with those seeking refuge here has been to cherry-pick those whose skills were useful to the economy, and to close the door on the rest.

The new sets of policies directed against anti-social behaviour have fallen particularly on the young; and since that behaviour is largely street behaviour, in practice these new policies have fallen most directly on the working-class young. In October 2002, Tony Blair said this about them:

> ...we will extend both the principle and the practice of 'on the spot' fines to tackle anti-social behaviour. We will bring forward measures to deal with parents of truants who refuse to cooperate with the schools. They will face a penalty. Far too many parents condone truancy by their children so we will make it far easier to impose those penalties. We need a new, simpler and tougher approach to anti-social behaviour. It is petty crime and public nuisance that causes so much distress to people: vandalism, graffiti, low-level aggression and violence. Anti-social tenants and their anti-social landlords can make life hell for their community. Families have a right to be housed. But they have no right to terrorise those around them. We will give local authorities new powers to license private sector landlords, ensuring that landlords and their tenants behave responsibly.[36]

By 2003 the government was proposing, in its anti-social behaviour White Paper, to do much more as well. It was proposing not only to give the police powers to seal crack houses permanently, but also to send wayward parents on residential parenting courses, to take persistent young offenders away from their families and place them with specially trained foster parents, and to introduce fixed penalty fines for a wide range of anti-social offences. Docking money from benefits, the greater use of injunctions to evict, the empowering of Environmental Officers to fine noisy neighbours – all these figured in a quite draconian array of proposals to tackle what David Blunkett, New Labour's Home Secretary in its second term, spoke of as a 'yobbishness' that 'changes the nature and culture of our society'. 'It creates instability and insecurity', he said, 'that leads law-abiding people to change their attitudes, losing trust.' And there were votes in it too, in his view. 'Britain has never been at a more insecure moment', he told the *Guardian* in March 2003, as British troops fought their way into Basra, 'I think my job is to provide some stability and order.'[37] So too did the Prime Minister, who backed his Home Secretary's introduction into the political lexicon of a new term – the *Asbo*, the anti-social behavioural order. In the five years that followed their creation in 1999–2000, 2,455 of these were issued – all designed to achieve one of New Labour's more bizarre performance indicators: a 15% reduction in bad behaviour by 2008![38] Historically in the UK, governments have been reluctant to legislate new moral codes into place, but apparently New Labour under first Jack Straw and then David Blunkett was prepared to do so.

In its second term the New Labour government also 'put some stick about' on another electorally popular issue: the issue of migration and asylum. Its first moves here were extremely liberal – quickly abolishing the Conservatives' primary-purpose rule challenging migrant spouses to prove they had a right to join their partners – but that liberalism did not last. By the end of New Labour's first term in office, and in the wake of the first of New Labour's two major pieces of legislation on migration and asylum-seeking, the policy stance had hardened and the administrative obstacles to entry had been raised. As Polly Toynbee and David Walker described the new situation faced by asylum-seekers:

In March 2000 the Home Office introduced tough new rules to try to deter economic migrants or refugees from choosing Britain. Straw copied a new German system, denying cash benefits to applicants, giving them instead food vouchers...worth only 70% of normal income support for people who often arrived with nothing but the clothes they wore....If they sought a judicial review of their case, they lost all benefits....From April 2000...every refugee newly arrived...had to fill in a twenty-page application form for asylum in English, without access to a lawyer, within fourteen days. If they failed this obstacle course they were deemed 'non-compliant', and automatically refused asylum.[39]

New Labour in power was always prepared to allow people in with skills of which the UK was short. Overseas-trained medical staff, for example, continued to play an essential role in many low-wage parts of New Labour's NHS. 'Nearly a third of UK doctors and 13% of nurses are non-UK born,' David Walker reported in 2001, 'and half the extra NHS staff employed over the past decade qualified abroad.'[40] There was even a time under this government when the UK was simultaneously funding AIDS assistance in South Africa and drawing South African nurses away from that vital work to staff wards in UK hospitals. Foreign-born workers without the requisite skills, however, remained less welcome. That was particularly so for economic migrants moving to the UK from *within* the enlarged European Union. Indeed it was entirely in line with general immigration policy that the government should have moved quickly, ahead of that enlargement in May 2004, to ensure both that new arrivals from Eastern Europe would have to work for a year before becoming eligible for benefits and that, as the Prime Minister said, 'if they can't support themselves, they will be put out of the country'.[41] That general policy on immigration, laid out in David Blunkett's 2003 White Paper – the one significantly titled *Secure Borders, Safe Haven* – established a legal route of entry for highly-skilled non-EU professionals and graduate students trained in such things as medicine and dentistry. It just omitted to do the same for non-EU workers with other skills, or without formal skills at all.

Where once the pace of reaction had been set by Conservative Home Secretaries, it was now set by Labour ones. It was David Blunkett, after all, and not some Thatcherite clone, who in 2003 proposed to strip failed asylum-seekers of their rights to state benefits, and 'as an absolute last resort' to take their children into care.[42] It was he who introduced, for the first time in UK migration law, compulsory citizenship tests and the taking of a loyalty oath, and it was he and not a Conservative Prime Minister who spoke of the children of asylum-seekers potentially 'swamping' local schools. Where once Norman Tebbitt had proposed the 'cricket test' as a measure of loyalty, it was now a New Labour Home Secretary who insisted on competence in English as a condition of citizenship. New Labour Ministers presented all this, of course, as impeccably radical and left-wing: as merely essential housekeeping to establish a framework for 'legal, managed, economic migration'.[43] 'Firm and fair', was how the Prime Minister described New Labour policy on immigration in April 2004: 'neither fortress Britain nor open-door Britain...controlled and selective immigration'[44] to fill skills gaps. But to many on the left it looked instead as a policy that, by pandering to right-wing sentiments, could only strengthen the presence of racism in British politics. Even Michael Howard, the leader of the Opposition and himself the son of Romanian Jews who had fled the Nazis in 1939, felt that, in his proposals on the children of failed asylum-seekers, David Blunkett had 'gone further than any civilized government should go',[45] and he was right.

Not surprisingly therefore in the light of all this, the longer New Labour has been in power, the more the prison population has grown. The UK is now, in consequence, the prison capital of Europe, with over 72,000 people in UK jails in 2004: a rate of incarceration (of 139 per 100,000 people) that is the highest in Western Europe and one that is now greater than that of countries such as Libya or Malaysia. Yet all this has occurred as recorded crime in the UK has fallen and as the social inequality that fuels criminal activity has continued unchecked. The full force of New Labour as a moralizing project has, in that sense, fallen unevenly in the society whose moral core New Labour claims to protect. Tony Blair, as we saw earlier,[46] likes to talk of his government as moving 'power, wealth and opportunity' downwards, making each more democratically available. But in truth no democratization of the distribution of wealth and power has yet occurred in New Labour Britain. Under Tony Blair's leadership, no less than earlier under Margaret Thatcher, it is apparently perfectly in order to be rich, powerful and self-serving. In the privacy of the club and the boardroom, self-indulgence remains the order of the day. But for those lacking access to such privileged spaces and obliged to take their more limited pleasures in more public arenas, the rules are tighter and the rules are enforced. New Labour came into power criticizing the Conservatives for presiding over a world in which there is one law for the rich and one for the poor. Stand on any Northern housing estate on a Friday night, or look out from one of the many holding areas that the government has created for people seeking refuge here, and it is quite clear that, in this regard at least, the world that New Labour inherited is also the world that they have chosen to reproduce.

Part 3

Setting Promise against Performance

8
Looking Back: The Auditing of New Labour

So the big questions that remain to be settled are whether all this New Labour activity has been worthwhile, and whether in consequence New Labour is worth supporting. These are in essence simple questions, of course, but they are also ones whose importance precludes the giving of simple answers. Many people will answer them simply – that is the downside of a democratic process that allows prejudice and reason equal measure in the exercise of the vote – but in an electorate as sophisticated as the one that New Labour faces, the government will find itself in 2005/06, as it did in 2001, not simply tested but also tested rigorously, against its own targets and the targets set for it by its political opponents. And so it should, for if there is one feature of this government that marks it out from all previous UK governments, it is surely New Labour's passion for performance indicators as the trigger to performance growth. Well, what is good for the goose is also presumably good for the gander: so if performance indicators are the flavour of the month, it is surely legitimate for us now to examine in detail just how well New Labour itself has so far performed?

Political performance indicators

That is, however, rather easier said than done, for judging political success is by no means a straightforward business. It is normally straightforward in a general sense, but it is rarely straightforward in the specifics of any particular case. In a general sense, the success of democratic political parties in power can and should be judged electorally, programmatically and strategically. Successful political parties are those that are able to retain and mobilize a solid electoral base. Successful political parties are those that come into power promising to do a range of discrete things, and then return to the electorate with those things done; and successful political parties are those that, in the process, move the society they govern in the broad general direction that they always said they would. Votes, policies and values all go together in a successful political party: the 'vision thing' informing the programme, and the programme consolidating the vote.

In practice, however, the matter is not quite so simple. To begin with, the longer a party is in power, the more its agenda is shaped by new issues and by developments in old areas that could not have been anticipated at the outset. It is hard then to test performance against promise, except by developing a rolling index of promises made, promises kept, and promises quietly discarded or re-specified. Moreover, the longer the party is in power, the more difficult it also becomes for its leaders to continually present themselves as champions of reform: for that call for reform must incrementally become a critique of the party's own previous inertia in power; or if it does not, if the party manages to generate a sense of permanent and unending reform, then elements of reform fatigue among even its most committed voters must eventually creep in to distort the electoral judgement. And those judgements are, in any case, always and of necessity provisional in nature, and based on incomplete data: for political projects – certainly political projects of the New Labour kind – are lengthy affairs. They have to be judged, not as something completed, but as something in train, and the very judgement itself then becomes a factor freeing up, or reducing, the political space available to the party for the continuation of its underlying mission. A political party returned with majorities of the scale that New Labour enjoyed in 1997 and 2001 can do a lot more – and can be expected to do a lot more – than parties returned with tiny majorities, or with no majorities at all. If Tony Blair's governments leave no bigger imprint on the UK sand that those of the Conservatives in 1992 or of Harold Wilson in 1974, then in immediate electoral terms they might still be judged successes, but in the longer sweep of things they must appear as lost opportunities of an unprecedented scale.

In any event, big majority or small, the impact of public policy is never easy to isolate, let alone to evaluate, for governments of necessity stand in the stream of things. They act through agents swimming in that stream; and they seek to change both the current and the swimmers by the insertion of policy-breakers and barriers (and occasionally water pumps). They invariably make big claims about changes in actor behaviour and in the flow of the water; but in truth, amid such movement it is hard to isolate the impact of public policy from the effect of private purposes and tidal forces. If a key variable changes, it is hard to tell the degree to which that change is the product of government initiatives; and even if no change occurs, it is hard to judge how far public policy at least prevented a move in the opposite direction to that desired. Behind the judgement on effectiveness, that is, have to stand other judgements too: on the logic of underlying trends; on what might have happened had other political forces been in charge; and on what might have happened had the political forces in power applied themselves with even more determination than was in fact the case. Judging the effectiveness of public policy in the UK since 1997 is therefore not a simple empirical matter. It requires the application of theory, the mobilization of explanation, and the willingness to think through how things might otherwise have developed had the balance of political forces, both inside and outside the Labour Party, been otherwise.

So judgement is not easy, but judgement can still be made. We can set trends against policy objectives, and trace the degree to which any redirection of those trends coincides with policy goals. We can set trends against stated goals. We can set trends against implicit goals. We can set trends against preferred goals – normally our own. We can compare trends, and changes in trends, comparatively and over time. We can use New Labour's own criteria of success. We can borrow or devise new ones. We can set New Labour thinking on the determinants of economic performance and social order against other theories of economic and social development and change. We can compare New Labour's stated goals with those of Old Labour, with those of other European social democratic parties, or with more socialist formulations. All that we can and should do, but what we cannot do is isolate one simple test of effectiveness. Instead we have to move forward incrementally and systematically, from a measurement of the immediately obvious and the persistently claimed, towards a more complex and deeper understanding of New Labour's impact on the forces operating on and around it.

New Labour's audit of itself

The New Labour government certainly believed that its narrowing of the gap between promise and performance could and should be measured: and indeed could and should be measured on a regular basis. To its immense credit, and in stark contrast to many of its predecessors, this was a government that asked to be judged against the detail of its commitments, and that then provided numerous opportunities for that judgement to be made.[1] The government even went so far as to develop, in 1998, a series of 13 (later 15) new indicators to measure the quality of UK life,[2] and during its first term at least, to publish an annual report on the fate of its 177 manifesto commitments. It reported 90 of them met by 1999 and 104 by 2000, with 71 still on course and two not timetabled. The reports were not entirely persuasive, however. They certainly failed to persuade the opposition, who ridiculed them as an expensive exercise in cliché and whitewash. The 2000 report was the last. It was hardly a bestseller – the government actually had to buy back 41,000 of the 100,000 copies of its predecessor – it was full of 'getting there', as the Conservative leader put it, with 'over 150 transitional verbs in a 65 page document'.[3] But at least the annual report enabled the serious voter to check pledge against performance in department after department, in what Tony Blair had initially hoped would come to be an annual 'state of the union' stocktaking on the American model. And at that specific level – of policy promise made and action taken – New Labour was in 2000, and has remained, very much a party of its word. Not all of its policy promises have been sustained, but the vast majority of them have, and the flagship ones – the five laid out as basic commitments in 1997 – those have been pursued vigorously and with considerable formal success. In 1997 the party promised, for example, that if elected it would 'get 250,000 young people off benefit and into work using money from the windfall levy on the public utilities'. That was a target it passed with ease on 30 November 2000, a success story marked with suitable ceremony and publicity by the Prime Minister, the Chancellor and the Secretary of State for Education and Employment all gathered together for that purpose in 10 Downing Street. There were 12,000 new bricklayers, the press was informed, 8,700 more sales people, and 12,800 more clerical officers. When New Labour audited itself, it did so in detail as well as in style.

In fact it was the annual budget statement that became, and has remained, a major moment of audit (and self-congratulation) for New Labour in power. Year on year, the Chancellor invariably opened up with a clear statement of achievements to date. The 2004 budget was a case in point. 'The purpose of this Budget', he told the House:

> ...is to lock in, for Great Britain, an economic stability that can and will endure. And it is a sign of the stability Britain has already achieved, and a tribute to the dynamism and hard work of the British people, that: even after the creation since 1997 of 1.8 million new jobs, 1.3 million in the private sector, and over 100,000 extra businesses; today

and every working day another 600 new businesses are starting up, 25,000 men and women each and every day are finding new jobs and an additional 10,000 new vacancies are each day being advertised – with new jobs being created at three times the rate of the 1970s, 80s and early 90s. For decades after 1945, Britain repeatedly relapsed into recession, moving from boom to bust. But I can report that since 1997 Britain has sustained growth not just through one economic cycle but through two economic cycles, without suffering the old British disease of stop go – with overall growth since 2000 almost twice that of Europe and higher even than that of the United States. Indeed in the Pre-Budget Report I told the House that Britain was enjoying the longest period of sustained economic growth for more than one hundred years. Mr Deputy Speaker, I have to apologize to the House. Having asked the Treasury to investigate in greater historical detail, I can now report that Britain is enjoying its longest period of sustained economic growth for more than 200 years...the longest period of sustained growth since the beginning of the industrial revolution.[4]

The longest period of sustained growth since the beginning of the industrial revolution: that was quite a claim! But then, the New Labour leadership has never been slow to point to its successes: both its general ones, as with the budget, and its more specific ones, as here, in 2004, in relation to the public services.

Public Sector workers fact sheet
- Teachers, doctors, nurses, police – more in post, more entering the profession and more pay...
- More teachers in post and in training....Better pay for teachers...
- More police in post...over the past 4 years police pay has risen faster than inflation...
- More nurses in post and in training...
- More doctors in post and in training...[5]

And so on: claim after claim after claim. In fact, both Gordon Brown and Tony Blair have become adept at squaring the circle of things done and things still to be done by talking the language of stages, and using the metaphors of building. Everything achieved is a 'foundation', everything to be done is 'the next stage', with the whole exercise as an 'ongoing' process, and with movement forward vital to avoid the danger of slippage back. When progress seemed slow, early on in New Labour's tenure of power, the Prime Minister talked the language of trust and of patience.

Later, when spending had soared and yet improvements seemed illusive, he talked the language of perception and potential. 'Keep faith, we will deliver', he told *Observer* readers in November 1997. 'We gave a contract to the people, and we will keep to it.'[6] 'The public sees the scars of underfunding', he told them in 2002, and:

> ...because of the way the NHS is covered by parts of the media, there is a bizarre disjuncture in public attitudes. Ask people if they personally had a good service, 10 to one say yes. Ask if the NHS overall is in good shape, they often answer no. The truth is the glass is half full. There are real problems. But the money and change and dedication of staff mean that the NHS is on the mend.[7]

If that failed to persuade, then the main New Labour leaders could always drop back onto the language of struggle and onto the virtue of toughness. 'There will be times when we will be unpopular', the Prime Minister told Michael White, particularly in what he called the 'post-euphoria, pre-delivery stage of the political cycle: there will be difficult decisions, but they will be taken for a purpose'. 'We thought change was a matter of will', he told a sceptical party conference in 2003, 'have the right programme, spend the right money, and the job is done. But experience has taught us: the job is never done.'[8] For the legacy was a tough one, and success would be necessarily slow in coming. After all, 'we are poor on innovation', the Secretary of State for Trade and Industry said in 1999, 'we have a long hours culture but we are not getting the rewards for it': and we were not to expect them soon. We would need to wait six or seven years, in his view, before the results of supply-side change would be there for us to see,[9] and in the meantime there would be periods of difficulty and doubt. 'I cannot recall a time', Tony Blair told the country in his New Year message in 2003, 'when Britain was confronted by such a range of difficult problems.'[10] But difficult or not, New Labour ministers remained convinced, of course, that under their leadership those problems could and would be transcended, and that without their leadership they would not. They also remained convinced that they, and not their critics, were right. 'More battered without, but stronger within', as Tony Blair had it in 2003:[11] and like him, only able to go one way, lacking a reverse gear.

The surface appearance of success

Anyway, on the surface of things at least, there was no call for this government to go into reverse gear. On the contrary: the battery of indicators to which it, and others, could turn to measure its success was, and remains, considerable. The *Financial Times* even had fun at the Chancellor's expense in the wake of the 2004 budget, finding his claim about 'the longest period of sustained growth for more than 200 years' to be too *cautious*! Their judgement was that the UK economy was 'currently enjoying the longest sustained expansion in its history', but that 'claiming "the most sustained period of economic growth since the dawn of time" might seem a little grandiloquent, even for Mr. Brown'.[12] Certainly the UK economy has continued to grow in a steady fashion under Gordon Brown's tutelage, and has so far avoided the worst of the recession to which first the US and then the rest of the main euro-zone economies have recently been prone. The annual growth rate of GPD in the UK has remained steady: at just over 3% in 1997, just under 3% in 1998, at 2% in 1999, and so on. It was still 2.2% in 2002–03, and probably 3.3% in 2003–04. That track record put the UK economy alongside the US for its first half-decade performance in the new millennium, and significantly ahead of the performance record of the EU-15 (*see Table 8.1.*)

Table 8.1   Real GDP growth (annual rate)

	UK	US	Japan	Germany	EU-15
2000	3.9	3.7	2.8	3.1	3.6
2001	2.3	0.5	0.4	1.0	1.7
2002	1.8	2.2	–0.3	0.2	1.0
2003	2.2	3.1	2.5	–0.1	0.8
2004	3.3	4.3	3.6	1.4	2.0

Source: NIESR, *National Institute Economic Review*, no. 189, July 2004, p. 8.

That rate of economic growth was achieved without a significant level of inflation. Gordon Brown was quite right to claim that New Labour had seen inflation drop to its lowest level for 42 years – 0.7% in December 2002 – and to point to the rate's presence *below* that set for it by the government (2.5%). It fell below that rate in late 1998, and remained within one percentage point either side of that target for the entirety of the period 1997–2004. He was also right to point out, as he regularly did, that price stability under New Labour stood in stark contrast to the inflationary explosions of the 1970s and 1980s, and was periodically significantly better than the governing European average. It was quite a moment for the UK economy when, in February 2000, its inflation rate was the lowest in Europe, and 'less than half the average of 1.7% for both the 15-nation EU and the 11-country single-currency zone'. That had happened only once before in all the years of UK membership of the European Economic Community,[13] and stood in stark contrast to the UK economy's dismal comparative record on price stability throughout the Wilson and Thatcher years.

The other major area of economic success relative to the European Union achieved under New Labour's leadership was employment and job creation. The number of people registered as out of work in the UK economy fell by 550,000 during New Labour's first term, to bring the total of those claiming benefit down to less than 1 million (950,300) in August 2001. That figure was lower than at any time since November 1975. Among the numbers removed from the unemployment register by as early as 1999 were 300,000 18–24-year-olds who found work/training under the New Deal. This departure from the unemployment rolls gave the UK a 3.2% claimant unemployment rate, down from 9.9% at the start of John Major's last term in office. (On the more demanding ILO Labour Force Survey count, the figure fell from 10.8% in 1993 to 5.2% in 2001.) From the election in 1997 until March 2001, as the Chancellor pointed out, the number of people claiming benefit fell by 40% (some 667,000 less), the ILO-defined unemployment total fell by 27% (down by 556,000), and employment rose by more than 1 million.[14] That pattern of success then continued, in more muted form, in New Labour's second term, so that by 2004 the number of claimants was down to 857,000 and the ILO unemployment rate to 4.7%. The comparable rate for the German economy for 2004 was 9.6% and for France 9.5%. With 200,000 new jobs created in just 12 months, the official October 2004 unemployment figure of just 1.39 million was hailed by the Minister for Works as a landmark achievement – and properly so.

A slight cloud on the horizon of the official figures, as New Labour approached its second bid for re-election, was the slight increase in the headline rate of unemployment in the spring of 2004, when slightly less than 1.5 million adults in the UK were still without paid employment. Yet the comparable figure for 1997 had been 30% higher. A deeper cloud was the persistence of regional pockets of long-term unemployment, and the continuing number of the potentially employed who were still 'parked' outside the labour market on incapacity benefits of various kinds and in premature retirement. It was estimated in 2002 that only one in four of the people on incapacity benefits was actually incapable of work,[15] and that in consequence the true numbers of the involuntarily unemployed in Gordon Brown's Britain was significantly higher than the claimant figures suggested.[16] But even with that 'hidden unemployment' factored in, the UK's job creation record under New Labour in its first two terms stood comparison to that of any leading industrial economy, including the American. In fact, the US unemployment rate in 2004 was still 0.8% higher than the UK's, even before the differential size of the prison populations in the two economies was brought into the equation, and by then the total number of people in paid employment of various kinds in the UK was nearly 2 million higher than it had been seven years before.

Moreover, for those in work, living standards continued to rise throughout New Labour's first years in office: on average by some 14% in real terms between 1996 and 2000,[17] and by a further 6% increment by 2004. 'For the first time in a generation, all parts of the society...enjoyed rapidly rising living standards',[18] and for the fortunate 40% of the UK population whose income was affected by mortgage payments, the cost of borrowing money – at 5% per annum in August 2001 – was the lowest for 40 years. The amount taken in taxes from that rising income was highly contested in the run-up to the 2001 election, but New Labour clearly benefited that year – as John Major had not in 1997 – from a 'feel-good factor' based on rising living standards for the majority of the UK electorate. This expansion in personal consumption brought UK GDP/head figures up by 2002 towards the best of the European economies: still 27% down on average living standards in the US, but (as Table 8.2 shows) close to those prevalent in Germany, France and Sweden.

Table 8.2   GDP/head for OECD countries (US$ 1999) 1960–2002

	UK	Germany (west)	Germany (united)	France	Sweden	Japan	US
1960	10,437	13,603		8,829	10,329	4,828	13,603
1979	15,894	22,562		17,522	17,502	15,938	22,562
1996	21,716	25,545	23,463	21,938	21,199	24,767	30,608
2002	24,771		25,549	24,808	24,880	25,128	34,076

Source: R. Dickens, P. Clegg and J. Wadsworth (eds), *The Labour Market under New Labour: The State of Working Britain 2003*, Basingstoke, Palgrave, 2003, p. 4.

That rising social wealth was no more equally distributed in UK society by New Labour policies than it had been by Conservative ones. Inequality remains a real feature of New Labour Britain, but at least with New Labour the poor did benefit in a sustained way from many aspects of public policy. New Labour was slow to start on this, held back, as we have seen, by its initial commitment to remaining within Conservative spending limits, but from 1999 a whole series of tax changes and policy initiatives cumulatively favoured the various constituent elements of the UK poor. The IFS calculated immediately prior to the 2001 general election that New Labour's first term had left the poorest 10% of the population better off each week by £8.62 and the richest 10% worse off by £4.74. The sums were trivial, derisory even: but the direction of change was not. The Chancellor's repeated if modest attempts to ease the burdens of child care for families with two working adults, his introduction of Working Families' Tax Credits and Child Tax Credits, his additional resources to pensioners, his determination to see off child poverty, even the miserably modest minimum wage, all helped to create the base for the Toynbee–Walker judgement that under New Labour 'the lot of the poor has improved more sharply than at any time since the foundation of the welfare state'.[19] New Labour should and could have done much more, of course: the UK remained towards the bottom of the European Poverty League through to the end of New Labour's second term. But at least things here were moving in the right direction: to the degree indeed that, by 2003, the Joseph Rowntree Foundation, the UK's premier monitor of these matters, found that the numbers of the poor were now back down to levels not seen since the late 1980s. This was successful social damage limitation indeed, and even something a little more.

Insecure foundations

However, unfortunately, New Labour's electorate between 1997 and 2004 did not simply bask in the glow of unprecedented levels of personal prosperity and marginally diminishing levels of poverty. They also gathered to themselves unprecedented levels of personal debt, and as they did so, they served to remind us of the fragile underpinnings of much of the UK's surface appearance of prosperity in Gordon Brown's economy. After 1997 New Labour presided over a consumer boom of Thatcherite proportions. It was consumer spending that freed the UK from the worst of the post-2000 global recession. It was also consumer spending financed on credit, lubricated by falling interest rates and underpinned by the collateral of secure salaries and exploding house prices. Between 1997 and 2004 New Labour's Britain increasingly lived on tick.

The figures on this are striking, and a cause for genuine concern. In January 1999, interest rates for personal borrowing stood at 6.25% and UK consumers already owed £29.7 billion on their credit cards. That was bad enough; but four years later, with interest rates at 3.75%, credit card debt had escalated to £52.7 billion. That £52.7 billion represented some 120% of personal disposable income, a mismatch made possible in part by mortgage equity withdrawal, by UK consumers using second mortgages to sustain a lifestyle that their salary and wage income alone could not begin to sustain. In 2003, for example, the scale of remortgaging was 57% higher than it had been the year before, for by then interest rates were at a 48 year low and mortgages cheaper than at any time since the late 1950s. Which is presumably why in 2004 the volume of consumer debt in the UK broke the £1 trillion barrier for the first time – with 80% of it in the form of loans secured against mortgages and remortgages – at the very moment when real incomes were actually falling under the impact of higher taxes, inflation and low salary settlements. That £1 trillion debt averaged out at a staggering £17,000 for every man, woman and child in New Labour Britain, or £46,600 for each of the UK's 2.17 million households.

The rising value of the housing stock fuelled this boom: house prices in the UK rose by 300% in the two decades after 1983, much of that rise occurring on New Labour's watch. House prices increased on average by 25% in 2002, 22% in 2003, and by a remarkable £1,100 a *week* in the first half of 2004: at rates of growth, that is, that completely outstripped the growth rates of wages and salaries. The Chancellor, for his part, hailed the housing boom as a Labour success story, telling the Labour Party conference in 2003 that

> ...while in world recessions in the Tory years Britain was first in, worst off, and last out – 10% inflation, 15% interest rates, 1.5 million in negative equity and 250,000 mortgage repossessions, Britain with a Labour Government and Labour policies has – even in a world downturn – the lowest inflation for 30 years, the lowest interest rates for nearly 50 years, there are 1 million new house owners and standards of living have risen faster than under the last Tory administration.[20]

What he did not tell the Labour Party conference, however, was that this dramatic inflation in house prices also came at a huge cost, particularly to the young and to the low paid. In fact, beyond its role as collateral on debt, the gain from rising house prices to existing house owners was entirely illusory – since a new house to be bought would have a price as inflated as the one to be sold – but for first-time buyers, and the person on average income, the cost was real enough.[21] Gordon Brown's gloss notwithstanding, New Labour cooked itself a major housing crisis as it engineered consumer-led economic growth after 1997: to the point indeed that by 2004 the Monetary Policy Committee of the Bank of England found itself trapped between contradictory imperatives: wanting to keep interest rates low to stimulate manufacturing investment, yet fearful of doing so because of overheating in the housing market, and knowing that a stiff rise in interest rates might trigger a housing price crash, negative equity and serious recession, as it had in the early 1990s.[22]

What Gordon Brown also failed to tell the Labour Party conference in 2003 was that, for a government committed to increasing social inclusion and guaranteeing uniform access to high quality public services, developments in the UK housing market since 1997 have been nothing short of a disaster. Soaring house prices do more than finance middle-class consumption. They also exclude working-class participation in the new affluence, and they do so to an intensifying degree. Where is the sanity in a housing market in which, according to the Halifax Building Society's 2004 survey of the UK's largest 634 towns, the average price of a house was more than a nurse could afford in 496 of them, more than a policeman could afford in 400 of them, more than a teacher could afford in 390, and more than a firefighter could afford in 251.[23] New Labour has presided over developments in the housing market which have left more and more public servants unable to live where they (and the government) want them to serve. Will Hutton's 40:30:30 society might be drinking more and eating more in 2004 than it did in 1997, but the inequalities in its consumption of housing remain firmly and stubbornly intact. So too do the numbers of people on the edge of personal bankruptcy, struggling and increasingly failing to restructure their personal debts.[24]

The post-1997 consumer boom did one other thing as well. It fuelled a record level of international debt, by sucking in imports of manufactured goods at a much faster rate than a shrinking UK manufacturing sector could pay for them with equivalent export orders. New Labour, that is, like the Conservatives before it, presided over a consumer sector that continued to grow rapidly and a manufacturing base that did not. The trade figures are striking. 'By coincidence, 1997 was the last year in which Britain had a trade surplus. It was only £1 billion, but it was the culmination of a steady improvement in which the hefty shortfalls at the end of the 1980s were eroded by a rebalancing of the economy following Britain's departure from the ERM.'[25] Thereafter, the economy moved into hock, and has remained there ever since. Indeed, since 1998 the deficit on the UK's overseas accounts has grown on a yearly basis: £8.5 billion in 1998, £15.9 billion in 1999, £19.6 billion in 2000, £27.6 billion in 2001, and £31.4 billion in 2002. By this dismal standard, the UK's trade performance in 2003 improved slightly: the deficit that year was only £20.4 billion; but thus far, at the time of writing, 2004 has seen a return to the by now standard rake's progress: with the economy racking up a deficit on its international trade of over £5 billion in the first three months of the year alone. Wobbling quarter by quarter between 0.8% and 3.5% of GDP, this trade deficit is reflective of the impact of an overvalued currency on a two-speed economy – one strong on services and weak on manufacturing – that New Labour has so far failed to rectify. The monthly figures for June 2001 were typical: that month a small surplus of £900 million for the service sector was more than swallowed by a deficit on trade in manufactured goods of £3.2 billion. It was an imbalance that helped to turn 2001 into a milestone of a particularly unfortunate kind, for 2001 was the first of the New Labour years in which the UK's deficit on its overseas trade was larger than at any time since records began: and those records have been kept without a break since 1697!

The continuing weakness of UK manufacturing

The weakness here is definitely one of manufacturing output and competitiveness; and in that sense is structural rather than cyclical. The signs of that structural weakness are everywhere in the figures. Manufacturing output since the recession of 1992 has grown at only half the rate of the economy as a whole. Gross capital employed in manufacturing has grown by only 2% per annum since 1995, while the import of manufactured components (a sign of relocation of industry abroad) has grown twice as quickly as it did between 1992 and 1997.[26] This hollowing out of UK-based manufacturing has continued apace through the New Labour years, and this in spite of repeated DTI strictures to the contrary. The DTI's survey of the 500 biggest UK spenders on capital investment in 2000 found the bulk of UK firms laying out less on new capital stock than their foreign competitors – the DTI was particularly critical of the pharmaceutical, aerospace and defence industries in this regard – in a context in which, because of past underinvestment, UK firms needed to invest *more* than their competitors merely to catch up.

The UK firms surveyed by the department increased their total investment spending by just 1.8% in 1999, compared to a 9.5% increase by their global competitors. Nor was 1999 merely a freak year. On the contrary, under New Labour the story has been consistent year on year: such that manufacturing investment as a percentage of manufacturing output peaked in the UK at just over 13% as New Labour arrived in power. By 2003 that figure had dropped to a little over 9%.[27] As a percentage of GDP, the trend in the figures for manufacturing investment was a rising one over the 1990s as a whole, but it was not a trend that was rising quickly enough. Nor was it one that was sustained under New Labour.

Manufacturing investment as a percentage of GDP was 2.4% in 1998. If Keith Marsden's figures are right, it had fallen to 1.4% in 2002.[28] In consequence, as the DTI pointed out ruefully in 2003, 'the level of business investment still remains below that of our major competitors despite an increase over the most recent cycle', and that was true too of 'business investment per worker'. The DTI had that figure at just over $6,000 per worker per year for the UK in 1990–2002, as against figures for France, Japan, the US and Canada that all exceeded $8,000.[29]

It is not that ministers were unaware of the importance of the manufacturing sector, or of the centrality of its performance to their ability to meet their other targets. There have been times when voices within the labour movement have reproduced Margaret Thatcher's old indifference to manufacturing – a widely-cited Fabian pamphlet in 1997 was certainly of that kind – but as we saw in Chapter 5, senior ministers knew full well just how important manufacturing was, and remains. 'To those who say we don't need manufacturing, all we need is services,' Patricia Hewitt replied in 2004,

> I say that's rubbish. When manufacturing employs three and a half million people, counts for three-quarters of all research and development, and produces the bulk of British exports, then Britain needs manufacturing, now as much as ever.[30]

It is rather, as Heather Stewart among others has noted, that New Labour has found that, in relation to business investment at least, 'you can lead a horse to water but you can't make it drink'.[31] In fact, New Labour in power has found it easier to attract new overseas horses than to galvanize local colts. Certainly reductions in barriers to foreign investment did at least initially stimulate the inward flow of foreign direct investment (FDI), to bring the total value of FDI stock in the UK by July 2001 to £500 billion.[32] In fact, only the US attracted more FDI in 1998 than the amount flowing into the UK, a flow greeted by the DTI as 'a clear vote of confidence in the UK economy and its workforce'.[33] But much of that inflow of investment funds went into mergers and acquisitions rather than into new capital stock, and was in any case more than offset, even during New Labour's first term, by the export of capital from the UK. So in the very same press release in which the DTI welcomed the 1998 record inflow of capital, it also had to concede that 'outward investment from the UK was also at record levels at the end of 1998: with the stock of UK direct investment overseas standing at £295.7 billion, a rise of £77.6 billion on the levels recorded in 1997'.[34] By that point indeed, British companies had replaced US ones as the major player in the cross-border mergers and acquisitions boom of the 1990s, accounting for some $199.3 billion of the total $800 billion involved in such transactions in 1999 alone.[35] That figure of nearly $200 billion of FDI by UK-based companies amounted to 39% of total EU outflows that year, and was three times as large as the FDI entering the UK in the same period.

Perhaps even more disturbing, recent OECD figures on UK R&D expenditure show it falling dramatically as a percentage of GDP over the last two decades of the twentieth century: from 2.4% in the early 1980s to 1.9% in 1997.[36] By the year 2000 indeed, the UK had 'the slowest rate of growth in the OECD in R&D spending', and the gap between the UK and top OECD performers was reportedly 'increasing every year'.[37] The 1990s were definitely 'a lost decade for UK private investment in R&D',[38] with UK-based firms only spending on average half as much per capita on R&D as were firms in Sweden and the US. Of course, New Labour's economic team was well aware of this shortfall, and strove mightily, as we have seen, to turn the tide around. In fact it remained the Treasury view throughout New Labour's first two terms that while skill deficiencies probably explained much of the productivity shortfall with Germany, 'innovation (proxied by R&D expenditure) appears very significant in accounting for the productivity gap with the US',[39] and required significant change in UK practices. The problem has been, however, that thus far at least no amount of government hectoring has managed to trigger any significant change in practice here. As the DTI stated in 2003:

UK business does not provide itself with the same level of technology resources as other leading industrial nations, with lower real expenditure per worker on R&D than most of its major competitors, and since 1991 the gap between spend per worker in the UK and its major competitors has widened. This pattern is also reflected in business enterprise R&D as a share of GDP. Although this ratio has stabilized in the last few years after a period of decline in the first half of the 1990s, this has to be seen against the increasing trend in other major industrial economies, notably the US and Germany.[40]

It is data like these that help to explain why, thus far at least, New Labour has failed to deliver on its core promise in 1997: that, if elected, it would generate a high-productivity, high-skill, high-wage economy.

Not that we, or the New Labour government, have been short of advice on how to lift the UK economy onto that higher and more desirable growth path. On the contrary, the UK manufacturing sector in particular has been the subject of regular reports and reviews since New Labour came to power, all full of recommendations for major change. As it arrived in office, the new government was greeted by an OECD report that recorded both a significant improvement in the productivity of UK manufacturing industry through the 1990s and the persistence of a continuing productivity shortfall. The OECD report was particularly sensitive to sectoral variations within UK manufacturing: recording world-class productivity levels in chemicals, and in paper and printing, but lower than average performance in a swathe of other sectors that included cars and aerospace, machinery, electrical machinery, food, drink and tobacco.[41] The CBI that year had workers in US-based firms 60% more productive than their equivalents in the UK, workers in Japan 26% more productive, those in France and Germany up to 11% more productive.[42] The later and more controversial McKinsey Report had the UK shortfall in output per capita relative to the US at 40% and Germany at 20%, and calculated labour productivity in the UK as only 73% of that in the US overall.[43] New Labour's own figures were slightly different: the numbers always depend in part on whether productivity is measured by output per worker or by output per hour, since long-hour economies like the US and the UK necessarily inflate that former figure. But both the Treasury and the DTI produced reports in 2001 that recorded the longevity and the persistence of the productivity gap, however measured.[44] As an earlier Treasury report put it in 1999, 'whichever measure of productivity is used...the UK has a sizeable gap compared with other major industrialized countries....Output per worker is highest in the US, with France and Germany just behind. The UK trails by some distance.'[45]

The critical thing to note here is that thus far under New Labour, that distance remains intact; and indeed on some measures may actually have widened. Certainly, the *Observer* carried a report in March 2001, ostensibly sourced from within the Treasury itself, that had the productivity gap actually increasing under New Labour 'by nearly a third'.[46] This report was probably alarmist: but it did underscore the Treasury's own awareness of the scale of productivity improvement still to be achieved as New Labour approached its second term in office. The DTI, for its part, simply reconfirmed in 2003 how intractable the problem was, and how little inroad into it New Labour policies were actually making. 'The picture of UK productivity performance,' it reported, 'whether considered in terms of output per worker or output per worker hour, remains broadly unchanged since the publication of the first edition of the *Indicators*' in 1999.[47] And that is costly to the UK economy, and to UK living standards.

On the Treasury's own figures, for example, if the UK were to match the productivity performance of the US, output per head in the UK would be over £6,000 higher.[48]

Responsibility for any widening of the productivity gap that the Treasury is now finding must in part be laid at its own door; for any growth strategy built, as New Labour's has been, on the expansion of service employment – where labour productivity is characteristically low – must intensify the problem of overall productivity underperformance, at least initially. The related failure of New Labour in power yet to find ways successfully and substantially to increase manufacturing investment, output and employment as a corrective to this service expansion, has then only compounded the problem. Even though particular UK firms continue to score well on the DTI's value-added scorecard and on other indicators of global and regional competitiveness, it remains the case that manufacturing output in the UK in total is currently stalled at its 2001 level – which is to say, no higher than its 1995 level – and that its employment total is in freefall: down 16% between 1998 and 2003, from 4.2 million as New Labour took office to 3.5 million by the middle of its second term. It would appear therefore that, thus far at least under Gordon Brown's tutelage, and in spite of the government's repeated productivity drives, UK-based 'manufacturing has neither the momentum nor the productive capacity to keep pace with the UK's demand for manufactured goods',[49] and that because it has not, the capacity of the UK economy to pay its way in the world and to lift its trend rate of growth is as far away as ever.

This weakness in the UK's manufacturing base then sits alongside, and compounds, at least two other 'sectoral' weaknesses in the contemporary UK economy: a weakness in the housing market and a weakness in the transport system. Each is weak in its own right, the product – as we saw earlier – of years of underinvestment that parallels that in the manufacturing sector. Each weakness is then compounded by its articulation with the others, so that together they increasingly threaten the capacity of New Labour in power to sustain the improvements in living standards on which the government's electoral viability ultimately depends. For that reason, if for no other, they too need dealing with, and quickly; and rather belatedly, ministers seem to have realized that. Suddenly there are plans on the table for major expansions in the housing stock and the road network over the next decade.[50] What ministers seem not yet to have realized, however, is the degree to which their planned resolution of housing shortages and transport bottlenecks will only compound the debt and trade deficit weaknesses that manufacturing underperformance in the UK has already created. For the building of new houses and the creation of new roads requires an army of skilled engineers and building workers that New Labour's investment in human capital has yet to generate, and the inflated wages of the skilled workers who are available for the task can only, during the immediate building period at least, suck in even more imports. Indeed, the better the roads, and the greater the number of houses, the easier it will be for imports to arrive and to be consumed.

The general situation appears to be this: that New Labour's failure thus far to generate a supply-side revolution in the manufacturing sector has created, for itself and for the country, an impasse whose physical manifestation is daily evident in the lines of stalled commuters on the country's overstretched road network. The government's consumer boom has filled the UK's transport system with cars it cannot easily absorb, and has generated a demand for housing that cannot easily be met. The result is less the creation of a balanced and sustained trajectory of economic growth than the generation of a gridlocked economy and society: gridlocked on interest rates because of the contradictory requirements of the manufacturing sector, the housing market and the trade deficit;[51] and gridlocked – literally gridlocked – on its road system by the very volume of imported cars that low interest rates and soaring house values have enabled UK consumers to buy. Deconstructing that gridlock is the key task facing New Labour in any third term, and yet, since the government has allowed itself to be trapped between a rock and a hard place here, quite how to do that is not immediately obvious.

The true character of New Labour Britain?

In truth it is never easy, as was noted at the start of this chapter, to isolate the impact of public policy, and certainly in New Labour's case, much of what is claimed as a product of policy often appears, on closer inspection, to be better understood as part of a longer story with a range of causal drivers behind it, of which public policy was only one. Indeed, that is true both for what New Labour has thus far achieved and, perhaps more awesomely, for what it has not.

It is certainly true that for the government's 'economic growth and job-creation story' to be fully understood, it is necessary to recognize that the trends New Labour inherited made its task easier than might otherwise have been the case. Economic growth was well underway, and unemployment was falling, well before it came to power. In fact the unemployment rate actually fell more slowly under New Labour during

its first term than it had under John Major's governments, as might be
expected as full employment came closer and closer. Moreover, the falling
number of claimants recorded under New Labour was part of a continuous
decline in unemployment from 1993, when the total had stood at nearly
3 million; and New Labour's economic growth performance (of steady
quarter by quarter growth) continued a pattern begun under John Major.
The OECD Survey on the UK in 2000 noted the by then 30 quarters of
uninterrupted economic growth,[52] but only half of those belonged to
New Labour. Likewise, the National Institute of Economic and Social
Research (NIESR) judged that year that all but 45,000 of the 300,000
placements in work made under the New Deal would likely have occurred
without it,[53] and other studies demonstrated that, for all New Labour's job
creating initiatives, *in*activity levels among UK workers remain stubbornly
unchanged. 21% of the available labour force was inactive in 1980. 21%
is still inactive today: all of which suggests that general growth forces
and the business cycle were the dominant elements in play here, and
that policy was not.

Which is presumably why, to date at least, the more grandiose of New
Labour's pre-1997 economic ambitions remain entirely unfulfilled. There
have been many discrete policy successes, and many long-term goals
– not least those relating to the abolition of child poverty – that remain
on track. But the trend rate of growth of the economy as a whole has
not been significantly and permanently lifted. A high-wage, high-skill,
high-productivity economy has not been created, nor has a German
or a Swedish model been brought into existence on the banks of the
Thames. In fact, in spite of its exposure to now more than seven years
of political control by one of Europe's leading social democratic parties,
UK economy and society remains very different from the core European
model in its main characteristics; and opt-outs from EU directives, and
the protection of the principle of subsidiarity, remain as central to the
New Labour relationship with the European Union as they were when
the Conservatives regularly said 'No! No! No!' to the introduction of
'backdoor socialism from Brussels'. Too large a segment of UK-based
manufacturing industry depends for what competitiveness it possesses on
the payment of low wages for work of long hours to allow the UK easily to
adopt the more progressive aspects of the EU labour codes; for even after
so long a period of New Labour government, UK *wage rates* remain low
(and unequal) by Western European standards, the *length of the UK working
week* remains long, *levels of stress* in UK offices and factories remain high,
and UK *skill levels*, by contrast, remain inadequate. This can hardly have
been the state of affairs that Gordon Brown wished to perpetuate when

he first took charge of the Treasury in 1997, but it is the state of affairs over which he has continued, however reluctantly, to preside.

Wages in the UK remain low by EU standards while the scale of income inequality remains high. The UK is an EU laggard on the first, and the EU leader on the second. CEOs in the UK are currently the highest paid in Europe, taking home an average annual pay package in 2001 of £509,019. UK manufacturing workers, by contrast, took home £20,475. The CEO package, though lower than the American, was 33% higher than that for France, the next highest EU payer, and higher than that in Japan. The pay of manufacturing workers in the UK was lower than that in Sweden (£23,034), France (£24,574), Germany (£26,124), the US (£31,603) and Japan (£36,779).[54] Nor is the gap between high and low pay in the UK narrowing. On the contrary, executive salaries rose by some 28% in the year 2000, six times faster than the rise of wages in general, as part of a decade-long process in which CEO salaries and bonuses in the top 100 UK companies rose by 288% while average earnings rose only by 45%.[55] Not surprisingly perhaps, New Labour ministers have therefore been obliged to concede that, thus far at least, the gap between the rich and the poor in the UK has not narrowed. It may yet begin to do so, when the cumulative effects of Gordon Brown's repeated budget moves on child benefit, pensions and income support really bite. But thus far they have not.

Moreover, at least 4 million people in the UK still regularly work more than the 48 hours a week ceiling set by the European Working Time Directive, and do so as a part of a labour force which enjoys (by EU standards) comparatively low levels of job flexibility. The UK remains the only EU country that allows its workers to surrender their right to work no more than 48 hours a week, and the TUC reports regularly on the many examples of private firms pressuring their employees to exercise that surrender. The New Labour government itself has been equally pressing in the case of both junior hospital doctors and teachers: to the point indeed, as we saw earlier, of triggering major industrial unrest among teachers in 2002–03, when their average working week touched 53 hours, and rising. In fact the TUC has recently calculated that UK workers put in about £23 billion of *unpaid* overtime each year, with 5 million workers averaging 7 hours and 24 minutes of such work each week![56] Much of that is work done at the weekend – recent surveys suggest that in practice four out of five employees now no longer enjoy the full traditional two-day break[57] – and this in an economy where nearly one worker in four still works nights. The government has now belatedly woken up to the adverse effects of this long hours culture on the quality of family life and child care, as well as on long-term labour productivity performance, and has started to strengthen the rights of parents to demand flexible working hours that are more compatible with a better work-life balance. This new line of policy is undoubtedly welcome; but it is also still very much a matter of too little, too late, of shutting the stable door long after the horse has bolted. For the UK remains way behind the best in Europe on the striking of that balance, and the 'progressive' dimensions of these new labour laws sit in direct contradiction to the government's much longer-established determination to increase productivity in the public services and to improve consumer rights there. 'Normal' hours of full-time work are at last beginning to come down in the UK – from 38.9 in 1994 to 31.8 in July 2004 – but still one father in three in the UK regularly works more than 48 hours a week, and a fifth of the entire UK workforce regularly put in 45 hours. The average figures are pulled down to the point of meaninglessness by the number of part-time workers and working mothers in the UK labour force, obscuring the fact that UK men in full-time employment still average a 43.5 hour working week, well above the EU norm. Indeed as the millennium turned, the average full-time UK worker was still putting in 1,737 hours of work a year. This was less than the 1,966 hours worked by the typical US worker but it was 175 hours more than the typical German worker and (amazingly) 336 more than the typical Norwegian.[58] 175 hours is four full weeks of work more per year than in Germany!

Not surprisingly perhaps in the light of that, and of the continued intensity of work in UK industry – there is no evidence of any easing of that, just the reverse in fact [59]– *stress levels* are disproportionately high in UK industry when studied comparatively and over time, and are now, according to the latest TUC data, 'the biggest threat to the health of the nation's workforce, costing the economy £7 billion a year in sick pay, lost productivity and NHS bills'.[60] According to the Health and Safety Executive in 2001, some 500,000 workers in the UK were currently suffering from work-related stress or depression, with nearly 150,000 of them haven taken at least one month off work sick because of stress-related illness.[61] In New Labour Britain, stress disproportionately affects managerial and technical jobs in the private sector, and hits hardest in the public sector among teachers, nurses and civil servants. Indeed the gap in job satisfaction between private and public sector workers, which was evident in the research data as late as 1990, seems now to have virtually evaporated, as public sector staff come under increasing workloads and bureaucratic regulation.[62] In 2003, one teacher in three was actually planning to quit the profession within five years, according to a major survey by the General Teaching Council, with more than half of those planning to go citing workload (including paperwork) as the main demotivating factor, and the government's own Audit Commission had earlier warned of an impending 'staff crisis' in the public services 'caused by stress and disillusionment among millions of workers'. Nearly 80% of those questioned 'blamed bureaucracy and paperwork. There were too many targets, and many felt that their work was increasingly driven by what could be measured, instead of what mattered to service users.'[63]

The centre-left think tank, Demos, even issued, in November 2004, a report on sleep deprivation in the UK – *Dream On* – *Sleep in the 24/7 Society* – which found that shortage of sleep was widespread, especially among managers and parents of young children.

> On any working day, a quarter of all managers in Britain are likely to be in a bad mood because they have not slept well, says Charles Leadbeater, author of *Dream On*. These sleep-deprived and shouty managers with a tendency to make mistakes are responsible for millions of British workers. It's hardly a recipe for good management.[64]

An earlier ILO survey of stress in the workplace in the UK, the US, Germany, Poland and Finland found work-related stress and anxiety on the increase everywhere: with between 15% and 30% of the UK's working population reporting work-related incidents of stress and depression, incidents reportedly costing the UK economy some 80 million working days a year and the NHS drug budget some 25% of its total.[65] After three years of New Labour's first term in office, and with a Chancellor self-admittedly inspired by a Calvinist enthusiasm for work, the *Work-Life Manual* published by the Industrial Society was still obliged to report that 'miserable, overworked, insecure – the British work the longest hours in Europe and express the least job satisfaction'.[66] This was hardly a recipe for a happy electorate.

Also, in comparative EU terms at least, not necessarily a *very skilled* electorate either. For all the programmes and spending on training over the years, and on education at its various levels, there is as yet no clear evidence of any significant narrowing of the skills gap between the UK labour force and those of its major industrial equivalents. Ministers quite properly say that this will take time to show through in the figures, and rightly point to the considerable progress made since 1997 in the numbers of students on basic literacy courses, taking intermediate skills programmes or gaining work-based training. All these numbers are significantly *up* since 1997, and that is all to the good. But by the same token, ministers are also obliged to concede that, even after a prolonged period of powerful New Labour initiatives,

> ...the UK continues to show weakness in terms of relative levels of human capital. Too many workers lack the key basic and intermediate skills. There have been improvements to the *flow* of workers into the labour force – through the reforms made to schooling – but weaknesses in the stock of skills remain...on many of the factors that seem to determine success in the knowledge economy...the UK continues to under-perform relative to other countries. The UK has lower skill levels than our competitors, with particular weakness in intermediate skills, and low levels of off-the-job training.[67]

There are important straws in the wind, of course – the number of young apprentices, for example, has risen by more than 750,000 since 1997, and the pool of workers with ICT skills continues to grow – but on the Treasury's own calculations, 'the UK's human capital stock [remains] deficient in comparison to the US in terms of the number of workers with higher skills (a degree or above) and in comparison to Germany in terms of intermediate and vocational skills'.[68] As the Executive Summary on the government's 2004 *Skills Strategy* document had it:

> We have particular skills gaps in basic skills for employability, including literacy, numeracy and the use of IT; intermediate skills at apprenticeship, technician, higher craft and associate professional level; mathematics; and management and leadership. Employers have long been concerned that they are not getting recruits with the skills they want.[69]

So serious indeed was the immediate skills shortage that New Labour ministers in 2001 actually explored whether immigration rules should be eased to facilitate the poaching of foreign-trained skilled workers, and the government's own National Skills Task Force produced tables of skill/general competence deficiencies in the labour force with figures of over 60% against technical/practical skills, and over 50% for computer/ IT competence, general communication skills and customer handling skills: this in an economy in which, by the Skills for Business Network's only calculation, 'about 80% of new jobs created between 2000 and 2010 will require skills equivalent to A-level or degree standard'.[70] Those numbers, on both the demand and the supply side of the skills equation, could not be 'hard' – judging such matters is extraordinarily difficult, and the danger of overvaluing credentialism in this area is huge – but their scale reinforced the view of report upon report from ministers, business organizations and the TUC: that the UK economy has entered the twenty-first century with a skills shortage so acute as to impact significantly on the competitiveness of firms based here.

From all this we can only safely conclude that the overall trend rate of growth for the UK economy is not likely to be qualitatively improved any time soon. And perhaps we should not be surprised: as we saw in detail in Chapter 1, the New Labour legacy here was a daunting one. The Blair government inherited an Anglo-American economy that was underperforming economically when compared to the US and in possession of social and training weaknesses when compared to Europe's best. In essence, it inherited a low-wage, long-hour, low-skill economy off the edge of a prosperous European market. Government policy has not yet qualitatively altered that inheritance – on either side of the equation. It has not yet narrowed the gap on US productivity, and it has not yet narrowed the gap on continental European levels of training and equality. New Labour ministers tend to present their achievements thus far as a job half done. They tend to say that they have spent the past years establishing a platform from which their policies will soon trigger significant improvements in productivity and training, and hence in economic performance and the social wage. We can only hope that they are right, and at this stage, who can definitely gainsay them? Of the nature of things, the jury has to be permanently out on claims and promises of that kind, but sadly we already have enough evidence to warrant a certain degree of scepticism among those of us called upon to judge. New Labour in power may score high for intention and for effort, but it has yet to match intention with outcome or effort with delivery; and until it does, how can it legitimately claim to have been successful?

9
Looking Forward: Unfinished Agendas and New Models

Nonetheless, honour must be given where honour is due, and it is definitely due here. Whatever else can and cannot be said about this New Labour government, one thing at least is very clear: this is a government of high intellectual capacity and moral purpose, one whose policies are sustained and underpinned by analysis of unprecedented quality and range. We are not dealing with stupidity here, or with the politics of soundbites, as arguably was the case in Labour governments in the past. There is real force in the arguments that New Labour politicians make about the novelty of the agenda posed by changes in the global economy, and by the rising expectations of an increasingly sophisticated and affluent electorate. There is real force in their ruminations on how best to modernize the provision of public services, the better to maintain public support for the social democratic principles underpinning their provision. There is real force in their argument that productivity growth holds the key to employment and affluence over time. Even its critics must concede that this is a government that has built its policies on the basis of careful and complex analyses of the origins and character of the problems that those policies are designed to redress; and that this is a government which, once it settled upon those policies, has demonstrated an unusually sustained capacity to hold to them, and to maintain their coherence over time.

If anyone doubts that, they should simply visit any departmental website and pull up whatever is available there as a background paper informing policy design. Or they should look in detail at the number and quality of the working papers emerging from the various centre-left think tanks that service this government as a source of long-term ideas; or they should read any of the reports produced by the myriad of task forces and working parties that the New Labour government called into existence as soon as it came to power.[1] As I write this, I have before me a Treasury Working Paper from November 1997. Headed rather laboriously *The Modernization of Britain's Tax and Benefit System, Paper No. 1: Employment Opportunity in a Changing Labour Market*, it runs to 25 pages of tightly argued analysis on the depth of the UK unemployment problem inherited from the Conservatives, and of the various labour market issues contributing to that problem. It draws on the latest academic research, and is extremely comprehensive in both its coverage and its detail. More readily available to a general readership might be the other volume that is sitting on the desk as this is written: Ed Ball and Gus O'Donnell's academically daunting explanation of the Treasury policy that they helped to shape – *Reforming Britain's Economic and Financial Policy*. This one was published by Palgrave in 2002, and comes with an introduction by Gordon Brown himself. Whether you or I agree with the content of these complex and sophisticated documents is not the point here, for regardless of their credibility they make one thing abundantly clear – that whatever New Labour did or did not do in power, it did not make core policy on the hoof, or build its proposals on the easy conventional wisdoms of either the golf club or the trade union branch. On the contrary, this New Labour government has been, to an unprecedented degree in modern UK politics, intellectually informed and academically sustained. If it has made mistakes, or failed to grapple with deep-rooted issues, it has not done so out of ignorance and lack of thought. Its failings, if that is what they be, derive from the quality of the thought processes sustaining policy, and not from any lack of thinking *per se*.

Half-full, half-empty: which way the sand?

Such seriousness of purpose deserves seriousness of response. It is no good judging progress against utopias, since they never arrive, or against non-existent governments that can never hope to be elected. Nor should policies be dismissed simply because their impact is slow and incremental. Policies have to be judged, as we saw in the previous chapter, against the general line of march that they help to sustain, and progress has to be judged against starting points, and assessed against the contradictions that block it, where that line of march creates them. Labour governments are only ever elected, in the wake of long periods of Conservative rule, if problems have so stacked up over the years as to make that Tory rule no longer sustainable. So the legacy for incoming Labour governments is invariably awful. It was this time, and legacies of that depth cannot easily be washed away. Poverty was inherited in 1997. Poverty remains. The UK's social capital was depleted. It still is. But is it as depleted as it was? Is poverty now more or less entrenched than in 1997? Will Hutton for one does not think so. It was his *The State We're In* that we used to chronicle the wastage of the Conservative years: so his judgement has a certain force when chronicling the years of New Labour too, and he is on record as seeing genuine progress since 1997. 'If the hourglass was half-empty and emptying a decade ago,' he has written, 'I would reverse the judgment today – it is half-full and filling.'[2]

Anthony Giddens, for one, more than agreed. 'This government is often criticized from the Left for having done nothing to counter inequality', he wrote in September 2004, yet in fact:

It is difficult to think of a single area of government intervention since 1997 which has not been related to questions of poverty and inequality. The child tax credit, working tax credit and pension credit; the minimum wage and the New Deal; the child trust fund and child benefit increases; Sure Start and the childcare tax credit; education action zones and a veritable maze of other programmes directed at deprived areas: large-scale investment in public services – the list goes on and on....This may be the first Labour Government actually to effect redistribution, rather than just talk about it.[3]

'Don't listen to the carpers,' David Aaronovitch, Will Hutton's colleague on the *Observer* has written, 'things are getting better in Britain...slowly.' It is just that the improvements are 'boring stuff; the stuff of slow change and gradual delivery'– but they are real nonetheless.

When Labour came in, I most wanted unemployment to continue to fall, and it has fallen and is lower than almost anywhere else in Europe. More selfishly, I wanted interest rates to be low, and they are now lower than at any time in nearly 50 years. I wanted more money spent on public services, and I wanted those services changed so that they were more effective. In fact the additional amounts being spent are greater than I had expected, not less, and there is now growing evidence of cultural change in the running of public services, even if this is very uneven. I wanted a minimum wage, more assistance for poor people, especially those with families. Those have all happened. There is a Parliament in Scotland, an Assembly in Wales, a mayor in London...and there is peace in Northern Ireland. These are not theoretical improvements....The state primary school of which I am a governor has had increased budgets for each of the past four years, next year's increase being nearly 12%....This is happening all over Britain.[4]

Changes like that keep politicians popular; and this Labour government remained popular far longer than most. It certainly totally transformed, for a decade at least, the political landscape of the UK: so effectively occupying the electoral ground once dominated by Margaret Thatcher that the Conservatives in 2001 were unable to make even a modest dent in New Labour's vast parliamentary majority. A Labour Party that before 1997 had never won two full terms in a row found itself by 2004 contemplating a third term, and possibly a fourth, and in the process kept stacking up political records that would have been unimaginable one or two decades ago. In August 2003 Tony Blair became the longest-serving Labour Prime Minister, passing Clement Attlee's 6 years and 92 days. In June 2004 Gordon Brown became the longest-serving Chancellor of the Exchequer in the twentieth century, passing David Lloyd George for that accolade. In 2001 the Labour Party won its second largest parliamentary majority of all time: second only, that is, to the one it won in 1997.

And yet such electoral dominance was, from the outset, built on shifting sands: some of New Labour's making and some not. For though the New Labour government remained more popular than the Conservative Opposition throughout the first parliament, and did not lose a by-election to it, it very quickly lost the moral high ground that it enjoyed in the heady days of May 1997. The quantity of its support stayed intact, but its quality did not. Within a year a government that had promised a new and cleaner form of politics was itself besmirched by scandals and controversy: scandals on party funding (the Bernie Ecclestone affair) and controversy (over planned cuts to benefit payments to lone parents and the disabled). Within a year too, Tony Blair's own standing in the polls had settled back into the range of the normal,[5] and by 2000 he was being barracked from the floor while addressing, of all things, the 10,000 conference delegates of the Women's Institute. And in 2001, though re-elected by a landslide in parliamentary terms, the vote itself was down. In 1997, 71.6% of the UK electorate went to the polls. In 2001 that figure was down to an all-time low of 59%, and of those who bothered to vote, only 42% voted Labour. That was only one potential UK voter in four.

For by then, even ahead of the crisis caused by the Iraq war, New Labour was running into a problem with its core electoral support. The problem was that its policies were more conservative than its core electorate, more acceptable to the floating voters of the English shires than to the hardened Labour support of the northern industrial towns. There were warning shots about that prior to 2001.[6] Peter Kilfoyle, the Liverpool MP, resigned from the government in 2000, claiming that New Labour had deserted its roots in the Labour heartland.[7] Labour conferences sent warning shots too – not least over pensions in 2000 and the renationalization of the railways in 2004 – as did rebel MPs within the Parliamentary Labour Party itself. In fact, backbench rebellions there grew in regularity and scale over time. In 1997, 47 MPs rebelled against the lone-parent benefit cut, 66 rebelled over disability benefits in May 1999, first 121 and then 139 voted against Blair's Iraq policy in February/March 2003, 62 opposed foundation hospitals in November 2003, and a huge backbench rebellion against university top-up fees in January 2004 brought the government's majority down, as we saw earlier, to a meagre five.

By then nearly two-thirds of all backbench MPs had rebelled against government policy at one time or another, but this New Labour government was not for turning: not on domestic modernization; nor, in 2003, on the invasion of Iraq itself. That invasion, so unpopular with party activists and increasingly over time with more and more of the electorate as well, then ate massively into New Labour's political base. Unease with the drift of domestic policy and fury over too close a foreign policy alliance with the most neo-conservative US administration since Ronald Reagan combined to gut the party of its membership. Membership in the Labour Party in the modern period peaked in 1997 at just over 400,000. By 2003/04 it was down by a half, to its lowest level for 70 years: 214,952 at the end of 2003, and falling.[8] Indeed, a reported 25,000 extra members left the party in the first six months of 2004 alone.[9] Unease with the drift of policy also cost the Labour Party heavily in a string of elections in 2003/04: by-elections, local government elections and eventually elections to the European Parliament. New Labour lost Brent East, once Ken Livingstone's constituency, in September 2003 on a 29% swing. In July 2004 it lost the previously rock-solid seat of Leicester East with a swing of support against it of almost the same proportion, and its overall vote in the European elections, just 23%, was even lower than Michael Foot's Labour Party suffered in the great Tory landslide of 1983. Labour did hold on to Peter Mandelson's old seat in Hartlepool in October 2004 – just – but again the swing against it was a staggering 18%.

So here was the paradox: a government presiding over a process of incremental improvement across a range of key social and economic indicators while experiencing a dramatic fall in its popularity, and in public trust in its leader. In 2003 an ICM poll found 51% of the UK electorate holding the Prime Minister trustworthy. By 2004 that figure was down to just 39%. By then, 20% more of the electorate were dissatisfied with his performance in office than were still satisfied with him – 58% dissatisfied, 38% satisfied – and the full March/April 2004 opinion polls suggested that, had the general election been held then, New Labour would have been lucky to scrape back to power with a majority of just 24. The poll numbers as the party gathered in conference in September 2004 remained the same. Iraq was the trigger of that fall in trust and support, of course, but it was not its sole cause. In the August 2004 polls, Iraq ranked tenth out of ten in issues considered to be key in voting, with only 12% saying it was the crucial deciding issue for them.[10] Foreign policy alienated party activists, but the electorate moved to a different and a deeper rhythm. In that same poll, 59% of those questioned put the NHS at the top of their priority list. In 2004 New Labour found itself less and less popular in the country not just because of its foreign policy but also because of its domestic record. It found itself less and less popular domestically because of a growing public sense of the existence there of a set of underlying contradictions in what it was about – contradictions and dilemmas that the kind of incremental and slow improvement noted by Hutton and Aaronovitch could do nothing to avoid.

The politics of squaring circles

At the heart of those dilemmas was New Labour's attitude to taxation. It is extraordinarily difficult for a party committed to the 'expansion of public services free at the point of use' simultaneously to fear the electoral consequences of a reputation for 'tax and spend'. That reputation, according to dominant mythologies these days, cost Labour the 1992 election and shedding it brought victory five years later. If the mythology is true – though it probably is not[11] – New Labour in power has an immense difficulty. It cannot raise taxes on a regular basis. At best, it can only look for windfall taxes that hit a narrow group of the overprivileged for a brief period of time and for an unambiguously popular cause: and only then occasionally, lest it alienate the business community whose investment is vital to the economic growth that the easy funding of New Labour's social policies require. If such windfalls are not available, New Labour can only tax in moderation and tax by stealth. In fact its leading figures cannot even discuss the possibility of raising taxes, as Peter Hain found to his cost when he did so in 2003 – he was immediately obliged by Number 10 publicly to recant, which he obediently did – for fear that even the contemplation of such tax rises will begin to erode, in the public mind, the difference between 'Old' Labour and 'New' that Tony Blair and his colleagues have worked so hard to create and sustain.

Yet New Labour still needs those tax revenues for the public sector goals it has set itself. Economic growth alone cannot generate sufficient revenues to enable New Labour to make up the accumulated shortfall in public investment that it inherited, let alone to expand the scale and quality of public service provision as it regularly promises to do. In its first term, the New Labour government avoided a large public sector deficit by combining sustained economic growth with limited public sector expansion, and was roundly criticized for its pains. But even that option is not available to it now, not least because ministers responded to that criticism by injecting large quantities of public money into service provision at a time of slowing economic growth. New Labour now governs with a large budget deficit that is forecast to continue. It also, by chance, governs with an electorate that regularly demonstrates its willingness to pay higher taxes in return for better public services. In fact, if the surveys are to be believed, two UK voters in three are now willing to be so taxed: a doubling of the proportion over a 20-year period.[12] New Labour's central policy problem is that its leading figures don't seem to believe that survey data. Instead they appear to cling to the view that potential taxpayers say one thing when answering questionnaires and another thing when voting, and so in consequence Blair, Brown and co. find themselves obliged to square the circle of low taxation and expanding public service provision in other and less progressive ways.

Those other ways then bring serious problems of their own, and that is true whether or not the way chosen is one of extracting more service from existing public resources or of looking outside the public sector for extra resources to sustain the service.

Squeezing more out of less is certainly one feature of New Labour's response to the tax and spend dilemma, and it is one that comes with a string of associated costs. The presentation of the case is always superficially persuasive: that New Labour wants public service provision that is consumer friendly and sensitive, that breaks away from the 'one size fits all' model of the past, and that steadily, year on year, provides not only more service, but service of a higher quality. Who could possibly be opposed to that? As end states, presumably nobody could, or would want to be. It is the daily reality of how New Labour chooses to get there that creates the resistance. Actually, there is some evidence that people in the UK care less about choice than about availability: that they are not as alienated from the 'one size fits all' welfare state as New Labour thinkers tend to assume.[13] But even if they are so alienated, the cost to the providers of New Labour's consumer-friendly public services remains high, and is in significant tension with other aspects of the New Labour project. New Labour as a government is fixated with performance indicators, and with performance indicators moreover that systematically raise the bar over time. The presence of those performance indicators – in education at least – then incrementally shapes the performance they are meant to measure, distorting it in the process in the minds of many of New Labour's critics.[14] It also locks more and more public service workers into what increasingly feels to many of them to be a 'regulatory juggernaut':[15] a veritable Leviathan of inspection, regulation, standard setting and audit that requires huge amounts of additional administrative effort simply to keep it at bay.[16]

Even if no distortion of educational output is in train – that claim, at least, has long been highly contentious, and a perennial milk cow for the Educational Right – what is certainly happening is that the pressure on people working in the public sector is being ratcheted up year on year. This ratcheting up is then forcing them onto a trajectory that is entirely at variance with New Labour's other recently emphasized work goal: which is to retreat from a long-hours, intensive-work economy, to alter the work-life balance in favour of more family time, and to ease the cross-pressures that come when work and child care coincide in families in which both adults perform paid labour. The contradiction between these two great imperatives is everywhere visible in the daily practice of New Labour in power.

There are times when Gordon Brown plays the Iron Chancellor, slashing 100,000 public service jobs and announcing public service agreements with new productivity thresholds. Then there are times when he – or some other major minister, especially Patricia Hewitt – sings an entirely different tune. New Labour is then suddenly all family-friendly, with ministers regretting how long and hard everyone is working, and linking excessive work-time to family problems, to crime and the like. Characteristically perhaps, the New Labour way of squaring this circle is not to reduce the length of the parents' working day: it is to increase the availability, while they work, of the labour of others, to tend their children for them. This is a classic 'paid labour' solution to a problem of child care that, in more progressive hands, would not give children over to the care of strangers but would enable one/both parents to spend more quality time with their children at home. The policy of the Iron Chancellor strives for a new, intensified work-effort bargain, and invites a strong and negative trade union response and a feminist critique.[17] That of the family-friendly Chancellor contains the embryo of a basic income for housework, and for all its limits is increasingly welcomed by the UK's overworked and overpressed families, as the survey data repeatedly shows.[18] Key sections of the UK electorate see the contradiction between these two powerful elements of the New Labour programme, even if ministers do not: and increasingly those sections at least are not buying the argument that public services can go on getting better and better without an enhanced flow of taxation to sustain them.

Yet when the taxation argument is put, sections of the New Labour leadership turn instead, and with enthusiasm, to the use of private funds for public sector investment projects. The enthusiasm is anchored, as we have seen, in more than the capacity it gives New Labour to square the circle of low tax–high spend. It is anchored also in a linked enthusiasm for the private sector itself, as a source of managerial skills and as a model of resource efficiency. Yet that solution is itself riddled with difficulties. Many of the joint ventures so far called into existence – beacon schools or foundation hospitals, for example, not to mention the long-privatized rail network – turn out, when audited, to be financed by highly expensive money and to be no more free of inefficiency problems than the rest of the public sector: which is presumably why, in September 2004, a remarkable 60% of the electorate – and 72% of potential Labour voters – when polled, actually favoured the reinsertion of a commitment to rail renationalization in the party's next election manifesto.[19] Too often, in the past at least, as the government's own OGC reported in 2002, the extra revenue accruing to firms participating in PFI schemes has come from cutting the pay and conditions of their workers;[20] though that at least is a distortion that New Labour has now moved formally to block. But still the issues remain of whether the circle of tax and spend is being squared now only by passing on an inflated tax burden to generations yet unborn – a political sleight of hand that will make the dilemma deeper for reforming governments in years to come – and of whether, in the process of doing so, commodification is creeping like a virus into the body of the welfare state.

Colin Leys has described the 'virus' in this way:

...when services become a source of profit – when they are 'commodified' – they immediately begin to undergo a transformation, following a distinctive logic. First they are 'Taylorised' – the work involved is broken up into its component parts and as much as possible is reassigned to the least qualified and lowest paid workers....Second, as many parts as possible of the service are cut...Third, people are made to do more and more of the work themselves...but fourth, the ultimate goal for all for-profit service provision is even more radical: to substitute the sale of a material commodity for the provision of services, because productivity levels in manufacturing are far higher than they can ever be in services....Producing Ritalin to 'calm down' disturbed children is highly profitable; employing social workers and therapists to help them overcome the effects of their confused, abused or just neglected childhoods will never be.[21]

Gordon Brown at least seems aware of some part of that danger. Alan Milburn, by contrast, seems not to see commodification as a danger at all. But if the critics of PFI are right, then with increased consumer-sensitivity and diversified institutions of public provision must also come significant increases in the *inequality* of public service consumption. If the critics are right, the outcome will be less an improved quality of welfare provision for all than a marked redistribution of existing quantities of welfare provision away from the poor. For markets are great generators of inequality as well as of growth; and the individualism endemic to them is necessarily corrosive of community. At the very least therefore, there is danger here and there may be disaster.[22] The danger is real enough for even Ed Balls to see: that in areas like health and education that 'depend upon an ethic of public service and a commitment to the services, if you go down that marketizing route, you run grave risks with that ethic of public service'.[23]

The manner in which at least the Blairites within New Labour frame the agenda facing the modern health service tells us much about the nature of their project and its direction. To talk of the problem as being the inappropriateness of a 'one shape fits all' structure to the requirements of the modern health consumer speaks to an understanding of the world in which progress comes through the empowerment of consumers and the extension of market relationships. Had they framed it otherwise – as say 'how best to guarantee universal access to high quality health care in a society scarred by social inequality' – then the existing balance of power between the centre and the localities in the existing health system might not have seemed so 'old-fashioned'. To empower consumers, to use markets as optimum allocators of health services, is a problematic strategy for parties of the centre-left who purport to care about equality of access and social justice, because for markets to empower all consumers equally, all consumers must be equipped with equal amounts of purchasing power. But in New Labour Britain they are not. New Labour inherited a society characterized by deep *inequalities* of income, and with it inequalities of access to resources by class, region, ethnic group and gender. Market forces alone can only reinforce those inequalities: markets are mechanisms for many things, but not for levelling playing fields. Those fields have to be levelled first. Yet as we have seen, the New Labour enthusiasm for using markets to trigger efficiencies extends to labour markets as well. This is not a government whose members act decisively to limit the pay of the privileged or to more than marginally lift the pay of the poor. But they cannot have it both ways. New Labour cannot run a health system that is consumer-sensitive, and tell us that this is the route to universal access to high quality health care, if some of the consumers it empowers are left rich and some remain poor. As Gordon Brown reminded the 2004 party conference, 45 million Americans currently lack health cover in the most marketized of health systems in the industrial world. New Labour is surely not set on reproducing that situation here, but it runs the risk of taking us off in that direction if its policies increase the marketization of welfare provision while doing nothing about the existing distribution of income and wealth.

Manufacturing a miracle

Presumably this would matter less if New Labour was able to generate a high rate of economic growth on the basis of sustained private investment in UK-based manufacturing industry: either by creating such a positive environment for business growth that companies voluntarily shifted onto a high-investment, high-wage, high-skill growth path; or, failing that, by direct government intervention to bring that growth path about. But New Labour has so far failed to trigger the voluntary route, and will not explore the more dirigiste alternative, and it will not do the second because of its understanding of the limited range of policy options that are now open to governments faced with the international markets of an increasingly globalized economy. There are state–market dilemmas in the New Labour project which underpin and amplify all the rest.

In a public discourse dominated by the categories and axioms of neo-liberalism – of the kind within which New Labour operates, and which its leading figures regularly replicate – economic growth is supposed to depend on the strength and competitiveness of market forces; and those forces are said to develop best if left free from heavy public regulation and government 'interference'. The argument sounds so wonderfully neutral and technocratic when put in that fashion, and yet, of course, the very sharpness of the term 'interference' gives the game away.[24] To leave the determination of the path and scale of economic growth 'to the market', in a capitalist economy, is in practice to leave all key economic decisions to the private choices of the owners and managers of capital. After all, it is free market capitalism, and not market socialism, that we are talking about here, and if the modern age is distinguished by any change in the space for the former, it is that parties of the centre-left have now systematically retreated from the earlier ambitions of similar parties to directly 'manage' that capitalism for socially desirable ends. Those socially desirable ends are still sought, but now – in the world of New Labour – these can only be attained on the basis of economic growth that is at best *teased out* of the private sector – urged, lubricated, facilitated – but *never directly triggered* by policies that contain sanctions against any section of the private sector that is falling down on the job.

New Labour's dilemma here is that it has denuded itself of the policy instruments of Old Labour's more active industrial policy without equipping itself with new and more potent ones, while simultaneously saddling itself with a monetary stance that has proved remarkably insensitive to the need for a competitive exchange rate. William Keegan's critique of Gordon Brown's 'prudence' is particularly potent on this point. By handing over the determination of interest rates to a Monetary Policy Committee of the Bank of England, the Chancellor won widespread praise for creating a climate of stable expectations that help to sustain steady economic growth, but he did so in such a manner that the previous Treasury practice – of monitoring interest rate movements 'in relation to sterling and what is happening to sterling'[25] – now no longer applied. In consequence, the already existing gap between the two faces of the UK economy – its booming service sector and its ailing manufacturing one – was intensified, as already beleaguered UK manufacturing firms found themselves exposed to cheap competition at home and high export prices abroad. William Keegan rightly traces that unwillingness actively to intervene in the currency markets, to a Treasury lack of confidence created by the events of Black Wednesday in 1992, and so to a policy stance that predated Gordon Brown's arrival in Number 11. But Keegan also rightly contrasts Conservative and New Labour policy here on either side of 1997, noting that Kenneth Clarke, John Major's last Chancellor of the Exchequer, 'had resisted advice from the Bank to raise rates on occasion largely because he was worried about making the pound even stronger and British industry's competitive position weaker'. Under Gordon Brown, by contrast, Keegan tells us, 'such concern was now largely swept aside from the point of view of operational policy, with potentially very damaging consequences'. For even though New Labour's Chancellor regularly asserted his belief that the 'exchange rate should be "stable and competitive", it was not obvious' – to Keegan at least – that 'over the following years, he was prepared in practice to do much about the pound's manifest loss of competitiveness'.[26]

Instead, Gordon Brown put at the core of the government's 'new' relationship with the business community in the UK policies of tax reduction and regulation-easement: but those were likely to work only if taxes and regulation were in truth the key barriers to investment in the previous period, as the peak organizations of business claimed them to be. And even if they were, such policies were inevitably bound to work with diminishing impact over time, as taxes fell and regulations were removed. In fact, the claims were always specious ones, and in consequence New Labour saw hardly any 'bounce' in investment as corporate taxation eased. All that Labour ministers were left with, to reinforce their pitch, was a new structure of Regional Development Agencies – each in competition with the others as it struggled with the local legacies of more than a century of uneven economic development in the UK – and a regular series of DTI White Papers and consultation documents that scored high on presentation and low on substance. Five years on from its first moment of power, still seeking a manufacturing miracle, New Labour's much-publicized *Manufacturing Strategy* is a case in point. Beautifully produced, and full of the latest managerial language and new growth theory assertions, what actually did that strategy amount to? Just these '7 pillars': and in truth very little indeed:

Pillar 1: *Macro-economic stability*...

Pillar 2: *Investment*...changes to the tax system which encourage entrepreneurship; assistance to investment in certain regions and by small companies; and encouragement of inward investment

Pillar 3: *Science and Innovation*...the recently introduced R&D tax credit for large firms, and the continued expansion of investment in the science base...

Pillar 4: *Best Practice*...we earmarked an extra £20m for best practice activity

Pillar 5: *Raising Skills and Education Levels*...

Pillar 6: *Modern Infrastructure*...we have set out a 10-year plan to modernize the transport network at a cost of £181 billion...strategy to increase broadband penetration

Pillar 7: *The Right Market Framework*...competition framework...free and fair trade...sensible minimum standards in the workplace. Action...to reform the planning system to meet business concerns.[27]

These pillars simply build a superstructure of incentives and a substructure of environmental supports. They are less a policy than a call to arms, directed at a business community that is to be 'lubricated' but not directed. But what if the business community declines to be called? What use is lubrication then? Tilting at windmills is no substitute for action, and there will be no action until this New Labour government resets its relationship to its local manufacturing class. New Labour would do well to remember R. H. Tawney's critique of an earlier Labour government's supine relationship to the dominant order. You cannot negotiate, he told them, while you are on your knees,[28] and yet to date, and with the exception of a few sticky moments around the 2002 budget process, the relationship between the government and the business community has been characterized by way too much deference on the government's part. It has in truth been one prolonged 'prawn offensive' since well before 1997: with New Labour leaders desperate not to offend, alienate, or otherwise discourage a local industrial entrepreneurial class whose extremely poor investment record, innovative capacity and managerial skills deserved tougher treatment.

For this is an industrial class whose performance is far poorer than that of the best of its Western European equivalents, and poorer still when set against the American industrial owning and managing class that the Chancellor is said to admire so much. In fact, the only truly outstanding thing that UK owners and managers are good at is paying themselves a lot for achieving little – we know that from the figures on directors' stipends and golden parachutes – and yet New Labour ministers have steadfastly refused to limit those, or to set up (as once, say, the South Korean government did, as the trigger to growth[29]) any system that might tie senior salaries in private industry to competitive performance. When in 2004 a Conservative MP and former businessman, Archie Norman, tabled a private member's bill designed to end 'rewards for failure', New Labour's Secretary of State for Trade and Industry immediately outflanked him on his right, explicitly ruling out any notion of new laws to end excessive boardroom pay. Taxing the wealthy, the Prime Minister told the *Guardian*, will simply encourage them to hire accountants and reduce the tax take![30] 'Do you believe an individual can earn too much money?' he was asked by Jeremy Paxman. 'I don't really,' was the reply,

> ...it is not – no, it is not a view I have. Do you mean that we should cap someone's income? Not really, no. Why? What is the point? You can spend ages trying to stop the highest paid earners earning the money but in an international market like today, you probably would drive

them away. What does that matter? Surely the important thing is to level up those people that don't have the opportunity in our society.
Paxman: But where is the justice in taxing someone who earns £34,000 a year, which is enough to cover a mortgage on a one-bedroom flat in outer London, at the same rate as someone who earns £34 million? Where is the justice?
Blair: The person who earns £34 million, if they're paying the top rate of tax, will pay far more tax on the £34 million than the person on £34,000
Paxman: I am asking you about the rate of tax.
Blair: I know and what I am saying to you is that the rate is less important in this instance than the overall amount of tax that people would pay...
Paxman: But Prime Minister, the gap between rich and poor has been widened while you have been in office....So it is acceptable for the gap to widen between rich and poor?
Blair: It is not acceptable for poor people not to be given the chances they need in life
Paxman: That is not my question.
Blair: I know it's not your question, but it's the way I choose to answer it....The way I choose to answer it is to say that the job of government is to make sure that those at the bottom get the chances.
Paxman: With respect, people see you are asked a straightforward question and they see you not answering it....Let's talk about tax. You promised
Blair: Why don't we talk about the poorest of society and what we are doing for them?
Paxman: I assume you want to be Prime Minister. I just want to be an interviewer. Can we stick to that arrangement?
Blair: Fine.[31]

So though New Labour as a government is heavily into performance indicators, it is not – it would seem – into performance indicators for the owners and managers of the UK's underperforming manufacturing sector. In relation to them, and in spite of regular ministerial protestations to the contrary, New Labour does not possess an active industrial policy of any substance.[32] It has a re-skilling policy that at best will generate results only in the long-term, and which actually looks inadequate to the scale of the problem even if given time to bite. It has a policy on public sector investment and productivity, but it does not even spend as much on industrial aid, and support for private sector R&D, as is the norm within the rest of the European Union. And it clearly does not think of the trade unions as its close allies in the modernization of the UK industrial base.[33] New Labour in power is consumer-sensitive rather than producer-sensitive on issues of efficiency and growth, and yet the industrial owning class by which ministers now put such store, and the private bankers on which they depend for finance, have a truly appalling record for industrial modernization without state incentives and pressure.[34] Gordon Brown talks of the 'lubricating' role of the state in relation to modern industry, and it is true that the smooth running of an engine requires that it be oiled. But for the engine to run at all, it requires fuel, and in the absence of an adequate supply of private fuel, in previous epochs that fuel would have come from the state. Not with New Labour: to its cost and ours. For in allying itself so closely with an underperforming UK industrial owning class, the Blair government has allied itself to the very source of the problem it is attempting to solve, and then for some reason is surprised when that alliance fails to generate the solutions it requires. Running with the wrong crowd has never been a good idea for parties of the centre-left, and yet here we are, running with the wrong crowd again.

The poor and the powerless

The weakness of New Labour as a government, in relation to the underperforming privately-owned industrial sector on which it depends for economic growth, has had two major social consequences. It has left New Labour in power tolerating levels of income and wealth inequality that have gone largely unreformed, and it has fed an incipient authoritarianism in the entire New Labour project, encouraging ministers to focus their disciplinary zeal on the casualties of prolonged underinvestment and low growth, and not on its agents of causality.

New Labour certainly came to power facing embedded systems of inequality which, so far at least, it has done precious little to penetrate. There has been some penetration: 'significant reductions in levels of poverty overall, and in levels of child poverty and pensioner poverty' were Giddens' chosen three in his recent defence of Gordon Brown's anti-poverty strategy,[35] and as we have seen, there certainly have been many policy initiatives aimed at poverty reduction. Yet perhaps not surprisingly in the light of Tony Blair's attitude to the taxing of high salaries, and in spite of these poverty programmes, 'inequality in disposable income (after tax and benefits) appears to have slightly increased since 1997'; 'the rich have continued to get richer'; and 'wealth distribution…has continued to get more unequal in the last decade'.[36] Overall, the 2004 IPPR report from which that data came gave the New Labour government a mixed score for achievement – and so, like Giddens himself, an agenda of action still to be addressed. The report, using as its benchmark the state of the UK when the original *Social Justice* report was prepared in 1994, found the UK a fairer society because of some of the things that New Labour ministers have done: it particularly mentioned progress on employment, child poverty, health and crime. But it also reported the modest nature of the achievement so far: that in 1998 the UK was bottom of the EU league, with the highest child poverty rate in the EU, and by 2001 had crawled its way up to position 11 out of 15. The report summarized the general position in this way:

> ..the Government has been good on poverty but not so good on inequality; better on income inequality than on wealth inequality; helped working families but done less for poor people without children; and cut crime but the poorest are still more likely to suffer crime and the fear of crime....Britain is still far from being a fair and just society. Parental social class and ethnicity still heavily influence life chances, while democratic participation is falling and political influence is polarized according to class and wealth. Women continue to be more likely to live in poverty while the percentage of wealth held by the wealthiest 10 per cent has increased from 47 per cent to 54 per cent over the last decade.[37]

Instead of triggering major income redistribution, the Blair government's enthusiasm for balancing rights with responsibilities has in practice focused on the urban poor. Its enthusiasm for squeezing more out of less has focused on the lower levels of the welfare bureaucracies, and its radicalism has stayed closer to the political class than to the owners and managers of capital funds. It is as though New Labour ministers feel more comfortable picking on those whose social and economic power is low than on those whose status and social clout is high, and that they feel more at home chasing the consequences of their love affair with the market than with limiting the market itself – chasing the consequences of individualism and competition, anti-social behaviour and the decline of 'community', but not corporate scandals and the mutual glad-handing of the director class.[38]

Hold an image in your mind of a pebble dropped into a still pond, and imagine the ripples moving out from the centre. Label them first political, then social and finally economic, and you have a map of New Labour's radicalism and impact. There has been definite radicalism, definite impact on the political circle nearest to the New Labour 'pebble': not fully radical even there – no proportional representation, only limited freedom of information, but nonetheless full devolution to Scotland and Wales, limits on election spending, a completely reshuffled political class. Come out to the next ring – the social one – and here New Labour has been active too, though only more patchily progressive: good on child poverty, helping pensioners, supporting families and the like, but also pushing welfare-to-work and punishing the young for truancy, drunkenness and loutish behaviour. It is the final ring – the economic one – where New Labour's record is much more talk than action: monetary stability for sure, but also income inequality, limited worker rights and deference to international capital. The further you go out from the centre to the edge – from the political through the social to the economic – the less decisive, radical and progressive New Labour appears to be. So far New Labour has moved the political class around in new institutions. It has imposed permanent reform on its own welfare providers and clients; but it has left the private sector largely untaxed and in many ways largely ungoverned. It is hard to avoid the judgement that, for all its progressive rhetoric at conference time and when elections loom, these days New Labour is actually tougher on crime than on the causes of crime, and that is a tragedy given the high hopes held by us all in the heady days of 1997.

The limits of 'third way' politics

This is all classic 'third way' stuff, New Labour style: full of reforming zeal, but highly selective about the targets on which that zeal is to be focused. New Labour's 'third way', as presumably is now obvious to anyone who has examined it in detail, is an extremely difficult thing to pin down. It claims not to be the same as the two 'ways' that preceded it – to be in some sense a synthesis of the best of the past, free of the weaknesses of both Old Labour and Thatcherism – and yet it is this very synthetic quality, and its associated lack of sharpness, that has so far prevented it from having the hegemonic impact on UK political life that first Keynesian welfarism and later neo-liberalism did so effectively years before. There is much talk these days in political circles of something called 'a third way' – and indeed we now possess a huge literature addressed to nothing less – but we still lack any sharp sense of what it is, what actual role it plays in policy design, and indeed whether, beyond the level of rhetoric, it even exists.

The sharpness has grown a little over time. The New Labour leadership seemed to require a second massive electoral victory in 2001 in order to shake off the old Wilsonian shibboleth of having to prove Labour's fitness to govern; and with that shibboleth gone, we do now occasionally come across senior party figures asserting the uniqueness and importance of what they are about. Even then, however, it is a uniqueness and importance that, in presentational terms, is more comparative than substantive in content. 'Britain is combining the best of the US and European models', New Labour's employment minister told a Nuffield College seminar in October 2000:[39] 'building a consensus that prosperity and justice for all can advance together'.[40] 'Some continents', Gordon Brown told the Social Market Foundation,

> ....are defined to the world as beacons of enterprise but at the cost of fairness; others as beacons of fairness or social cohesion at the cost of efficiency. In our time, Britain can be a beacon for the world where enterprise and fairness march forward together. It is a very British idea.[41]

British it may be, and a consensus too, but sharp it is not. As we first observed in Chapter 3, Margaret Thatcher was the last major British politician who knew the importance of political sharpness, and who in consequence was brilliantly effective in repositioning the entire political debate in the UK on territory of her own choosing. As we saw then, like all good hegemonic politicians, Margaret Thatcher took a single and simple idea – in her case, the idea of the 'market' – and embedded it institutionally in one policy area after another: such that long after she had left the political stage, her legacy had not. It remained, locked in, part of the daily experience and common sense of an entire electorate. New Labour has yet to find that single organizing idea, or to fully embed its organizing philosophy in a new set of institutions. As we saw earlier, 'stakeholding' played that potentially hegemonic role briefly in the last years of opposition, but ultimately its implementation required too radical a confrontation with the existing distribution of industrial and social power for a New Labour leadership keen to reform everything but the way private industrialists made their investment decisions. The idea of the UK as a 'meritocracy' has since been periodically rolled out – by the Prime Minister if not the Chancellor – as a possible alternative organizing pole; but for many in the party, that notion sits ill with an older social democratic vision of the UK as a society compassionate to its weaker brethren and driven by a sense of community rather than by individual ambition. 'Stakeholding' didn't play well with the Institute of Directors, and was consequently dropped. The idea of the UK as a 'meritocracy' is equally unpopular among the party's own rank and file, and is likely to experience a similar fate.

Anthony Giddens has recently suggested that Labour should renew its commitment to something he terms 'a New Equalitarianism': but it certainly hasn't yet, and it is significant that the hunt for New Labour's big idea is still on. In its absence, a government which inherited a political discourse dominated by the axioms and categories of neo-liberalism has yet to break free of that inheritance. It has yet to break from a public discourse in which taxation is presented, not as a welcome source of a valuable social wage, but as an unwelcome extraction from an entirely private one. It has yet to break free from a discourse in which public ownership, public funding and the public direction of economic and social activity have to justify themselves in ways that private ownership, private funding and private direction do not. It has yet to break from a discourse that treats the private ownership of the means of production as a guarantee of enterprise, growth and efficiency, rather than of inequality, instability and overproduction; and it has yet to break free of the glibbest and most optimistic of the current characterizations of globalization.[42] There has been no 'great moving left show' to correct the 'great moving right show' that the Conservatives triggered once Margaret Thatcher has ousted Edward Heath in the 1970s. Instead there has been what Stuart Hall called 'a great moving nowhere show' – a continuation of what Will Hutton once described as 'New Labour's Achilles' heel': that, lacking an 'economic theory which is critical of capitalism, it is wide open to simple business definitions of the public interest because it has no other reference point'.[43] There is a new vocabulary, of course – that of a 'third way' – but there is no new organizing philosophy to replace what was there before; and that is why the election victory of 2001 tells us less about the likely longevity of New Labour in power than might otherwise be the case. The Conservatives could not break out of their parliamentary ghetto in 2001, less because New Labour had shifted the political centre of gravity away from them and more because New Labour had so positioned itself on traditional Conservative territory that the Tories as a party could find no clear blue space. Electorally the space still has its supporters, and if New Labour falters, they may yet defect back.

Whether they do will turn in part on the adequacy of the 'model' that New Labour policies are bringing into existence into the UK, and therefore on the accuracy of the claim made by Gordon Brown and others that we are witnessing the emergence of a unique fusion, across the UK economy and society as a whole, of efficiency and fairness. On this, of course, the jury must still be out, and the lines of march are still in dispute. All the proposed ways forward will claim to be radical. All will come talking the language of 'empowerment', 'renewal', 'social solidarity', 'democratization' and 'global justice'.[44] All will claim to be left-wing, but in truth the Blair way will not be a progressive one, and the Brown way, though better, will – unless it alters – remain deeply flawed.

A third-term New Labour government marching to a Blairite rhythm will, at most, create a meritocratic society in which the rhetoric of opportunity and community, and of balanced rights and responsibilities, will mask a deepening of inequality and the entrenchment of a minimum social floor. How high that floor will be set will be determined by public toleration of taxation, and the odds are that in a climate of growing individualism and the extended use of market mechanisms to allocate education and health, that toleration will decline over time. When Tony Blair and his allies talk of their vision, it is much more egalitarian and desirable than this, of course: they project an image of a society opening up at the bottom, full of educational opportunity, skill training and urban renewal – an image

> not of a society where all succeed equally – that is utopia, but an opportunity society where all have an equal chance to succeed...where nothing in your background, whether you're black or white, a man or a woman, able-bodied or disabled, stands in the way of what your merit and hard work can achieve.[45]

But it is just an image. The routes to it, and the possibility of it, remain unclear and uncertain. What is certain is that, in a Blairite future, no levels of taxation, or degrees of redistribution, will be allowed to disturb the incentives for private investment and the taking of profit: so that, over time, the UK will again increasingly resemble the Conservative country that New Labour inherited: more prosperous perhaps, and with a slightly stronger social net to catch the poor than the Tories might have funded, but only quantitatively different, not qualitatively transformed by New Labour in power.

When we discussed the national minimum wage in Chapter 5, we found Tony Blair promising the TUC in September 1997 that his way, the New Labour way, would not be 'the Tory way – inequality, insecurity and low wages for the many, very high rewards for the few'.[46] But what else is a meritocratic society but that, when its economic base has been weakened and its social capital depleted by generations of neglect.[47] Roy Hattersley had it entirely right:

> Meritocracy removes the barriers to progress which block the path of the clever and industrious. But the notion of social mobility on which it is based is, to most of the children of the inner cities, a joke. A Labour Government should not be talking about escape routes from poverty and deprivation. By their nature they are only available to a highly-motivated minority. The Labour Party was created to change society in such a way that there is no poverty and deprivation from which to escape. Meritocracy only offers shifting patterns of inequality.[48]

These days, Tony Blair presents his social radicalism as an agenda to extend 'opportunity and security to all hard-working families'. The very formulation seems to divide the world into the hard-working and the feckless, and so plays into that right-wing discourse on 'free-riders' and 'scroungers on the public purse' that then demonizes the most vulnerable victims of a free market capitalism. The Blair formulation also slides over the issue of whether the returns for hard work are the same for everyone in a world of unregulated and unequal labour markets. Richard Branson may be able to fly millionaires to the moon, but a whole string of Bransons will not deliver a social democratic version of 'trickle down economics', no matter how strongly Tony Blair argues that it might. 'I doubt the public will be keen to support this new Labour approach of excellence for the few and a safety net for the many', the retiring General Secretary of the TGWU said in 2002: and he spoke for many when he did so.[49]

That is perhaps why a version of the Gordon Brown show is so popular among more left-wing, or 'old-fashioned' social democrats, inside the now tense Labour coalition. I say 'a version' because Gordon Brown himself is as difficult to read as is the New Labour project he has done so much to shape. Brown is also the arch modernizer, as we saw earlier: tough on the unions, micro-managing public sector productivity, critical of European labour market regulation, supportive of PFI. Yet he is also the stealth socialist, the family-supportive Chancellor, the provider of much-needed funds to the education system and the health service, the thinker defending public provision against the full play of the market. It is this second Brown who now attracts so much left-wing hope within the Labour coalition, and it is this second Brown whose policies do offer help directly to key sections of the poor: to pensioners certainly, and to families in poverty, if not yet to the childless poor. It is to this second

Brown that the thinking left tend naturally to gravitate with their various specifications for how a third term ought properly to be used.

Yet care is essential here, for 'Brown has become the past master at allowing people to project on him views that he does not hold' and as we have just noted, his 'public service vision exists alongside his commitment to the British model of "competition, liberalization and reform"'.[50] Care needs to be taken too because it is also this second Brown that seems pre-programmed to run into the standard buffers experienced by all left social democratic parties in power. He seems pre-programmed to meet the tension between his economic ambitions (geared to a healthy private sector) and his social ones (that require the heavy taxation of a successful private sector), and like his leader, and just as bizarrely, he seems to believe that a meritocratic Britain without losers is a genuine possibility. He seems to believe, unless this is pure rhetoric adopted only for conference purposes, that New Labour can create

> ...a Great Britain of aspiration and ambition where there are no barriers to achievement, no ceilings on talent, no cap on success and where the common sense of the age is that not just a few but everyone has the chance to fulfil their dreams and potential.[51]

Like many left social democrats, Gordon Brown seems convinced that growth and justice can go together, so long as UK industry can out-compete industries based elsewhere, and so long as capital can be attracted from them to us because of the superiority in the UK of the tax regimes and skills supply available to foreign-owned firms. Yet that is not so much a growth strategy as a treadmill: it commits the UK workforce to a perennial battle to run harder, just to stand still, as every other competing economy does the same.[52] In fact, as far as I can tell, there is simply nothing in Gordon Brown's existing strategy to enable the UK, historically behind in that race, to leap forward with sufficient speed even to catch up, let alone to pass its key competitors. Moreover, in the process of trying, the Brown strategy, behind a rhetoric which in his case is often intensely nationalistic, runs the risk of actually perpetuating an even more acute version of the long-hours, low-wage economy that New Labour inherited and promised to replace.[53]

Even that part of the Brown agenda that so appeals to progressive opinion – the redistribution by stealth, particularly to the children of the poor – is not without its serious critics from the left, and properly so. That criticism has been directed in part at the 'stealth' of the redistribution project, and in part at the premises of the 'redistribution' itself. For redistributing income *sotto voce,* as Ruth Lister and others have noted, has the disadvantage of 'doing good' while 'not being seen to be doing good'; and when coupled, for cover, with tough language on unemployed claimants and the like, actually 'sends out messages which could undermine the...popularity of the welfare state' by helping to create 'a negative image of the welfare dependent which is damaging to the self-respect of those on benefit'.[54] Moreover, redistributing in small slices, also in order to remain under cover, creates additional complexities in the tax and benefit system – complexities which then both increase the degree of non-take-up of the changes on offer, and ensure that whatever individual changes do occur will only have the most marginal of impacts on the lives they are meant to improve. And by directing all its reforming fire at the children of the working poor, by using entry into paid labour as the key route out of poverty, and by setting up the problem as one of 'hard-working families', the entire New Labour social project carries with it fundamental premises that may themselves be false. It certainly carries the premise that 'paid work within a profoundly unequal labour market can be equated with social inclusion', and it also carries the premise that 'paid work represents the primary obligation for all those of working age' – in the process discounting 'the value of community and voluntary activities and the unpaid work of reproduction and care carried out in the home, mainly still by women'.[55] The problematic nature of those premises, the marginal impact of the many tiny reforms so far introduced and the depth of the processes locking children into poverty, have collectively led many commentators to counsel caution here. 'We will not rest until we have banished child poverty from the face of Britain', the Chancellor has often insisted, but as David Piachaud and Holly Sutherland have rightly noted, given how 'much remains to be done' that rest may actually 'be a long time in coming'.[56]

The choice: three ways or four?

There is a judgement to be made here – a weighing of possibilities and potentials, and a decision. All of us need to decide whether New Labour policies are staging posts on a trajectory that over time will indeed produce a more efficient and a fairer society, or whether it is the case that, in order to reach such a society, policy will have to be reset and trajectories altered. If it is the first, then progressive elements in the UK electorate can safely vote Labour with enthusiasm. If it is the second, they can only vote Labour without illusions, while working inside and outside the party for the injection of radical change. So which it is to be?

As towards the end of New Labour's second term a general election again loomed, key ministerial figures regularly, and for understandable reasons, asserted the former case: that no resetting of basic policy trajectory was necessary, that progress so far had been impressive, that much remained to be done, and that doing it was what New Labour's third term would be all about. The party's 2004 conference was in that sense the moment at which the New Labour leadership attempted to reconnect the government to its political and electoral base – a reconnection that was much needed after the detour through the war in Iraq – by launching a new set of policies, and by launching them as a veritable crusade. Vote New Labour, the Prime Minister said, and you will get the policies promised to the trade unions at Warwick, you will get new policies to help first-time homebuyers, new policies to give working parents child care from 8.00 a.m. to 6.00 p.m. all year round, new choices on schools to go to and hospitals to use, and so on. It was the Education Secretary who presented his part of this new package as a 'crusade' – a crusade 'worth fighting for, worth working for, worth voting for' – and as such, a set of changes that would make 'a fundamental difference to all our futures':[57] and he was not alone in thinking that. That decision on wrap-around child care from 8.00 a.m. to 6.00 p.m. was rightly hailed, even by commentators often critical of New Labour, as a huge step forward: indeed as even possibly 'the first great extension of the welfare state in 50 years, at last embracing the upbringing of children as the shared social responsibility of all'.[58]

Given that sort of response, it may seem churlish to complain, but – conference hyperbole notwithstanding – complaint, or at least immense caution, is still in order here. Wrap-around child care is a welcome but still limited response to a real set of tensions at the heart of the New Labour project; but it does not take those tensions away. This is still a project that seeks to combine rising labour productivity with improvements in the quality of family life within an economy whose success and failure the Chancellor continues to measure in the old-fashioned, narrow and commodity-focused way. There is no evidence that the quality of life indicators developed by New Labour early in its period in office have shaped the trajectory of policy in Gordon Brown's Treasury, or even that success is being sought/measured against that wider set of tests. Yet it needs to be, if New Labour is to effect a qualitative transformation in the working lives of the people who voted for it, and through them, of the entire fabric of UK society as a whole. Paying new parents to stay at home is significantly preferable to having them forced back into paid work before they want to, as even the Independent Childcare Commission chaired by Harriet Harman recognized in the report that it published immediately prior to Ms Harman's return to government in 2001,[59] and paid-for child care is better than no child care at all. But a working day short enough to allow parents to care for their children is a whole deal better. As Madeleine Bunting has correctly argued, 'only if we begin to get a grip on the problem of Britain's 3.75 million long-hour workers will we trigger the reshaping of working time required to ease the oppressive strain of an outdated work culture (built on the assumption of a stay-at-home wife) on today's two-earner family'.[60] New Labour's wrap-around child care proposal is a welcome Band-Aid to a deepening cut in UK economic and social life: but it is a response to a problem. It is not a resolution of the problem itself.

Maybe the problem is impossible to solve. Maybe the UK economy has fallen so far behind that only a 'civilized' version of a sweatshop economy is all that the future can hold. Maybe UK workers will always have to work long hours, and wrap-around child care is all we can do to alleviate it. But presumably the New Labour leadership doesn't think that, and certainly nobody wants the UK's long-term future to be of this kind. As far as I can tell, the goal of a low-hours, high-investment, high-productivity economy remains – and quite properly remains – the working target of New Labour in power: and because it does, it behoves all of us to face honestly the scale of the resetting of policy that actually stepping up to such an economy still now requires. The detail of that resetting is not easily available to us – there is still much serious planning work to be done in the think-tanks of the radical left – but the scale of the required rupture with present policy is clear, as is the general direction that such a rupture will need to take.[61]

To break free of the economic legacy left to New Labour by two decades of Thatcherite neglect of the UK's manufacturing base, policy will have to change dramatically and rapidly across a series of key fronts: not least on sources of investment, on attitudes to Europe, and on the stance on trade. For private investment will not generate that change alone, nor will companies be able to compete in a world of unmanaged trade when obliged to dilute their existing work-pay bargains, and the EU will not be able to defend existing levels of job protection and welfare provision by the processes of internal incremental erosion of benefits and the external lowering of trade barriers that New Labour ministers (including Gordon Brown) are prone to advocate. The future for the UK left does not lie in a deconstruction of the European welfare model. On the contrary, it lies in a defence and a deepening of that model, a defence that will be possible only if the UK genuinely positions itself at the very heart of the

European project. In consequence, it also lies in an active protection of the global space necessary for the European model to continue to flourish. We cannot afford to surrender that space. No one – in or out of Europe – would benefit from a race to the bottom, of the kind now released upon workers worldwide by the institutionalization, at the level of the global system, of the free trade fantasies of the neo-liberal right. And because they would not, the key task facing centre-left policy-makers of a genuinely progressive kind is the design of policies at the global level that can trigger a generalized 'ratcheting up' of living standards across the world system as a whole. Relying on free trade to do that will simply not be enough.

In consequence, and though difficult as it will be to effect, a progressive future for the UK left lies through a programme of WTO reform: trade policy has to become central to radical politics in the manner suggested by the protesters at Seattle and since. Even Stephen Byers, who at the Seattle WTO meeting defended the UK's free trade stance, has since recanted, and he is not alone in now recognizing that 'free market trade policies hurt the poor' and that 'a different approach is needed: one which recognizes the importance of managed trade with the objective of achieving development goals'.[62] The left needs to create a trade policy for the UK and the EU that, at the very least, privileges the protection of labour standards, introduces controls on capital flows, and encourages the bilateral negotiation of special trading terms with newly developing economies that pay higher wages. It needs one that replaces the economic maxims of free trade with the social concerns of fair trade, and one that actively manages demand at the global level – in true Keynesian style – in order to undermine the otherwise persistently reproduced inequalities that flow from the unregulated exchange of goods between unequal trading partners. And at home, the future of the UK left does not lie in yet more UK-focused 'prawn offensives' on the local business community. It lies in the re-equipping of the UK state with policy instruments that really bite (including public ownership and state finance). It lies in the use of the size of the EU as a bargaining tool with large multinational capital – the state is not impotent before global capitalism, it must simply raise its level of operation to meet the new capacities of multinational firms – and it lies in a reconstitution of the links between the political and industrial wings of the UK labour movement that New Labour has done so much to undermine. New Labour's 'third way' currently contains far too much of Margaret Thatcher's 'second way', and far too few of the policy instruments of Old Labour's 'first way', effectively to reset the growth trajectory of UK plc. Accordingly Labour ministers would do well to re-examine the Labour Party's own past, rather than that of the Conservatives, when designing future Labour policy, and this time they would do well to undertake that re-examination in a more sympathetic manner than was fashionable in the leadership circles of the Labour Party in the 1990s.

In fact, if New Labour is to flourish as a progressive government of a unique kind, it could do no better than make the big idea of its third term not 'personalized services' – as seems likely – but instead the pursuit of greater individual and collective 'happiness'. It could do no better than to replace all its performance indicators with a single measure of 'public satisfaction' – in the Canadian manner – and to do its homework on the new economics of hedonism. If it did that, it would find that GDP is a poor indicator of success in terms of happiness, at least after per capita income gets above about £15,000, when other factors kick in: job security, employment, a stable family environment and good health. As Michael Kitson has observed:

> The policy agenda that focused on happiness would attach a high priority to increasing jobs, reducing work insecurity and reducing stress in the workplace. Additionally, hours worked would be reduced and geographical labour market flexibility discouraged to improve family life. Public expenditure would be increased in areas of health and education, and redistribution would be important to increase social cohesion and to improve the welfare of those on low incomes (whose happiness is linked to income). This is a policy agenda that is very different to the modern orthodoxy, which focuses on increasing GDP through increasing labour market flexibility, encouraging risk taking and limiting the role of the state.[63]

What would be wrong, for example, in New Labour establishing for itself a benchmark of progress for its third term that was based, not on GDP growth, but on the most basic of the value commitments of the UK labour movement: the commitments to equality and social justice? The Blairites could even give that benchmark a religious anchorage if they so chose, as the rest of us went forward on a purely humanistic basis: arguing that we should work for a world organized around the principle of '*do unto others as you would have them do unto you*'. The world we live in now is not so organized. We as consumers enjoy low-priced commodities whose cheapness is the product of the underpayment of their producers in societies whose labour movements lack the strength and the presence of ours. We as taxpayers regularly consume public services whose availability requires the underpaid labour of fellow-citizens whose private deprivation is hidden from us behind a rhetoric of 'overmanning and the lack of market discipline'. It may be that some public services – now, or in the past – were so overmanned, and that in consequence Gordon Brown was right to impose rigorous sets of public service agreements that triggered productivity growth year on year. But eventually, and arguably now, a point must be reached where services can grow and taxes can be contained, only if public sector workers are obliged to operate under terms and conditions of service that the rest of us would rightly refuse to tolerate for ourselves. That is the point at which productivity drives should cease and higher taxation should kick in. For if it is to last, and while in office to be worth the candle, a progressive government needs from the outset to build a constituency of moral worth: one that refuses to live well off the exploitation of others: one that in consequence insists on paying proper levels of tax for proper services, and proper prices for the goods and services that the market, rather than the state, brings to the table. A trade policy based on generous labour standards, and a welfare policy based on generous funding, will eventually create a society here in the UK, and help to create societies elsewhere, that are genuinely fair and free. Policies built on free trade and welfare retrenchment will not. The UK is not such a society now – nor is the global order in which it trades – but both at home, and to a lesser degree abroad, New Labour is in a position to move us towards such an end-state if it so chooses. Because it is, by that chosen direction of movement we, its electorate, ought now to begin to hold it to account.

To my mind, and in spite of all the difficulties involved in the process, the future of the UK left lies through a systematic and incremental radicalization of New Labour's 'third way' into a *fourth* one that can indeed combine growth and prosperity for all, and that can in consequence move us towards a genuinely egalitarian social order. If I am right, the issue before the Labour Party now is not simply who will lead it and who will not. That is an important matter, but it is not the key question. The key question before the Labour Party now concerns the recalibration of its entire project. It is about the direction in which the party (and its electorate) will and should be led.

Notes

Preface

1. The outstanding example is S. Driver and L. Martell, *Blair's Britain*, Cambridge, Polity Press, 2002.
2. The focus of this volume is on economic and social policy. Constitutional reform is only lightly touched upon, and the discussion of foreign policy is entirely left to the companion volume, David Coates and Joel Krieger (with Rhiannon Vickers), *Blair's War*, Cambridge, Polity Press, 2004.

Chapter 1

1. Andrew Rawnsley, 'We are a nation reborn', *Observer*, 3 May 1997.
2. Tony Benn in conversation with the author, for the Open University Social Science television programme, *The 1997 Election:Traditions, Failures and Futures* (interview, 20 October 1997).
3. L. P. Hartley, *The Go Between*, Harmondsworth, Penguin Books, 1967, p. 1.
4. P. Armstrong, A. Glyn and J. Harrison, *Capitalism since World War II: The Making and Break Up of the Great Boom*, London, Fontana, 1991, pp. 167–8.
5. See for example, B. Supple, 'British economic decline since 1945', in R. Floud and D. McCloskey (eds), *The Economic History of Britain since 1700*, volume 3, Cambridge, Cambridge University Press, 1994, pp. 318–46; and S. Wilks, 'Conservative governments and the economy 1979–97', *Political Studies*, vol. XLV, 1997, pp. 689–703.
6. Michael Barratt Brown, *What Really Happened to the Coal Industry*, Nottingham, Institute for Workers Control, 1972, p. 5.
7. The term given to the systems of semi-automated mass production that spread through consumer industries in the UK after 1945, and first pioneered by Henry Ford. On this, see D. Coates, *Running the Country*, London, Hodder and Stoughton, 1995, pp. 23–6.
8. G. Rhys, 'The transformation of the motor industry in the UK', in R. Turner (ed.), *The British Economy in Transition*, London, Routledge, 1995, p. 147.
9. R. Church, *The Rise and Decline of the British Motor Industry*, Cambridge, Cambridge University Press, 1994, p. 54.
10. By June 1999, employment in UK-based manufacturing firms had fallen to 4.2 million (Employment Policy Institute, *Employment Audit*, Issue 12, Winter 1999, p. 5).
11. P. Gregg and J. Wadsworth, 'Economic inactivity', in their *The State of Working Britain*, Manchester, Manchester University Press, 1999, p. 56.
12. D. Coates, 'UK under-performance: claim and reality', in D. Coates and J. Hillard (eds), *UK Economic Decline: Key Texts*, Hemel Hempstead, Prentice Hall/Harvester Wheatsheaf, 1995, p. 7. The bulk of those excluded by this process were male workers in the second half of their working career. Job

creation in the UK between 1979 and 1997 was heavily skewed towards part-time work so that overall the numbers of hours worked in the UK economy actually fell: from 850 million a year in 1984 to 780 million in 1994.

13. The 1960 figures, in 1998 US dollars (using data based on purchasing power parity exchange rates) were 4,672 for Japan, 9,842 for West Germany, 8,546 for France, 7,286 for Italy and 10,503 for the UK. The 1998 figures were 24,170 for Japan, 24,868 for the western part of Germany, 22,255 for France, 22,234 for Italy and 21,502 for the UK. By the same token, hourly wage rates in manufacturing in the UK were on average 81% of those prevalent in the US. The equivalent figure for Germany was 132%, for France 87% and for Italy 96% (L. Mishel, J. Bernstein and J. Shmitt (eds), *The State of Working America 2000–2001*, Ithaca, Cornell University Press, 2001, pp. 374, 381).

14. Employment Policy Institute, *Employment Audit*, Issue 11, Summer 1999, p. 1. 'While we observed a compression in the working week, when overtime was included the working week clearly lengthened. In 1998 only 16% of men worked fewer than forty hours a week, while 30% worked more than fifty hours (this compares with 27% and 24% respectively a decade earlier). Among women too, the working week was longer. In 1998 45% of women worked over forty hours a week, and 10% worked over fifty hours (compared to 27% and 4% respectively in 1988). There is also an important gender difference in patterns of overtime work. Ten years ago women worked little overtime compared to men, but by 1998, while women were as likely as men to be working overtime, it was much more likely to be unpaid' (S. Harness, 'Working 9 to 5?', in Gregg and Wadsworth, *The State of Working Britain*, p. 107).

15. Mishel et al., *The State of Working America 2000–2001*, p. 400.

16. House of Commons Select Committee on Trade and Industry, Second Report, *The Competitiveness of UK Manufacturing Industry*, London, HMSO, 1994, p. 20. On the Government's own figures that year, the UK had slipped to 17th in the international league table of per capita income (*Competitiveness: Forging Ahead*, Cmnd 2867, London, HMSO, 1994, p. 13.)

17. Ibid., pp. 17, 18.

18. '...the crucial fact is that Britain has had a low, and sometimes a very low, level of output per unit of investment (for much of the post-war period it was almost half the amount enjoyed by West Germany). Correspondingly, the returns to investment, the level of demand for capital and the rate at which the capital stock has grown have all been relatively low' (Supple, 'British economic decline since 1954', p. 344).

19. House of Commons Select Committee on Trade and Industry, *The Competitiveness of UK Manufacturing Industry*, p. 20.

20. M. Porter, *The Competitive Advantage of Nations*, London, Macmillan, 1990, pp. 484–94.

21. W. Walker, 'National innovation systems: Britain', in R. Nelson (ed.), *National Innovation Systems: A Comparative Analysis*, Oxford, Oxford University Press, 1993, pp. 160–1.

22. House of Commons Select Committee on Trade and Industry, *The Competitiveness of UK Manufacturing Industry*, p. 20.

23. Porter, *The Competitive Advantage of Nations*, p. 494.

24. House of Commons Select Committee on Trade and Industry, *The Competitiveness of UK Manufacturing Industry*, p. 22.

25. For a full discussion of the academic literature on this, see D. Coates, *The Question of UK Decline*, Hemel Hempstead, Harvester Wheatsheaf, 1994.
26. For an accessible extract from the report of the House of Lords Select Committee on Overseas Trade, see D. Coates and J. Hillard (eds), *The Economic Revival of Modern Britain: The Debate between Left and Right*, Aldershot, Edward Elgar, 1987, pp. 183–203.
27. These were *Competitiveness: Helping Business to Win* (1994) and *Competitiveness: Forging Ahead* (1995). Both emerged from Michael Heseltine's Department of Trade and Industry (DTI) and stand comparison, as we will see later, to similar reports and White Papers emerging from the DTI after 1997.
28. 1979 is always the nadir year in these reports. Things declined to then, and stabilized or even improved afterwards, but never to such a level as to have yet made up all the ground lost. The DTI's *Competitiveness: Forging Ahead* spoke of 'a competitiveness gap' that had 'opened up over the best part of a century and had been particularly marked since 1945' (p. 7).
29. The later Institute for Public Policy Research (IPPR) report, addressing the controversy on the degree of UK underinvestment in machinery and equipment relative to key overseas competitors, insisted that 'UK investment, excluding residential construction, has been *lower* than that of all our major competitors, except the United States... [this] persistently low level of investment, particularly in manufacturing, has resulted in a relatively low level of capital stock and equipment per worker. UK industry is much less capital-intensive than industry elsewhere.' The report recorded the percentages of GDP going to investment in manufacturing and equipment between 1960 and 1993 in the UK as 8.4%, but as 12.4% in Japan, 9.8% in Italy, 8.7% in Germany, 8.9% in France and 7.6% in the US. (IPPR, *Promoting Prosperity: A Business Agenda for Britain*, London, Vintage Books, 1997, pp. 25–7).
30. There is now a huge research literature on the underskilling of core workers in the UK economy prior to 1997, and on the associated deficiencies in both the education and training systems. For a fuller discussion, see D. Finegold and D. Soskice, 'The failure of training in Britain: analysis and prescription', *Oxford Review of Economic Policy*, vol. 4(3), 1988, pp. 21–53; D. H. Aldcroft, *Education, Training and Economic Performance 1944–1990*, Manchester, Manchester University Press, 1992; D. Ashton and F. Green, *Education, Training and the Global Economy*, Cheltenham, Edward Elgar, 1996; and D. Coates, *Models of Capitalism*, Cambridge, Polity Press, 2000, pp. 107–20.
31. 'Although we have many world beating companies, average productivity levels in manufacturing have not yet risen to those of our major competitors...our productivity shortfall is less in services.' DTI, *Competitiveness: Helping Business to Win*, p. 13. The DTI's *Competitiveness: Forging Ahead* similarly spoke of 'a significant gap [that] remains overall' and of a 'lag behind the US, Germany and France in some areas of service productivity, although the gap is less than in manufacturing'. Broadberry calculated the gap in output per employee in 1989 between the UK and the US as a staggering 77% in the manufacturing sector and 31.5% in the economy as a whole. The equivalent figures for the economy as a whole were, for Germany 16% and France 29% in 1989. He also found that this shortfall hadn't changed much in the twentieth century (S. Broadberry, *The Productivity Race: British Manufacturing in International*

Perspective 1850–1990, Cambridge, Cambridge University Press, 1997, pp. 66, 52, 395).

32. The problem of skills was very deep-rooted and general in the UK inherited by New Labour. The new government actually commissioned a report on basic literacy and numeracy in the UK from Sir Claus Moser. He found 7 million adults without basic literacy skills, and up to twice that number struggling with numeracy. His report, *A Fresh Start*, was published by the Department for Education and Employment (DfEE) in March 1999; and its findings were in line with those of the OECD's international adult literacy survey, *Knowledge Skills for the Knowledge Society*, published in 1997.

33. Two in particular: the already cited IPPR's *Promoting Prosperity* and the Institute's earlier *Social Justice* report. *Promoting Prosperity* was very much in the spirit of the age, isolating four main problems: a long tail of underperforming companies; too many undereducated and undertrained people; too little investment and too many shifts in government policy. On this, see the report, p. 20.

34. House of Commons Select Committee on Trade and Industry, *Competitiveness of UK Manufacturing Industry*, 1994, p. 13.

35. For a fuller discussion of these, see D. Coates, 'Labour Governments: old constraints and new parameters', *New Left Review* 219, September/October 1996, pp. 62–77.

36. In 1950 there were 408,033 marriages in the UK and 33,074 divorces. In 1997 there were 310,218 marriages and 161,057 divorces. As late as 1971, couples accounted for 92% of all family units in the UK. By 1997 that figure was down to three families in four; and by then the proportion of dependent children growing up in single-parent homes was 21%. In 1971 it had been just 7%.

37. The basic structure of privilege at the top of society remained unchanged. On the structures of privilege inherited by New Labour, see J. Paxman, *Friends in High Places: Who Runs Britain?* London, Michael Joseph, 1990; J. Scott, *Who Rules Britain?* Cambridge, Polity Press, 1991; and D. Coates, *Running the Country*.

38. This was partly a result of entrenched attitudes, and partly of the lengthening of the male working day. As David Brindle reported in 1996, 'more than one in four earning fathers is putting in more than 50 hours a week at work, and almost one in ten more than 60. Such men are markedly less likely to help with child care, or take part in family activities' (David Brindle, 'The Mythical "new man" is hard at work', *Guardian*, 4 November 1996, p. 2). As late as 1995, surveys recorded that women still tended to 'prepare the evening meal, do the washing and the ironing, and cleaning, while men are responsible for household repairs. In 84% of the households surveyed in 1995, women remained mainly responsible for the ironing, and in 70% of them for preparing the evening meal as well' (*Guardian*, 9 August 1995, p. 4).

39. S. Walby, *Gender Transformations*, London, Routledge, 1997, p. 27.

40. By 1994 the labour force was pretty much 50:50, men:women – 10 million of each. But over 9 million of the men worked full-time as against under 5 million of the women. By then 81% of men of working age were in employment as against 69% of all women of working age, but that 11% gap, though still substantial, was significantly less than the 32.9% figure for the gap in employment rates by gender from as late as 1975. On this see T. Desai

et al., 'Gender and the labour market', in Gregg and Wadsworth, *The State of Working Britain*, p. 170.

41. On this, see C. Creighton, 'The rise and decline of the "male breadwinner family" in Britain', *Cambridge Journal of Economics*, vol. 23, 1999, pp. 519–41. The wage gap between men and women was narrowing in the 1990s, but at 75% was still substantial. (Desai et al., 'Gender and the labour market', p. 176).

42. 'As a consequence of these changes in married women's labour market participation, households supported by a single male earner are now a minority, comprising, in 1991, 34% of all two-adult households below retirement age' (Creighton, 'The rise and decline of the "male breadwinner family"', p. 526).

43. J. K. Galbraith, *The Affluent Society*, Boston, Houghton Mifflin, 1969.

44. 66 Ecus per head in Germany and France, 32 in the UK (*Observer*, 5 November 1995, p. 18).

45. The Third International Maths and Science Study ranked Scotland 16 and England 17 in a league table on numeracy for nine-year-olds; and 24th out of 40 for numeracy at age 14. That same year, an Office for National Statistics (ONS) survey of people aged 15–65 found a higher proportion of Britons with basic literacy problems than their equivalents in Germany, Sweden, the Netherlands and the US (*Financial Times*, 26 January 1998).

46. J. Doward, 'Jam Tomorrow', *Observer*, 3 July 2003, p. 12.

47. J. Walters, 'Gridlocked UK: now its official', *Observer*, 25 November 2001, p. 16.

48. Quoted in the *Guardian*, 1 March 2001, p.15.

49. *Financial Times*, 20 May 1997, p. 15: figures from the Joseph Rowntree Foundation.

50. Gregg and Wadsworth, *The State of Working Britain*, p. 225.

51. Cited in the *Guardian*, 10 February 1995, p. 7.

52. For this, see the *Guardian*, 14 August 1998, p. 4.

53. W. Hutton, *The State We're In*, London, Cape, 1994, p. 23.

54. W. Hutton, 'Led astray by the moral crusaders', *Observer*, 3 November 1996, p. 28.

55. As Ian Hargreaves observed just two weeks before New Labour came to power, 'Will Hutton is probably the most influential writer on the left in British politics. His latest book, *The State We're In*, has sold more than 200,000 copies, turning Hutton into a one-man road show, sometimes performing at three or four events a week, not to mention the television documentaries and the Will Hutton website [Hargreaves could also have added the regular Monday column in the *Guardian*]' (Ian Hargreaves, 'Test your Will-power', *New Statesman*, 18 April 1997, p. 44).

56. W. Hutton, *The State to Come*, London, Vintage Books, 1997, p. 9.

57. W. Hutton, 'It's society, stupid', *Observer*, 23 March 1997, p. 29.

58. Hutton, 'Led astray by the moral crusaders', p. 28.

59. Hutton, *The State to Come*, p. 12.

Chapter 2

1. For a more general discussion of political parties as living traditions, see D. Coates, 'Strategic choices in the study of New Labour', *British Journal of Politics and International Relations*, vol. 4(3), 2002, pp. 479–86.

2. The original Clause 4 was very short, and formally committed the party 'to secure for the workers by hand or by brain the full fruits of their industry and the most equitable distribution thereof that may be possible, upon the basis of the common ownership of the means of production, distribution and exchange, and the best obtainable system of popular administration and control of each industry and service'. Such a full-blooded commitment to a socialist future had been adopted, largely for electoral reasons, in the immediate wake of the Russian Revolution, but it actually played very little part in the reality, as distinct from in the symbolism, of Labour Party policy-making in the years that followed. Labour's political opponents made much of it, again for electoral reasons, but Labour policy-makers did not. Which was why in 1959 Hugh Gaitskell tried to replace the original constitutional statement with one that cautiously recognized that 'both public and private enterprise has a place in the economy'. Unfortunately for Gaitskell, however, symbolism still counted for much in the Labour Party of his day, and in the end he was forced by fierce internal party opposition to settle for a compromise document that merged the old constitution with his new 'amplification' of it. Blair took the Old Clause 4 on again in 1995, and this time successfully replaced it with a much longer statement that committed the party to, among other things, working for 'a dynamic economy, serving the public interest, in which the enterprise of the market and the rigour of competition are joined with the forces of partnership and co-operation to produce the wealth the nation needs…a thriving private sector and high quality public services'.

3. Neil Kinnock, in conversation with the author, for the BBC/OU programme *The 1997 Election: Traditions, Failures and Futures*, Brussels, 23 October 1997.

4. The calculation is Royden Harrison's, in his *New Labour as Past History*, European Labor Forum, Pamphlet no. 8, 1996, p. 2. The term 'new' appeared 107 times in New Labour's draft manifesto, *Labour's Road to the Manifesto*, in 1996. The term 'socialism', by contrast, appeared once (*Guardian*, 5 July 1996, p. 13).

5. Tony Blair was clear on this even before he became party leader, telling Philip Stephens that 'the role of government is not about picking winners or whatever. It's about government enabling industry to make the best use of things like technology and research and development' (Philip Stephens, 'A marketable Danger Man', *Financial Times*, 11/12 June 1994, p. 8).

6. Tony Blair to the Trades Union Congress (TUC), 9 September 1997.

7. Tony Blair, quoted in Stephens, 'A marketable Danger Man'.

8. Tony Blair, *New Britain: My Vision of a Young Country*, London, Fourth Estate, p. 18.

9. How genuinely novel New Labour was, or would be, quickly became a matter of intense academic dispute. Partly it was a dispute about the relative elements of continuity and discontinuity in the policies proposed, a dispute that often turned on the period of the party's history singled out as the comparator. Partly it was a dispute on the extent to which New Labour was, or was not, Thatcherite beneath the surface. For the argument on continuity with Old Labour, see S. Fielding, *The Labour Party*, Basingstoke, Palgrave, 1996; and D. Rubenstein, 'A new look at New Labour', *Politics*, vol. 20(3), 2000, pp. 161–7. For the argument on continuity with Thatcherism, see C. Hay, *The Political Economy of New Labour*, Manchester: Manchester University Press, 1999; and

R. Heffernan, *New Labour and Thatcherism*, Basingstoke, Palgrave, 2001. For the argument on discontinuity from both Old Labour and Thatcherism, see S. Driver and L. Martell, *New Labour: Politics after Thatcherism*, Cambridge, Polity Press, 1998, and *Blair's Britain*, Cambridge, Polity Press, 2002. For an earlier Coates view, written as a corrective to the hype surrounding New Labour in 1995 and 1996, see his 'Labour governments: old constraints and new parameters', *New Left Review* 219, September/October 1996, pp. 62–77, reprinted in D. Coates (ed.), *Paving the Third Way*, London, Merlin Press, 2003.

10. Harold Wilson, *The New Britain: Labour's Plan Outlined*, Harmondsworth, Penguin, 1964, pp. 21, 9–10.

11. Blair, *New Britain*, pp. xii–xiii.

12. Labour Party, *Let Us Work Together – Labour's Way Out of the Crisis*, February 1974.

13. But not, it should be noted, in 1959, when the manifesto was overwhelmingly concerned with the use of the surpluses generated by successful economic growth. The economic background to the first wave of post-war revisionists in the Labour Party was significantly different to the background experienced by the second.

14. Neil Kinnock, in his introduction to the Labour Party's 1992 election manifesto.

15. By, among others, N. Thompson, *Political Economy and the Labour Party*, UCL Press 1996; M. Wickham Jones, *Economic Strategy and the Labour Party*, London, Macmillan, 1996; Heffernan, *New Labour and Thatcherism*.

16. Tony Blair, in the introduction to the 1997 Labour Party manifesto, *New Labour: Because Britain Deserves Better*, London, Labour Party p. 1.

17. Ibid., pp. 3–4.

18. Labour Party, *New Labour: Because Britain Deserves Better*, p. 11.

19. Ibid., p. 15.

20. On this, see D. Coates and C. Hay, 'The internal and external face of New Labour's political economy', *Government and Opposition,* vol. 36(4), 2001, pp. 442–71.

21. Tony Blair, speech to the Keidanren, Tokyo, 5 January 1996, p. 2.

22. Gordon Brown, to the conference on 'New Policies for the Global Economy', September 1994, p. 1.

23. Ibid., pp. 4, 6–7, 7–8.

24. To the point indeed, in 1996, of persuading the Shadow Cabinet and the National Executive Committee jointly to issue a special 'manifesto for business' that promised, among other things, no increase in the top rates of income tax, and full consultation with the Confederation of British Industry (CBI) over the agenda for the UK's six-month presidency of the EU in 1998.

25. Brown, to the conference on 'New Policies for the Global Economy, p. 1.

26. Ibid., pp. 4, 15. The case for the importance of 'new growth theory' to New Labour politics is fully laid out in D. P. Dolowitz, 'Prosperity and fairness? Can New Labour bring fairness to the 21st century by following the dictates of endogenous growth?', *British Journal of Politics and International Relations*, vol. 6(2), 2004, pp. 213–30.

27. Brown, to the conference on 'New Policies for the Global Economy, pp. 4, 7.

28. Tony Blair, The Mais Lecture at City University, London, 22 May 1995, p. 7.
29. Blair, speech to the Keidanren, p. 6.
30. Tony Blair, speech to the European Socialists Congress, Malmo, Sweden, 6 June 1997.
31. On capitalist models and UK politics, see D. Coates, 'Models of capitalism in the new world order: the UK case', *Political Studies*, vol. 47(1), September 1999, pp. 77–96; and 'Capitalist models and social democracy', *British Journal of Politics and International Relations*, vol. 3(3), 2001, pp. 284–307.
32. N. Thompson, 'Supply side socialism: the political economy of New Labour', *New Left Review*, 215, 1996, p. 39.
33. On Blair's January 1996 Singapore speech, with its radical stakeholder moment and its rapid abandonment, see Ibid., pp. 38, 50–2; D. Coates, 'Placing New Labour', in B. Jones (ed.), *Political Issues in Britain Today* (fifth edition), Manchester, Manchester University Press, 1999, pp. 357–8; and G. Kelly et al. (eds), *Stakeholder Capitalism*, London, Macmillan, 1997.
34. Tony Blair, 'The Third Way: Part 2', *Prospect,* March 2001.
35. Thompson, *Political Economy and the Labour Party*, p. 273.
36. Anthony Giddens, who wrote and edited a series of rethink documents from 1994, was particularly important here: notably *Beyond Left and Right: The Future of Radical Politics*, Cambridge, Polity Press, 1994; *The Third Way: The Renewal of Social Democracy*, Cambridge, Polity Press, 1996; *Globalization: Runaway World*, London, Profile Books, 1999; *The Third Way and its Critics*, Cambridge, Polity Press, 2000; and *Where Now for New Labour?*, Cambridge, Polity Press, 2002.
37. Robert Reich published a number of influential books in the 1980s and 1990s, including *The Next American Frontier* (1983) and *The Work of Nations* (1992).
38. In fact *The Economist* once likened 'trying to pin down an exact meaning in all this to...wrestling an inflatable man. If you get a grip on one limb, all the hot air rushes to the other' ('Goldilocks politics', *The Economist*, 19 December 1998, p. 73).
39. In intellectual matters, impact and quality are not the same thing. Nor is one necessarily the guarantor of the other. Whatever this emerging 'third way' argument was, it was not rocket science. It was always nearer to cliché and platitude than that, often building its claims for newness by over-generalizing contemporary economic and social trends, and polarizing simplistic and historically misleading alternatives: left against right, state against market, public against private, and so on. We will have occasion later to reflect on the real dilemmas to which the best of the 'third way' thinking was an important response, but for more general critiques of what was weak and misleading in this new centre-left orthodoxy, see A. Callinicos, *Against the Third Way*, Cambridge, Polity Press, 2001, and J. Petras, 'The third way: myth and reality', *Monthly Review*, March 2000.
40. Stuart White, 'The Ambiguities of the Third Way', in his edited collection, *New Labour and the Progressive Future*, London, Palgrave, 2001, p. 14.
41. Anthony Giddens, 'Did they foul up my Third Way?', *New Statesman*, 7 June 2004.
42. Christopher Henning, 'Old style Thatcherism with a new fig leaf', *Sydney Morning Herald*, 12 October 1998.

43. 'Goldilocks politics', *The Economist.*
44. Hélène Mulholland, 'Blair unfazed despite gloomy poll', *Guardian*, 8 June 2004.
45. This was Robin Cook, doing his bit for the 'third way', at the Social Market Foundation in 1998. He enumerated six New Labour principles in that speech: strong communities are the foundation of freedom and opportunity; social exclusion nurtures economic inefficiency; open politics sustains progress; responsibilities and rights go hand in hand; globalization means interdependency; policy must modernize as fast as society changes (*Guardian*, 23 April 1998, p. 8).
46. *Guardian*, 19 March 1996, p. 18.
47. Tony Blair and Gerhard Schroeder, *Europe: The Third Way/Die Neue Mitte*, London, Labour Party, June 1999.
48. Ibid., p. 2.
49. Anthony Giddens, 'Is three still the magic number?', *Guardian*, 25 April 2003.
50. Robert Reich, 'We are all Third Wayers now', *The American Prospect*, vol. 10, issue 43, March 1999.

Chapter 3

1. Tony Blair's remarks at the launch of the party's manifesto, as captured in the BBC/OU programme *The 1997 Election: Traditions, Failures and Futures*, 20 October 1997.
2. On this, see A. King, 'The night itself', in A. King et al., *New Labour Triumphs: Britain at the Polls*, London, Chatham House, 1998, pp. 7–9.
3. Ibid., p. 10.
4. S. Fielding, 'Labour's path to power', in A. Geddes and J. Tonge (eds), *Labour's Landslide*, Manchester, Manchester University Press, 1997, p. 33.
5. A. King, 'Why Labour won – at last', in King, *New Labour Triumphs*, p. 186.
6. Ibid., p. 187.
7. Ibid., p. 194.
8. On this, see S. Hall, 'The great moving right show', reproduced in his *The Hard Road to Renewal*, London, Verso, 1988.
9. Will Hutton, interviewed for the BBC/OU Programme *The 1997 Election: Traditions, Failures and Futures.*
10. There is clear evidence of this in the election studies that followed Labour's victory. Typical is this passage from Anthony King: 'There is a good deal of evidence that by 1997 the trade-off in most voters' minds between improved services and tax increases had tilted, to some degree at least, in favour of tax increases. The most popular single manifesto pledge made by any party was the Liberal Democrats' pledge to put a penny on the standard rate of income tax to fund educational improvements. Fully 85% of voters said they would approve of such an increase' (King, 'Why Labour won – at last', pp. 196–7). Sam Brittan also reported that shift: that in May 1997 'more than 60% favour "tax and spend" and only 5% support the reduction of taxes' (*Financial Times*, 4 May 1997, p. 17).
11. P. Toynbee and D. Walker, *Did Things Get Better? An Audit of Labour's Successes and Failures*, Harmondsworth, Penguin, 2001, p. 232.

12. Tony Blair, *The Third Way: A New Politics for the New Century*, London, Fabian Society, 1998, p. 7.
13. Tony Blair, cited in the *Guardian*, 8 April 1997, p. 1.
14. David Miliband, 'The new politics of economics', in C. Crouch and D. Marquand (eds), *Ethics and Markets,* Oxford, Oxford University Press, 1993, p. 26. Miliband was initially head of Blair's Policy Unit, later Schools Minister and now Minister for the Cabinet Office.
15. Quoted in D. Coates, 'Placing New Labour', in B. Jones (ed.), *Political Issues in Britain Today*, Manchester, Manchester University Press, 1999, p. 357.
16. Tony Blair, *New Britain: My Vision of a Young Country*, London, Fourth Estate, 1996, pp. xii, 208, 218.
17. Ibid., p. 261.

Chapter 4

1. Labour Party, *New Labour: Because Britain Deserves Better*, London, Labour Party, 1997, p. 11.
2. Gordon Brown, House of Commons, 15 July 1998.
3. Tony Blair, election statement, quoted in the *Guardian*, 24 June 1994, p. 8.
4. Gordon Brown, to the conference on 'New Policies for the Global Economy', September 1994, p. 3.
5. Tony Blair, 'The stakeholder speech', Singapore, 7 January 1996, p. 2.
6. Blair, election statement.
7. Labour Party, *New Labour: Because Britain Deserves Better*, p. 10.
8. Ibid, pp. 10–11.
9. Gordon Brown, to the Institute of Fiscal Studies, 29 May 1999.
10. Labour Party, *New Labour: Because Britain Deserves Better*, p. 15.
11. Ibid., p. 9.
12. Tony Blair, to the conference on 'New Policies for the Global Economy', September 1994, p. 8.
13. Tony Blair, *The Third Way: New Politics for the New Century*, London, Fabian Society, 1998, p. 8.
14. Labour Party, *New Labour: New Life for Britain*, London, Labour Party, 1996, p. 12.
15. The term appears on page 12 of the 1997 election manifesto, *New Labour: Because Britain Deseves Better.*
16. Gordon Brown, 'The conditions for full employment', The Mais Lecture, City University, London, 19 October 1999.
17. Not least James Naughtie's *The Rivals*, London, Fourth Estate, 2002, and Andrew Rawnsley, *Servants of the People: The Inside Story of New Labour*, London, Hamish Hamilton, 2000.
18. A claim made by Gordon Brown himself on many occasions, including to Faisal Islam in the *Observer* interview, 15 April 2001, Business Section, p. 3. The Chancellor's enthusiasm for, and commitment to, his 'welfare-to-work' programme is well documented.
19. Gordon Brown, House of Commons, 3 July 1997.
20. The key example here is Gordon Brown's February 2003 address to the Social Market Foundation, on which we will comment more fully later. See also the text of his Labour Party conference address in September 2003, in which he

said: '...while markets are the engine of prosperity, there is and always must be a public realm upholding the non-material values – reciprocity, care and concern – that are the soul of our society...the town square is more than a marketplace, the city centre more than where people buy and sell, community more than a collection of individuals...we owe obligations to each other that go beyond calculation, contract and exchange.'

21. Gordon Brown, 'Radical reforms are on the way', the *Guardian* interview, 1 June 2001, p. 21.

22. The exchange can be found in two articles in the *Guardian* (25 July and 2 August 1997). It contained this defence of New Labour thinking by Gordon Brown. 'We reject equality of outcome not because it is too radical but because it is neither desirable nor feasible....The equality of opportunity I support is recurrent, life-long and comprehensive: employment, educational and economic opportunities for all...with an obligation on government to pursue them relentlessly....Our modernization of the welfare state will create work, make sure that work always pays, and provide recurring opportunities for life-long learning.' For a fuller statement of Brown's views, see his lectures in 1994 (the Smith lecture) and 1997 (the Crosland lecture), and his May 2000 address to the CPAG.

23. Because of space constraints, this is not part of our story here, but it is an important part of the overall New Labour one. The impressive work of Clare Short, and now Hilary Benn, and the sustained effort of Gordon Brown to both ease the burden of debt on the poorest of Third World countries and to bring the UK aid budget up to 0.7% of GDP, are among the finer parts of the New Labour record. It is notable in this regard that in the 2004 Comprehensive Spending Review the Department of Overseas Development saw its budget increased by more than 9% a year between 2005 and 2008 when other departmental budgets were being constrained. Periodically, the Prime Minister also joined in: with a messianic statement on world justice to the 2001 party conference, and with the 2004 Commission for Africa. The Blair touch here smacked of liberal imperialism. The Brown initiatives seemed more like global Keynesianism. The role of the UK at the World Trade Organization (WTO) and International Labour Organization (ILO) has yet to be charted fully, and needs to be. On the downside of the Prime Minister's propensity for liberal imperialism and unanchored moralizing in foreign affairs, see D. Coates and J. Krieger's *Blair's War*, Cambridge, Polity Press, 2004. For a sympathetic but ultimately critical account of the early stages of Brown and Short's foreign aid policy, see R. Dixon and P. Williams, 'Tough on debt, tough on the causes of debt? New Labour's Third Way foreign policy', *British Journal of Politics and International Relations*, vol. 3(2), 2001, pp. 150–72.

24. For a full statement on this, see Gordon Brown's Joseph Rowntree centenary lecture, 8 July 2004, at <http://politics.guardian.co.uk.print/0,3858,4966610–110366,00.html>

25. 'Still dodging the bullets', *Guardian*, 24 April 1999, p. 26.

26. Mansion House address, 15 June 2000.

27. 'Brown wants Treasury to focus on jobs and growth', *Financial Times*, 29 April 1996, p. 8.

28. Gordon Brown, 'Modernizing the British economy: the New Mission Treasury': speech to the Institute for Fiscal Studies, 27 May 1999.

29. Will Hutton, 'Time for cheese-parers to become toast', *Observer*, 28 September 1999, p. 26.
30. Nigel Wicks, former deputy permanent secretary at the Treasury, quoted in the *Guardian*, 16 April 2002, p. 10.
31. 'Inside the Treasury', *Guardian*, 15 April 2002, p. 10.
32. Gordon Brown, quoted in the *Guardian*, 28 May 1999, p. 6.
33. This summary by Stephen Timms, Financial Secretary to the Treasury, speaking at the 'Creating the Entrepreneurial Economy' conference, 9 May 2000.
34. Tony Blair, to the 2000 CBI annual dinner.
35. From the text of the letter from the Chancellor of the Exchequer to the Governor of the Bank of England, reproduced in *The Financial Times*, 7 May 1997, p. 10.
36. Gordon Brown, first budget statement, House of Commons, 7 July 1997.
37. Ibid.
38. For a very comprehensive exposition of the thinking behind these initial policy moves, by two of their key architects, see Ed Balls and Gus O'Donnell, *Reforming Britain's Economic and Financial Policy: Towards Greater Economic Stability*, Basingstoke, Palgrave, 2002. For two views of the adequacy of it all, see M. Artis and M. Sawyer, 'The economic analysis of the Third Way', *New Political Economy*, vol. 6(2), 2001, pp. 255–78, and S. Buckler and D. Dolowitz, 'Can fair be efficient? New Labour, social liberalism and British economic policy', *New Political Economy*, vol. 9(1), 2004, pp. 23–38.
39. Brown, first budget statement.
40. Brown, 'The Conditions for Full Employment'.
41. On this, see N. Carter, 'Whither (or wither) the euro? Labour and the single currency', *Politics* vol. 23(1), 2003, pp. 1–9.
42. W. Keegan, *The Prudence of Mr. Gordon Brown*, London, John Wiley, 2003, p. 286.
43. Figures from R. Brooks, *Pay and the Public Sector Workforce*, London, IPPR, 2004, p. 2.
44. Statement to the House of Commons, 12 July 2004.
45. Ibid.
46. Labour Party, *New Labour: Because Britain Deserves Better*, p. 11.
47. This was a cull of 104,000 jobs in a civil service of half a million people (84,000 from Whitehall departments, 20,000 from the staff of the devolved assemblies in Scotland, Wales, Northern Ireland and local government), to save £20 billion by 2008. By then Gordon Brown was using 'administrative savings' as the third great source of extra funds for front line services, to supplement the sources created by reduced unemployment and a reduction in debt payments. A total of 40,000 jobs were to go at the Department for Work and Pensions (DWP), 1,460 at the Department for Education and Skills (DfES), 10,500 at the Inland Revenue and Customs and Excise, and so on.
48. Pre-budget statement, 4 November 1998.
49. *Guardian*, 19 July 2000, p. 1.
50. Gordon Brown to the House of Commons, 15 July 2002.
51. In this instance Jo Magee, aviation officer of the Institution of Professionals, Managers and Specialists, in the *Financial Times*, 12 June 1998, p. 9.
52. Pre-budget statement, 4 November 1998.
53. Figures in the *Guardian*, 3 October 2002, p. 24.

54. Ibid.
55. Ibid.
56. Budget statement, 21 March 2000.
57. Pre-budget statement, 4 November 1998.
58. Blair, *The Third Way*, p. 10.
59. 2002 Pre-budget report, chapter 3, p. 11 of 16.
60. Statement to the House of Commons, 12 July 2004.
61. Gordon Brown to the Institute for Fiscal Studies, 27 May 1999.
62. Labour Party, *New Labour: Because Britain Deserves Better*, p. 15.
63. Gordon Brown, 'No quick fixes on jobs', *Financial Times*, 17 November 1997, p. 16. He was not alone in this view. David Blunkett put it this way: 'We believe that employment is the path out of social exclusion. More people in productive employment will bring huge bonuses for individuals, their families, the communities in which they live, and our economy. It will release resources to increase skills and improve employability and reverse the spiral of dependence, economic inactivity and poverty that results from isolation from the labour market' (DfEE Press Release, 20 February 1998).
64. David Blunkett, 'Cutting-edge jobs programme works twice as fast', DfES Press Release, 28 February 2001.
65. Brown, first budget statement.
66. The choice to train for work with a new cash payment of £15 a week on top of benefit; the choice of a few hours' work a week, with the first £20 of earnings allowed with no reduction in benefit at all; the choice of part-time work with a guaranteed £155 for 16 hours, or the choice of full-time work on a guaranteed £214 a week.
67. Brown to the House: 'In return the Government has decided that from next year all lone parents on income support, including parents with children under five, will be required to undertake interviews about work choices at regular intervals' (budget statement, 7 March 2001).
68. When the Conservative government had first introduced this allowance, the Labour Party in opposition had strenuously opposed the use of this sanction!
69. David Blunkett, 'No hiding place for fraudsters', *Observer*, 14 January 2001, p. 31.
70. Pre-budget statement, 9 November 1999.
71. Labour Party, *New Labour: Because Britain Deserves Better*, p. 15.
72. Gordon Brown, second budget statement, House of Commons, 17 March 1998.
73. Gordon Brown, to the Labour Party conference, 29 September 2003.
74. Figures from the *Guardian*, 4 November 1998, p. 15.
75. Quoted in the *Guardian*, 28 November 2001, p. 16.
76. 'He is making money follow the children, going to parents rather than to married people or to particular types of parent', one said; 'it is not conditional on either employment or marital status, and that is good'. Holly Sutherland, Director, Microsimulation Unit, Cambridge University, quoted in the *Financial Times*, 10 March 1999, p. 11.
77. Pre-budget statement, 10 December 2003.

Chapter 5

1. *Guardian,* 19 June 2001.
2. *Observer,* 30 July, 2000, Business Section, p. 5. This absence of a mission is less surprising if it is set against the overall history of industrial policy in the UK. On that see D. Coates and P. Reynolds, 'Industrial policy: conclusion', in D. Coates (ed.), *Industrial Policy in Britain,* London, Macmillan, 1996, pp. 241–68.
3. On this, see D. Coates, 'New Labour's industrial and employment policy', in D. Coates and P. Lawler (eds), *New Labour in Power,* Manchester, Manchester University Press, 2000, pp. 133–4.
4. Peter Mandelson, to the TUC, 17 September 1998.
5. The Institute of Directors was a persistent critic. 'Secretaries of State come and go with the regularity of third century Roman emperors', its business policy executive said in September 2002, giving the department a 'Jekyll and Hyde' feel, with 'frequent changes of policies' (*Guardian,* 2 September 2002). Even the normally more sympathetic CBI criticized the DTI for putting too much of its energy into business regulation, not enough into standing up for business interests against the policies of other government departments. 'It is not doing enough', the CBI director general told the BBC, to 'push the wealth creation message' (BBC News, 10 September 2001). The CBI issued its own very careful review of DTI priorities and structure in August 2001, and was involved in the inquiry that Patricia Hewitt launched, on arriving at the DTI, into the views of the department held by its various stakeholders. On the back of that review, Wilf Stevenson reported, 'the DTI has been reorganized to focus on four main objectives: supporting successful UK businesses; driving innovation and promoting science; establishing and championing fair markets; and creating a sustainable energy policy'. Stevenson gave this reorganized DTI high marks and a clean bill of health (*New Statesman,* 20 September 2004).
6. Labour Party, *New Labour: Because Britain Deserves Better,* London, Labour Party, 1997, p. 14.
7. Tony Blair, addressing the biennial conference of the German employers' organization in Bonn, cited in the *Financial Times,* 19 June 1996, p. 1. He made a similar point to the Socialist International meeting in Malmo, Sweden, a year later. 'We need minimum standards of fairness at work as an essential part of a civilized society, but they don't guarantee job protection. Employability – knowledge, technology and skills, not legislation alone – is what counts.'
8. Labour Party, *New Labour: Because Britain Deserves Better,* p. 14.
9. It was the UK, for example, which led the charge in Europe for opt-outs from the European Working Time Directive, particularly for junior hospital doctors. The NHS couldn't cope with them working less than 58 hours a week. They normally averaged 73! In this charge, the UK was supported by, of all countries, Germany: to produce the bizarre sight of Europe's two largest centre-left governments allying to restrict worker rights. On this, see the *Telegraph,* 21 March 2004, p. 2, and the *Financial Times,* 29 March 2004, p. 6.
10. To the point indeed that by 2004 the EU Commission took the UK government to court for its failure adequately to integrate and implement the Working Time Directive into UK law and industrial practice. On this, see BBC News, 7 March 2004.

11. So the UK took the lead in torpedoing Lionel Jospin's employment plan at the EU summit in June 1997, persuading EU members to favour moves towards the deregulation of labour markets. New Labour used its six-month EU presidency in 1998 to push a jobs programme 'Getting Europe to Work' that emphasized measures to increase labour market flexibility, reduce the burden of bureaucracy on small businesses, and complete the Single Market by 1999. Roy Hattersley followed this with an account of an exchange between Blair and the French President, Jacques Chirac, when the former pushed for UK exceptions from the European Social Chapter that added to unit costs. 'Blair pursued the case for flexibility until the President put a paternal hand on his arm "Remind me,", he said, "You are leader of the British Left and I am leader of the French Right. Or is it the other way round?" To his credit, Blair smiled' (*Observer*, 3 May 1998, p. 23).

12. Tony Blair, speaking to the World Economic Forum at Davos, 28 January 2000.

13. Tony Blair, speech at Malmo, Sweden, June 1997.

14. 'We will not let EU weaken Thatcher union laws, says Straw', the UK Foreign Secretary, to the CBI annual dinner, quoted in the *Guardian*, 19 May 2004, p. 2.

15. Not least Silvio Berlusconi of Italy and Jose Maria Aznar of Spain, in 2002 two of Europe's leading right-wing prime ministers. Outflanking even Jacques Chirac on his right, Tony Blair wrote in the Italian newspaper *Corriere della Sera* that 'Europe's labour markets need to be more flexible. Businesses are still encumbered by unnecessary regulations', and he and the Spanish Prime Minister then jointly pushed for 'more flexible types of labour contracts', the replacement of labour laws with 'soft regulation', and moves to increase 'the effectiveness of public employment services' by 'opening this market to the private sector' (*Guardian*, 19 February 2002). The UK government even took the unusual step of publishing a White Paper on this in the run-up to the Spanish presidency of the EU in the first half of 2002.

16. 'where a clear majority of employees wishes to be represented' and 'where a ballot shows that a majority of those voting and at least 40% of those eligible to vote are in favour of recognition'. *Fairness at Work*, paragraphs 4.16, 4.18.

17. Ibid., paragraph 2.12.

18. Ibid., Foreword.

19. Ibid., paragraph 1.13.

20. On this, see P. Smith and G. Morton, 'New Labour's reform of Britain's employment law. The Devil is not only in the detail but in the values and policy too', *British Journal of Industrial Relations*, vol. 39(1), 2001, pp. 119–38.

21. The DTI under Patricia Hewitt launched a campaign in March 2002 against the long hours culture in UK industry, extolling the virtues of better balance between home and work. It was largely an advertising and advocacy campaign, supplemented by a small fund of public money to assist employers introducing changes to make work hours more flexible, and by a voluntary coalition of business leaders. The only 'teeth' in the initial proposal were the granting of the right of parents of young children to request flexibility of their employer and the parallel obligation on the employer to offer evidence if that request

was declined. Once the request had been declined, however, no other sanction applied.

22. *Financial Times* editorial, 'Unions and Employers', 22 May 1998, p. 17.
23. *Financial Times*, 16 March 1999, p. 1.
24. *New Statesman*, 13 February 1998, p. 12.
25. Quoted in the *Guardian*, 18 November 1998, p. 14.
26. Wood and Godard's assessment, cited in Smith and Morton, 'New Labour's reform of Britain's employment law', p. 124.
27. I am grateful for this quotation, and much else here, to the important work of Smith and Morton, ibid.
28. Quoted in the *Financial Times*, 18 December 1998, p. 1.
29. Quoted in the *Guardian*, 29 January 1999, p. 2.
30. There was a second, in 2001, which the unions also found profoundly disappointing, but which did extend the eight-week cushion for lawful striking without dismissal to 16 weeks.
31. Tony Blair, addressing the TUC, Brighton, 9 September 1997.
32. Labour Party *New Labour: Because Britain Deserves Better*, p. 14.
33. Margaret Beckett, DTI Press Release, 27 November 1997.
34. DTI Press Release, 31 December 1998.
35. DTI Press Release, 28 October 1997.
36. Labour Party *New Labour: Because Britain Deserves Better*, p. 14.
37. Professor George Bain, quoted in the *Financial Times*, 19 June 1996, p. 10.
38. Quoted in the *Guardian*, 28 May 1998, p. 2.
39. John Monks, commenting on what he referred to as 'a substantially changed mood in Whitehall after 18 years of systematic exclusion', hailed his first post-election meeting with Tony Blair as signalling 'the dawn of social partnership Britain' (quoted in 'TUC back at No. 10 after years out in cold', *Guardian*, 22 May 1997, p. 10).
40. John Monks embodied this 'new unionism', seeking to reposition the TUC as a key 'social partner' in a national campaign to improve competitiveness. 'The days when trade unions provided an adversarial opposition force are past in industry', he told Robert Taylor in 1997; but 'it has become too easy for companies to modernize working practices by trampling on their own workforces'. What was needed was 'a new settlement based on partnership which provides employees with basic minimum workplace rights' (*Financial Times*, 3 September 1997, p. 16). What could be more New Labour than that?
41. Mandelson was not alone in presenting the issue in this way. Under New Labour, all the DTI Secretaries of State seemed to have seen their role to be that of union 'modernizer': by which they meant both the retention of a residual union role 'in protecting their members against arbitrary and unfair treatment' and the acquisition of new roles 'helping members develop the skills they need to survive and prosper in an ever more challenging labour market' and 'working with business to promote business performance' (This was Stephen Byers, to the TUC Partnership Conference, May 1999. It could have been any of them).
42. Cited in the *Guardian*, 24 December 2001.
43. *Observer*, 17 March 2002.

44. The TUC was reportedly furious with Patricia Hewitt's refusal to amend this part of the 1998 Act. The internal TUC paper said: 'Under international laws, supported by the UK Government, workers have a right not to suffer detriment as a result of taking industrial action. This was not a qualified right and the UK Government should not make it one' (*Guardian*, 24 December 2001).
45. For details, see the *Guardian*, 18 May 2004, p. 7, and 7 August 2004, p. 12.
46. The firefighters staged 15 days of industrial action in 2002/03 in pursuit of a 40% pay rise that would restore their position in public league wage tables to the slot they occupied after their last national stoppage, also against a Labour government, in 1977. They eventually settled with their local authority employers for 16% over two years, but even this was not enough for a Labour government that wanted fewer firefighters, less shifts and a ban on second jobs.
47. A *Guardian*/ICM poll in September 2002 found 63% of the electorate in favour of a moratorium on public–private sector partnerships, and that included 65% of all Labour voters and even 61% of Conservative ones (*Guardian*, 26 September 2002, p. 1).
48. Seumas Milne, 'Blair gives modernity a bad name', *Guardian*, 5 December 2002, p. 24.
49. BBC News, 16 May 2001.
50. Tony Blair, speaking at Labour's spring conference, Cardiff, 1 April 2002.
51. Respectively Dave Prentice, Derek Simpson, Kevin Curran, Tony Woodley, Billy Hayes, Bob Crow and Andy Gilchrist.
52. BBC News, 7 March 2002.
53. That the T&G and Unison welcomed, but the GMB scorned (see the *Guardian*, 27 March 2002, p. 1).
54. We have two remarkable guides to all of this: Robert Taylor and Steve Ludlam. For the Ludlam corpus, see his chapters in the two volumes edited with M. J. Smith, *New Labour in Government*, London, Palgrave, 2001, and *Governing as New Labour*, London, Palgrave, 2004; the article jointly written with M. Bodah and D. Coates, 'Trajectories of solidarity: changing union-party linkages in the UK and USA', *British Journal of Politics and International Relations*, vol. 4(2), 2002, pp. 222–44; and S. Ludlam and A. Taylor, 'The political representation of the Labour Interest in Britain', *British Journal of Industrial Relations*, vol. 41(3), 2003, pp. 727–50.
55. Tony Blair, to the Knowledge 2000 Conference, SOAS London, 7 March 2000.
56. Labour Party, *New Labour: Because Britain Deserves Better*, passim.
57. Gordon Brown, to the TUC, 12 September 2000.
58. David Blunkett, 'Reskilling the key to stable growth', DfEE Press Release, 20 January 1998.
59. The National Skills Task Force issued four reports between 1998 and 2000, and a comprehensive set of research papers.
60. By 2001, 73 NTOs had been created, covering 90% of the UK labour force. Their core functions were to identify training needs, set standards of occupational competence, actively promote training opportunities, and carry out regular audits on progress. In the view of a later Lifelong Learning Minister, Malcolm Wicks, their creation meant that 'not since the days of the full Industrial Training Board system have employer sector interests been so well placed

to drive training arrangements in the UK' (DfEE Press Release, 20 October 1999).

61. Blair, to the Knowledge 2000 Conference.

62. Lord Sainsbury, speaking in London, 26 March 2003.

63. This figure from Sir Claus Moser's 1999 report for the DfEE, *A Fresh Start: Improving Literacy and Numeracy*. As we noted earlier, the equivalent figure for people with numeracy difficulties was probably double that for those with reading difficulties.

64. DfEE Press Release, 25 February 1998.

65. As David Blunkett said when responding to the Moser report: 'We recognize the crucial importance of raising basic skills standards among adults as part of our agenda to widen participation in learning and to improve skills in our working population. Basic skills education has a key place in the initiatives we have already launched...all major Government training initiatives from the New Deal to our National Training Organizations include a focus on provision for adults with poor basic skills' (DfEE Press Release, 25 March 1999).

66. David Blunkett, DfEE Press Release, 25 February 1998.

67. Gordon Brown, to the TUC, 12 September 2000.

68. DfEE Press Release, 17 February 1998.

69. Gordon Brown, in a lecture to the Royal Economic Society, 13 July 2000.

70. The Treasury produced a regular analysis of the productivity gap in each budget's background papers. It published *Productivity in the UK: The Evidence and the Government's Approach* in November 2000 and *Productivity in the UK: Enterprise and the Productivity Challenge* in June 2001. At the Treasury's behest, the CBI and TUC then produced a joint submission in October 2001, building on reports that they had generated separately on a regular basis. The TUC, for example, issued a report in 1999 on the impact of the skills gap on UK productivity levels, and one in 2002 on the similar impact of what it termed mediocre management in many UK firms. The government also commissioned reports from private sources. The McKinsey Global Institute produced one in 2002. Michael Porter from the Harvard Business School produced another in 2003, and the DTI itself regularly issued *UK Productivity and Competitiveness Indicators*.

71. Treasury, *Productivity in the UK: The Evidence and the Government's Approach*, p. 17. Convinced that the DTI documents produced under the Conservatives had been too much an exercise in public relations, the DTI under Margaret Beckett immediately launched a benchmarking investigation of seven key sectors, and found some pretty depressing data. As she told the CBI in November 1997, it wasn't just a matter of the UK having 'a long tail of under-performing companies'. On the contrary, the investigation's findings suggested that 'it was not just the weakest companies that had to catch up. It may be that all our firms need to benchmark themselves against the best in the world' since 'our overall performance on several counts – innovation, skills, productivity – remains behind that of other developed countries. The common weaknesses identified included: relatively low levels of investment, a failure of small and medium size companies with growth potential to succeed; a failure by too many businesses to adopt best practice; low levels of skill; and weakness in exploiting export markets' (report on *Benchmark for Business* document, and Margaret Beckett's response to it, from the *Financial Times*,

12 November 1997, p. 9. For the earlier literature on UK underperformance, see D. Coates, *The Question of UK Decline*, Hemel Hempstead, Harvester Wheatsheaf, 1994).

72. Patricia Hewitt, to the TUC, 9 September 2003.
73. Gordon Brown, to the CBI Annual Conference, 2000.
74. Ibid.
75. 'Chapter 3: Meeting the Productivity Challenge', Budget Papers 2002, paragraph 3.3.
76. Margaret Beckett, 'Message to businesses large and small, business support organizations and to trade unions', 3 May 1997.
77. Stephen Byers, in speeches of February and October 1999.
78. To a degree, this was partly a presentational issue. In the DTI's depleted budget, as we will see, funds were set aside for support for industries or firms in trouble, but nonetheless spending there was projected as flat 1998–2001 while that set aside for the encouragement of 'knowledge transfer and collaboration' was doubled (see the *Financial Times*, 1 April 1999, p. 16). But it was also reflective of a new reluctance, among Labour Industry Secretaries, for extensive intervention. Stephen Byers put it this way: 'We should restrict support to the following areas: to help industry through a period of change which has come about because of a government policy decision....to provide support in areas where there are potential net economic benefits which would not be realized by the private sector on its own...to secure investment in geographical areas of greatest need (however this should not be just about job creation or retention but will increasingly be linked to raised productivity and improvement in the skills base)...[and, given] the international environment...[to ensure that] UK companies [are] not put at a competitive disadvantage...but our primary objective – within the European Union and more widely – is to achieve this goal by arguing for cuts in state aid by others. These must now be seen as very much the exceptions' (speaking to the IPPR, 22 September 2000).
79. Quoted in the *Financial Times*, 11 December 1998, p.20
80. Stephen Byers, to the German/British Chambers of Commerce, 13 April 1999.
81. *Our Competitive Future: Building the Knowledge-Driven Economy*, London, DTI, 1998, p. 6.
82. Interview in the *Guardian*, 16 May 2002, p. 22.
83. He and H. Ketels published *UK Competitiveness: Moving to the Next Stage*, as a DTI Economics Paper (no. 3) in 2003.
84. Larry Elliott, 'Byers tells business to shape up', *Guardian*, 13 December 1999, p. 26.
85. It also, in July 2002, issued its own response to a highly critical report from the House of Commons Select Committee on Trade and Industry.
86. The science minister, Lord Sainsbury, put it this way: 'The Government recognizes that it has a central role to play in the health and well-being of the science and engineering base...three roles...a key role in funding basic and strategic research...a crucial role to play in encouraging the exploitation of knowledge and new technologies....[and] to help the customer...to ensure that people can be confident about the new products which science can deliver.' The government was particularly keen to encourage basic research in genomics, 'e' science, and basic technology; and to strengthen science

teaching in schools (speech at Imperial College, 12 September 2000). The Prime Minister threw his own weight behind a strengthening of the UK's science base, and the greater commercial exploitation of its output, in a major policy speech in May 2002.

87. The small business sector has its own minister. The government upgraded the Business Links system of advisory centres inherited from the Major government, legislated against late payments, lowered the small business rate of corporation tax, gave tax credits for small business R&D and rewarded successful small-scale innovators with extra financial assistance, cut its own regulatory burden on small firms, and triggered the creation of small-business friendly venture capital firms. It launched a Small Business Service in April 2000 to maximize the opportunities for start-ups and small business growth across the country as a whole. The Regional Development Agencies were particularly important in all of this. So too was the Treasury, 'creating one of the most favourable tax systems for small firms', as the Small Firms Minister put it as early as July 1997.

88. According to the TUC, settling between 1996 and 1998 at just 30% of the EU average: at 334 euros per person employed in the manufacturing sector, as against an EU average of 1113 euros, and figures for Italy of 1995 euros, Germany 1434 and France 1131 (*Observer*, 16 July 2000, Business Section p. 3). Indeed in 2002 the European Commission issued figures showing that Britain spends less on ailing industries as a percentage of GDP than the rest of the EU taken together: 0.5% in the UK case, 1.5% for the EU as a whole. Between 1997 and 1999, the UK spent £175 per employed person on this, as against £445 in Germany, £483 in France and £352 for the EU as a whole. By 2003, however, the DTI was setting aside a record £6.1 billion for industrial aid, and the Ministry of Defence was quietly sustaining, through purchases and grants, a strong military-industrial complex in the UK, around firms like British Aerospace, GEC, Vickers, GKN and Rolls-Royce. This was hardly surprising, given the inheritance by New Labour from the Conservatives of an arms industry employing 400,000 people (mostly in Labour-held constituencies), one bringing into the UK £2 billion a year in export earnings.

89. Quoted in the *Financial Times*, 4 November 1998, p. 1.

90. Blair, to the Knowledge 2000 Conference.

Chapter 6

1. The distinction is Mario Cuomo's, often cited by Tony Blair as a description of New Labour in power (see, for example, his speech to the 1998 party conference).

2. Gordon Brown's Mansion House speech, 26 June 2002.

3. Quoted in the *Guardian*, 15 May 1997, p. 1.

4. Gordon Brown, 'A modern agenda for prosperity and social reform', 3 February 2003. For an associated and fuller Treasury-drafted discussion of the strengths and weaknesses of markets, see chapter 2, 'Understanding the Public Services Productivity challenge', in the Treasury discussion document, *Public Services: Meeting the Productivity Challenge*, April 2003.

5. Tony Blair, speaking to the Labour Party conference, 2 October 2001.

6. Press conference, 24 April 1997.

7. Speech to the Labour Party conference, 1 October 2002.
8. This formulation was Peter Mandelson's, cited in the *Observer*, 4 May 2001, p. 27.
9. Speech by the Prime Minister on the Reform of Public Services, 16 July 2001.
10. Tony Blair, to the *Guardian*, 20 December 2002, and to the IPPR/Demos conference, October 2004.
11. Interview in the *Guardian*, 11 September 2001, p. 7.
12. Ibid.
13. Ibid.
14. Interview in the *Guardian*, 20 December 2002, p. 4.
15. Speech by the Prime Minister on the Reform of Public Services.
16. Tony Blair, *The Courage of Our Convictions: Why Reform of the Public Services is the Route to Social Justice*, London, Fabian Pamphlet, 2002, pp. 21–8.
17. Tony Blair speech at Local Government and Women's Conference, Cardiff, 3 February 2002.
18. Brown, 'A modern agenda for prosperity and social reform'. On unease with this development within sections of the party and government, see J. Ashley, 'Who'd buy a personalized service from this lot?', *Guardian*, 10 June 2004, p. 24.
19. Quoted in the *Guardian*, 24 June 2004, p. 1.
20. 2001 pre-budget report, paragraph 6.7.
21. Gordon Brown, the House of Commons, 15 July 1998.
22. Gordon Brown, introducing the 2002 Comprehensive Spending Review to the House of Commons, 15 July 2002.
23. *Public Services: Meeting the Productivity Challenge*, London, HM Treasury, 2003, paragraph E.2.
24. Brown, Mansion House speech, 26 June 2002.
25. Labour Party, *New Labour: Because Britain Deserves Better*, London, Labour Party, 1997, p. 13.
26. *PFI: Meeting the Investment Challenge*, HM Treasury, 2003, paragraph 1.6.
27. Defined, in paragraph 3.4, as 'where the public sector contracts to purchase quality services, with defined outputs, from the private sector on a long-term basis, and including maintaining or constructing the necessary infrastructure...'.
28. Ibid., paragraphs 1.8, 1.9.
29. To the extent indeed that the Labour Party chairman was actually jeered by party activists when defending PPPs at the party's spring conference in 2002 (see BBC News, 4 February 2002).
30. The key text here is Colin Leys, *Market-Driven Politics*, London, Verso, 2001.
31. This fears were well founded. Even the government's own watchdog, the Office of Government Commerce (OGC), found 'contracting out had led to a reduction in numbers employed, some change in the terms of transferred public sector workers, and new workers being offered different terms and conditions to transferred employees' (cited in the *Guardian*, 3 August 2002, p. 2).
32. *Guardian*, 3 October 2002, p. 24. The IPPR report, *Building Better Partnerships*, published in June 2001, called for major changes to the way PPPs were organized, but did not argue against their use as a matter of principle.

Their judgement was a balanced one, captured in this quotation from Peter Robinson, their chief economist: 'To date, two economic rationales have been offered for PFI:one potentially serious, one spurious. The potentially serious argument is that in the right circumstances PPPs can offer significant value-for-money gains. At the moment the evidence of this is variable across sectors – PFI seems to be offering significant gains in roads and prisons but not in hospitals and schools. The spurious argument is that using private finance to pay for capital investment allows governments to undertake more projects than would otherwise be the case. Because all PFI projects are publicly funded and incur future liabilities for the Treasury, they don't lead to "extra" schools or hospitals being built' (IPPR Press Release, 25 June 2001).

33. David Taylor MP, to the House of Commons, July 2001.

34. David Walker, 'Never-Never Land', *Guardian*, 9 October 2002. See also R. Ball, M. Heafey and D. King, 'PFI – a good deal for the public purse or a drain on future generations?', *Policy and Politics*, vol. 29(1), 2001, pp. 95–108.

35. Geoffrey Robinson, Paymaster General (*Financial Times*, 22 October 1998, p. 10).

36. *Guardian*, 11 September 2001, p. 1. This commitment is now enshrined in chapter 6 of the Treasury's *PFI: Meeting the Investment Challenge* document, and in paragraph 1.23, namely, 'The value for money that PFI provides should not be achieved at the expense of staff terms and conditions.' Among the detailed elements in that commitment, there is this: 'The code ensures that new employees terms and conditions that are "overall, no less favourable" than their transferred colleagues, and requires that employers provide a pension to a given standard.'

37. Brown, 'A modern agenda for prosperity and social reform'.

38. Cited in the *Guardian*, 11 September 2001, p. 1.

39. Speech by the Prime Minister on Reform of Public Services.

40. Figures in this paragraph from R. Brooks, *Pay and the Public Service Workforce*, London, IPPR, July 2004.

41. On this, see the parallel volume to this one, *Blair's War*, co-written with Joel Krieger, with the help of Rhiannon Vickers (Cambridge, Polity Press, 2004).

42. His clearest defence of them was to the Social Market Foundation in an address on 30 April 2003.

43. The fear was not so far off the mark. The original title proposed by Alan Milburn for these foundation hospitals was 'foundation *companies*', apparently a title too far even for Number 10 (see the *Guardian*, 12 March 2003, p. 11).

44. Frank Dobson, to the Catalyst fringe meeting at the 2003 TUC, where he argued that 'Ministers have started to redefine the NHS as a health insurance system not a health care system. They want to set hospital against hospital competing for patients. Foundation hospitals will compete against non-Foundation hospitals. All NHS hospitals will have to compete with private diagnosis and treatment centres. Hospitals the Government decides are "failing" will be handed over to private management....And the competition is going to be rigged. Foundation hospitals will have more money, more staff and more freedom than non-Foundation hospitals' (Press Release, Catalyst, 11 September 2003).

45. Brown, 'A modern agenda for prosperity and social reform'.

46. Quoted in the *Guardian*, 12 February 2003, p. 13.

47. Tony Blair, quoted by BBC News, 6 May 2003.
48. This was replaced in 2004 by the Healthcare Commission, auditing health care standards across both the NHS and the private sector.
49. *The New NHS: Modern and Dependable*, London, Department of Health, 1997, chapter 3, paragraph 1.
50. The best guides here are Leys, *Market-Driven Politics*, pp. 167–77, and A. Pollock, *NHS:plc*, London, Verso, 2004.
51. Commissioned by the Treasury, this report reviewed health care systems across the advanced capitalist world, and gave a ringing endorsement to the underlying principles of the NHS. 'There is no evidence,' the report concluded, 'that any alternative financing method to the UK's would deliver a given quality of health care at a lower cost to the economy. Indeed other systems seem likely to prove more costly...the UK system of financing appears to be relatively efficient and equitable. It delivers strong cost control and prioritization and minimizes economic distortions and disincentives. A further key advantage of the UK's funding system is its fairness, providing maximum separation between an individual's financial contributions and their use of healthcare' (Interim Report, November 2001, paragraphs 2.18, 2.24: the full report came in April 2002).
52. *The NHS Plan: A Plan for Investment, a Plan for Reform*, London, Department of Health, 2000.
53. *Delivering the NHS Plan*, Cm 5503, April 2002, pp. 4–6.
54. Which is presumably why the ONS announcement in October 2004 that productivity in the NHS had probably *fallen* by up to 1% a year since New Labour came to power so annoyed the Secretary of State for Health. 'Absurd' was the way he described it (see the *Guardian*, 17 October 2004, p. 16).
55. *Guardian*, 28 July 2000, p. 9.
56. His successor was apparently less impressed. Press reports in April 2004 talked of a planned scrapping of the concordat, because of overcharging by private health care providers (see the *Guardian*, 6 April 2004, p. 6).
57. Quoted in the *Guardian*, 10 January 2002, p. 7.
58. *Guardian*, 14 November 2003.
59. Quoted in the *Guardian*, 26 November 2003, p. 10. On the promise of a moratorium, John Reid said: 'I will ask the Commission for Health Care Audit and Inspection to conduct the review before autumn 2005. Obviously during that period I would not pass any new application for a new NHS foundation trust onto the regulator' (House of Commons, 19 November 2003)!
60. *Guardian*, 19 November 2002, p. 12.
61. This was well captured in this remark by an unnamed backbench MP. 'Even if Tony Blair offers £20,000 a year and free flights to the Bahamas to every poor student, I'll still vote against him. We've got to get the bastard out' (*Guardian*, 20 January 2004, p. 22).
62. It also came unstuck politically, not least because as soon as education policy in Scotland was devolved to the new Scottish Assembly, that assembly abolished the fee (even though the majority party in that assembly was Labour).
63. 'Blunkett sets new Labour school rules', *Guardian*, 28 December 1994, p. 2.
64. DfEE Press Release 318/98, 23 June 1998.
65. Quoted in DfEE Press Release 351/97, 5 November 1997.

66. Chris Woodhead himself became a deeply unpopular and controversial figure across the teaching profession and educational policy-making community – the 'witchfinder-general', the chairman of the Commons education sub-committee once dubbed him. His forced resignation in 2000 was widely welcomed, and opened a new career for him in right-wing journalism from which to criticize New Labour policy.
67. The figures are Howard Glennester's, from the LSE, cited in the *Guardian* 4 September 2001, p. 1.
68. 'Blair pledges schools spending boost', BBC News, 12 July 2002.
69. 'Blair signals landmark shift in schools policy', *Financial Times*, 13 February 2001, p. 10.
70. David Miliband, quoted in the *Guardian*, 24 June 2002, p. 6.
71. Question and Answer session with delegates after his speech, reported in the *Guardian*, 30 September 2004, p. 11.
72. Of the teachers voting, 86% supported the boycott, but the 34% participation rate in the ballot was too low, under the NUT's own rules, to trigger the action.
73. Of the 30,000 teachers surveyed by the NUT in 2003, 80% thought the testing regime was stressful to children. The test regulating body, the Qualifications and Curriculum Authority, claimed otherwise (BBC News, 24 November 2003).
74. Blair, *The Courage of Our Convictions*, p. iv.
75. Andrew Rawnsley, 'It's not the fee, it's the principle', *Observer*, 7 December 2003, p. 29.
76. Blair, *The Courage of Our Convictions*, p. iv.

Chapter 7

1. Labour Party, *New Labour: Because Britain Deserves Better*, London, Labour Party, 1997, pp. 19–20.
2. Tony Blair, speaking at the Aylesbury estate, Southwark, 2 June 1997.
3. Tony Blair, to the 1997 Labour Party conference, cited in the *Guardian*, 1 October 1997, p. 8.
4. Blair at the Aylesbury estate.
5. Tony Blair's introduction to an essay collection by Giles Radice, reproduced in P. Richards (ed.), *Tony Blair in His Own Words*, London, Politico's, 2004, pp. 147–8.
6. *Observer*, 7 December 1997, p. 24.
7. Social Exclusion Unit, homepage: <www.cabinetoffice.gov.uk/seuhome.html>. For an illuminating discussion of the concept and its relationship to poverty, see Ruth Lister, *Poverty*, Cambridge, Polity Press, 2004, pp. 74–98.
8. Cited in the *Guardian*, 27 March 1998, p. 10.
9. Andrew Taylor attached paramount importance to a 'continuing prime ministerial role in overseeing the SEU's activities' in his analysis of the Unit's power resources, and as early as 1999 was wondering 'what would happen if prime ministerial attention was to shift'. His report was eventually published as 'Hollowing out or filling in? Taskforces and the management of cross-cutting issues in British government', *British Journal of Politics and International Relations*, vol. 2(1), 2000, pp. 46–71.

10. Social Exclusion Unit, *Breaking the Cycle: Taking Stock of Progress and Priorities for the Future*, London, September 2004, pp. 4–5.
11. Social Exclusion Unit, *Tackling Social Exclusion: Taking Stock and Looking to the Future*, London, March 2004, p. 13.
12. Ibid., p. 2.
13. Ruth Lister and 55 other leading professors of sociology and social work, in 'Government must reconsider its strategy for more equal society', a letter to the *Financial Times*, 1 October 1997.
14. Speaking to the IPPR conference, January 1999, quoted in the *Financial Times*, 15 January 1999, p. 7, and the *Guardian* of the same date, p. 3.
15. Tony Blair, speaking at a North London comprehensive, 8 February 2001.
16. Tony Blair, to the IPPR, 11 October 2004.
17. Tony Blair, 'A Britain in which nobody is left behind', speech in Hackney, London, 18 September 2002.
18. Gordon Brown, *The Social Justice Priorities of Labour's Second Term*, London, Bevan Society, 2002, p. 9.
19. Gordon Brown, Joseph Rowntree centennial lecture, 7 July 2004.
20. Ibid.
21. Tony Blair, speaking at Toynbee Hall, 18 March 1999.
22. *Guardian*, 20 August 2004, p. 8.
23. On this, and much else here, see Madeleine Bunting, 'A job is not enough', *Guardian*, 11 October 2004, p. 17.
24. Gender and politics in the New Labour project is a vital issue in its own right, inadequately covered here. See Sarah Childs, *New Labour's Women MPs: Women Representing Women*, London, Frank Cass, 2004; and J. Squires and M. Wickham-Jones, 'New Labour, gender mainstreaming and the Women and Equality Unit', *British Journal of Politics and International Relations*, vol. 6(1), 2004, pp. 81–98.
25. On this, see R. Hattersley, 'A weakness for wealth and power', *Guardian*, 1 November 2004, p. 16.
26. S. Machin, 'Wage inequality since 1975', in R. Dickens, P. Gregg and J. Wadsworth (eds), *The Labour Market Under New Labour: The State of Working Britain*, Basingstoke, Palgrave, 2003, p. 193. The Gini coefficient for female wage inequality moved in the other direction, from .403 in 1997 to .391 in 2001.
27. All this in a Cabinet Office paper, reported in the *Guardian*, 3 July 2003.
28. Ruth Lister, 'The social cost of the Middle Britain ethos', *Guardian*, 25 May 2001, p. 18.
29. Jack Straw took some persuading on this, but by 2000 was under pressure, from the Police Federation charity among others, to reclassify cannabis, so removing the threat of imprisonment for possession. It was left to his successor as Home Secretary to reclassify cannabis as they suggested, but even he retained laws making trafficking in cannabis a custodial offence.
30. It is perhaps significant here that, in the free vote on the various options – from a fully appointed House of Lords to a fully elected one – the Prime Minister should have voted for the fully appointed one. So much for the 'redistribution of power...to the many, not the few'. For a full evaluation of the 'Jekyll and Hyde' quality of the constitutional changes and governing style adopted by the New Labour government, see D. Beetham et al., *Democracy*

under Blair: A Democratic Audit of the UK, London, Politico's, 2002; and the earlier S. Weir and D. Beetham, *Political Power and Democratic Control in Britain*, London, Routledge, 1999.

31. Tony Blair, to the Labour Party conference, 1 October 1997.
32. BBC News, 25 July 2004.
33. Nick Cohen, 'Turning right to wrong', *Guardian*, 1 August 2004, p. 27.
34. Martin Kettle, 'New Labour is creating a whole new category of victim', *Guardian*, 10 August 2004, p. 20.
35. Tony Blair told the *Guardian* in November 2003 that 'summary justice, which will allow the police to impose fixed penalty fines for a far wider range of offences, could become a centrepiece of Labour's third term agenda' (28 November 2003, p. 1).
36. Tony Blair, 'My vision for Britain', *Observer*, 10 November 2002.
37. *Guardian*, 12 March 2003, p. 11.
38. *Guardian*, 1 September 2004, p. 6.
39. P. Toynbee and D. Walker, *Did Things Get Better?* London, Penguin, 2001, pp. 170–1.
40. David Walker, 'Welcome to Britain', *Guardian*, 29 January 2001.
41. Quoted in the *Financial Times*, 24 February 2004, p. 2. The Prime Minister was speaking on BBC Midlands.
42. David Blunkett, defending his policy in his 'I am not King Herod' piece in the *Guardian*, 27 November 2003, p. 25. The legislation that followed did not include that proposed power.
43. David Blunkett, quoted in the *Guardian*, 26 February 2004.
44. *Guardian*, 27 April 2004, p. 1.
45. Michael Howard, speaking in the House of Commons, 26 November 2003.
46. See page 148.

Chapter 8

1. For a full discussion of the seriousness with which policy evaluation is taken by this government, see P. Meadow and H. Metcalf, 'Special issue on policy evaluation: introduction', NIESR, *National Institute Economic Review* no. 186, October 2003, pp. 57–9.
2. The 13 were: economic growth, social investment, employment, health, education and training, housing quality, climate change, air pollution, transport, water quality, wildlife, land use, and waste. By 2004 they had expanded to 15 headline sustainable development indicators, used as a 'quality of life' barometer, supplemented by no less than 132 indicators of sustainable development! For this, see DTI, *UK Productivity and Competitiveness Indicators 2003*, DTI Economic Paper no. 6, pp. 23–4.
3. William Hague, quoted in the *Guardian*, 15 July 2000.
4. Gordon Brown, to the House of Commons, 17 March 2004.
5. Press Release, Prime Minister's Office of Public Service Reform, 12 June 2004.
6. *Observer*, 23 November 1997, p. 25.
7. Tony Blair, 'NHS: we can do it', *Observer*, 14 April 2002.
8. Tony Blair, Labour Party conference, 30 September 2003.
9. Quoted in the *Guardian*, 13 December 1999.

10. Quoted in the *Guardian*, 1 January 2003.
11. Tony Blair, to the Labour Party conference, 30 September 2003.
12. *Financial Times*, 9 June 2004, p. 13.
13. Larry Elliott, 'UK inflation lowest in EU', *Guardian*, 16 February 2000.
14. Gordon Brown, in the *Guardian*, 15 March 2001.
15. The figures are Steve Fothergill's, cited in the *Guardian*, 29 October 2002.
16. For 2004 as a whole, the official unemployment figure will be somewhere near 900,000 (based on those claiming the Jobseeker's Allowance) or 1.4 million (using the ILO figure). That latter figure would rise to 2.5 million if some of those on incapacity benefit were included, on the lines suggested by the Sheffield Hallam University study. On this, see 'The Disgrace of Incapacity Benefit', *New Statesman*, 17 September 2004.
17. <http://news.bbc/vote2001/facts/Are we better off?>
18. R. Dickens, P. Clegg and J. Wadsworth (eds), *The Labour Market under New Labour: The State of Working Britain 2003*, Basingstoke, Palgrave, 2003, p. 2.
19. *Guardian*, 19 February 2001, p. 17.
20. Gordon Brown, Labour Party conference, Bournemouth, 29 September 2003.
21. As Martin Weale, director of the NIESR, put it, 'Sharp increases in house prices crowd out productive investment. The country as a whole cannot become better off by pushing up house prices, whereas it can by building roads and factories and things like that....It's nice for the people who own their homes, but not those who haven't bought them yet – including those who have not been born. In a sense it's paying for the present by robbing the future' (quoted in the *Guardian*, 30 December 2003, p. 3).
22. A leading member of the Bank of England's Monetary Policy Committee warned UK householders in September 2004 to brace themselves for a possible fall in house prices of up to 30% (*Guardian*, 15 September 2004, p. 2).
23. The survey was issued in February 2004, by which time the government had its £250 million 'Starter Home' policy in place, giving key public sector workers help with house purchase via shared ownership schemes, equity loans and grants.
24. Citizens' Advice reported a 44% increase in the number of people seeking help with debt problems between 1998 and 2004 (BBC News, 7 August 2004).
25. Larry Elliott, 'It's downhill all the way for UK trade traffic', *Guardian*, 16 February 2004, p. 23.
26. M. Swift, 'We ignore the trade gap Cassandras at our peril', *Guardian*, 23 July 2001.
27. Data in the *Observer*, 24 August 2003, Business Section, p. 7.
28. K. Marsden, *Gordon Brown and British Competitiveness: A Statistical Analysis*, London, Centre for Policy Studies, 2003, p. 26.
29. DTI, *UK Productivity and Competitiveness Indicators 2003*, pp. 4, 29.
30. Patricia Hewitt, speaking to the Labour Party conference, 27 September 2004.
31. Heather Stewart, 'Brown's struggle with business over investment', *Guardian*, 21 April 2003, p. 21.
32. *Financial Times*, 12 July 2001, p. 8.
33. DTI Press Release P/99/1029, December 1999.
34. Ibid.

35. M. Atkinson, 'Britain's $200bn leads global takeover boom', *Guardian*, 4 October 2000.

36. *Observer*, 30 July 2000, Business Focus, p. 5. US data confirms this. In 1981 the US spent 2.32% of its GDP on total R&D, 1.73% on non-defence R&D. The UK figures that year were larger: respectively 2.37% and 1.84%. By 1997 the US figures were 2.60% and 1.87%, the UK's only 2.16% and 1.65% (National Patterns of R&D resources: 2000 Data Update, on <www.nsf.gov/sbe/srs/nsf01309/start.html>

37. *Guardian*, 21 May 2000.

38. CVCP, *Talent, not Technology: Publicly Funded Research and Innovation in the UK*, SPRU, Sussex, 2000, p. 13, available from <www.sussex.ac.uk/spru/index/html>

39. HM Treasury, *Productivity in the UK: The Evidence and the Government's Approach*, 1999, pp. 16–17.

40. DTI, *UK Productivity and Competitiveness Indicators 2003*, pp. 44–5.

41. OECD, 'Labour productivity levels in OECD countries', *Financial Times*, 17 April 1997, p. 12.

42. *Guardian*, 23 September 1997.

43. McKinsey Global Institute, *Driving Productivity and Growth in the UK Economy*.

44. HM Treasury, *Productivity in the UK: Enterprise and the Productivity Challenge*, 2001; DTI, *Opportunity for All: A White Paper on Enterprise, Skills and Innovation*, 2001.

45. HM Treasury, *Productivity in the UK: The Evidence and the Government's Approach*, p. 6.

46. Citing Mary O'Mahoney, from the NIESR, on her background paper to the Treasury. (*Observer*, 4 March 2001). In fact the O'Mahoney and Crafts calculation for the Treasury of the productivity gap in output/worker had the UK lagging the US by 35%, France by 27% and Germany by 26%. When allowance is made for hours worked, the gaps shift slightly: 33% for France, 29% for Germany and 26% for the US (cited in the *Observer*, 29 October 2000, Business Focus, p. 2).

47. DTI, *UK Productivity and Competitiveness Indicators 2003*, p. 19.

48. HM Treasury, *Productivity in the UK: Enterprise and the Productivity Challenge*, p. 1.

49. Swift, 'We ignore the trade gap Cassandras at our peril'.

50. The government commissioned in 2003, and received in 2004, Kate Barker's report *Review of Housing Supply* which laid out various scenarios for housing stock expansion. The government has had a ten-year transport plan in place since July 2000, covering road, rail and bus services. In fact, policy changed over time, favouring road-building far more than New Labour had initially intended, and culminated in a huge new road-building programme announced in December 2002. New Labour had initially intended to build new roads only 'as a last resort' but was obliged to reset policy in line with the UK commuters' commitment to the car over the train. By 2004 the Deputy Prime Minister was proposing that 500,000 new homes be built in the English East, this only three years after the house-building sector as a whole recorded its lowest number of starts for 75 years: just 162,000 new homes built in 2001. The Prescott plan met predictable but pointed resistance – the leader

of the Hertfordshire County Council pointing out, quite rightly, that 'the M25, M1, A1 and M11, all key trunk roads that cross the county, are already full to capacity [and] that the region's railways were full, with no investment planned' (*Guardian*, 14 October 2004, p. 1).

51. On these, see C. Hay, 'Credibility, competitiveness and the business cycle in "Third Way" political economy: a critical evaluation of economic policy in Britain since 1997', *New Political Economy*, vol. 9(1), 2004, pp. 42–63.
52. OECD, *Economic Survey: The UK*, Paris, 2000, p. 21.
53. R. Riley and G. Young, *The Macroeconomic impact of the New Deal for Young People*, NIESR Discussion Paper no. 184, December 1999. A later four-year assessment by Richard Blundell and others concluded that the New Deal for Young People had raised employment by 17,000 a year, rather than the 375,000 figure used by the government (Dickens et al., *The Labour Market under New Labour*, p. 17).
54. BBC News online, 'UK bosses the best paid in Europe', 30 July 2001.
55. *Guardian*, 29 August 2001, p. 1; BBC News, 10 October 2003.
56. BBC News online, 'TUC say workers are abused', 2 December 2003.
57. Martin Wainwright, 'Four in five staff work weekends', *Guardian*, 7 September 2004, p. 9.
58. L. Mishel, J. Bernstein and J. Schmitt, *The State of Working America*, Washington, DC, Employment Policy Institute, 2000, p. 400.
59. On this, see Dickens et al., *The Labour Market under New Labour*, pp. 143–5; and for the pre-1997 data, see F. Green, 'It's been a hard day's night: the concentration and intensification of work in Late Twentieth Century Britain', *British Journal of Industrial Relations*, vol. 39(1), 2001, pp. 53–80.
60. Cited in the *Observer*, 31 October 2004, p. 9.
61. BBC News online, 'Stress causes 6.5 million sick days', 25 June 2001. For more details, see Madeleine Bunting, *Willing Slaves*, London, HarperCollins, 2004, pp. 177–207.
62. Research by Oswald and Gardner at the University of Warwick, cited in the *Observer*, 22 April 2001.
63. Cited in the *Guardian*, 3 September 2002, p. 1.
64. Demos Press Release, 1 November 2004.
65. Cited in the *Guardian*, 12 October 2000, p. 15.
66. Cited in the *Guardian Weekly*, 20–26 January 2000, p. 13.
67. DTI, *UK Productivity and Competitiveness Indicators 2003*, pp. 54, 11.
68. HM Treasury, *Productivity in the UK: The Evidence and the Government's Approach*, p. 17.
69. DfES, *Skills Strategy*, London, 2004, p. 12.
70. This, in their own advertising promotion, 'UK facing severe skills gap', 13 April 2003.

Chapter 9

1. In August 1997 we were awaiting reports from, among others, the Task Force on Youth Justice, the Welfare to Work Task Force, the School Standards Task Force, the Literacy Task Force, the Numeracy Task Force, the Creative Industries Task Force, the Task Force on Tax and Benefits, the Private Finance Task Force, the NHS Efficiency Task Force, the Better Regulation Task Force,

the Football Task Force, the Advisory Group on Competitiveness, the Export Forum, the Special Educational Needs Group, the Working Group on Teacher Bureaucracy...even the Review on Surrogacy Law. These were committees set up, not to bury issues as often in the past, but to clarify them quickly and to expedite policy (see Caroline Daniel, 'May the task force be with you', *New Statesman*, 1 August 1997, pp. 27–32).

2. In 'Britain just gets better', *Guardian*, 21 February 2004.

3. Anthony Giddens, *New Statesman*, 24 September 2004.

4. *Observer*, 13 July 2003, p. 25.

5. The *Guardian*/ICM poll for September 1998 brought his initial high scores on personality (80% in 1997), trust (54% in 1997) and arrogance (only 21% in 1997) to 60%, 34% and 29% respectively. The 'Blair bubble bursts' was how the figures were reported, 'with a disaffected electorate...beginning to view him as just another politician' (*Guardian*, 9 September 1998, p. 1).

6. But not many: for the relative quiescence of the PLP during that first Parliament, see P. Cowley and M. Stuart, 'In place of strife? The PLP in Government 1997–2001', *Political Studies* vol. 51(2), 2003, pp. 315–31.

7. Kilfoyle was right. The major defections from Labour in 2001 did come from its heartland: from abstentions by council house tenants, trade unionists and unskilled manual workers. Margaret Hodge found genuine alienation in her London constituency. 'This wasn't apathy', she reported, 'the non-voters expressed anger...they just felt that nobody with power listened to them' (*Guardian*, 3 November 2002).

8. The *Guardian*/ICM poll of party members in 2004 found only 28% who had joined in the previous decade. The rest had a longer party membership: suggesting that those attracted by New Labour in the 1990s were the first to leave. Even the pro-modernizing *Renewal* magazine carried an editorial in August 2004 warning of a potential 'melt-down' in the party, and calling for both a new direction of policy and a new leader.

9. *Guardian*, 3 August 2004, p. 2.

10. Alan Travis, 'Iraq given a low priority by voters', *Guardian*, 18 August 2004, p. 1.

11. Certainly the 1992 election study team, on the basis of a survey carried out just after the election, 'concluded that voters swung away from Labour in 1992 because of a lack of faith in the party's ability to improve services such as health and education, rather than because of its position on taxation. That fact, coupled with the perception that more voters saw Labour – rather than the Conservatives – as a divided party explains its 1992 defeat. The tax bombshell is an urban legend: it has no substantial evidence' (Paul Whiteley, *Guardian*, 27 June 2003, p. 22). But legends are remarkably impervious to evidence, however substantial. Roy Hattersley reported Tony Blair telling him, immediately before the 1997 election, that John Smith's 1992 tax-raising 'alternative budget' had 'given legs to the Tory lie about the certainty of a massive tax hike' (*Observer*, 23 June 2003, p. 18). Both Whiteley and Hattersley were drawn to set the record straight because of the Hain climb-down (on which, see later).

12. The twentieth British Social Attitudes Survey, taken in 2003, found 63% of those questioned thought taxes and spending on the welfare state should be higher. In 1983 the figure had been 32%.

13. For data on the latest focus group trends on this, see Martin Kettle, 'Why too much choice is bad for us and bad for Blair', *Guardian*, 30 March 2004.

14. See, for example, Jenni Russell's 'Drilled, not educated' piece in the *Guardian*, 20 August 2004, p. 21. A scathing critique of the A-level system, and of the Schools Minister's defence of it, she wrote of a system 'which has drilled children through their school lives, at the expense of teaching them to think, learn and create', one that is 'not producing what we need: a meritocracy of highly skilled, motivated people who have developed their talents. It delivers impressive statistics rather than students with impressive educations.'

15. *Financial Times*, 12 August 1999, p. 11.

16. That message at least seems to be getting through to ministers. The press carried reports in February 2004 of plans to scale back Ofsted inspections from 2005 and to launch in the NHS in 2006 a 'bonfire of targets' (see the *Guardian*, 10 February 2004, p. 1).

17. The best of which is that of Madeleine Bunting, on which more later.

18. The *Guardian*/ICM Poll for August 2004 is typical, showing widespread support for Brown's 'family-friendly' policies (for details, see the *Guardian*, 17 August 2004, p. 1).

19. The *Guardian*/ICM Poll for September 2004, reported in the *Guardian*, 22 September 2004, pp. 12–13.

20. The report was leaked to union leaders, and by them to the rest of us: see the *Guardian*, 8 March 2002; and also S. Sachdev, *Paying the Cost: PPPs and the Public Service Workforce*, London, Catalyst, 2004.

21. C. Leys, *What Works: Public Services Publicly Provided*, London, Catalyst, 2001, p. 2.

22. See on this Allyson Pollock, *NHS:plc*, London, Verso, 2004.

23. Quoted in the *Guardian*, 4 November 2002, p. 1.

24. 'Neo-liberalism is in that sense a class project as well as a theoretical argument, and needs to be recognized as such' (David Coates, *Models of Capitalism*, Cambridge, Polity Press, 2000, p. 104).

25. Sir George Blunden, to the Treasury and Civil Service Committee of the House of Commons, 20 October 1993, quoted in William Keegan, *The Prudence of Mr. Gordon Brown*, London, John Wiley and Sons, 2003, p. 212.

26. Ibid., p. 181.

27. *Summary, Government's Manufacturing Strategy*, May 2002.

28. Tawney's famous essay 'The choice before the Labour Party' was first published in *Political Quarterly* in 1932. It is worth reading in its entirety even now, including this often cited piece. 'Onions can be eaten leaf by leaf, but you cannot skin a live tiger paw by paw: vivisection is its trade, and it does the skinning first. If the Labour Party is to tackle its job with some hope of success, it must mobilize behind it a body of conviction as resolute and informed as the opposition in front of it. The way to create it, and the way when created, for it to set about its task, is not to prophesy smooth things. Support won by such methods is a reed shaken by every wind. It is not to encourage adherents to ask what they will get from a Labour Government, as though a campaign were a picnic, all beer and sunshine. It is to ask them what they will give. It is to make them understand that the return of a Labour Government is merely the first phase of a struggle, the issue of which depends on them.' A

fuller extract can be found in D. Coates, 'Social democracy and the logic of party traditions', *Economy and Society*, vol. 15(3), 1986, pp. 422–4.

29. On the South Korean growth model and the 'disciplining of capital', see Vivek Chibber, 'The politics of a miracle: class interests and state power in Korean developmentalism', in D. Coates (ed.), *Varieties of Capitalism, Varieties of Approaches*, Basingstoke, Palgrave, 2005, pp. 122–38.

30. *Guardian*, 22 January 2004, p. 22.

31. BBC interview with Tony Blair, 6 June 2001.

32. There is often posturing instead of policy, as when for example, Patricia Hewitt summoned Ford to talks about the closure of Jaguar production in Coventry, with the loss of 1,150 jobs. Talks, but still job losses. Just talks.

33. For an argument that it *should*, see Robert Taylor, *Social Democratic Trade Unionism: An Agenda for Action*, London, Catalyst, 2003. For an earlier debate on whether it *could*, see Perry Anderson, 'Figures of descent', *New Left Review* 161, 1987, pp. 20–77, and D. Coates, *The Question of UK Decline*, Hemel Hempstead, Harvester Wheatsheaf, 1994, pp. 123–7.

34. On this, see the UK economic decline literature cited earlier, including the citations in the note above.

35. Anthony Giddens, *New Statesman*, 24 September 2004.

36. Will Paxton and Mike Dixon, *The State of the Nation: An Audit of Injustice in the UK*, London, IPPR, 2004, p. 60.

37. IPPR Press Release, 2 August 2004, *A Decade of Tackling Poverty, but Britain's Far from a Fair Society*.

38. I am grateful to Nev Kirk for this.

39. Tessa Jowell, DfEE Press Release, 26 October 2000.

40. Gordon Brown, to the 2004 Labour Party conference.

41. Gordon Brown to the Social Market Foundation, February 2003.

42. For the adverse impact of New Labour world views on foreign policy issues, see D. Coates and J. Krieger, *Blair's War*, Cambridge, Polity Press, 2004, p. 125.

43. The Stuart Hall argument is reproduced in A. Chadwick and R. Heffernan, *The New Labour Reader*, Cambridge, Polity Press, 2003, pp. 82–7; that of Will Hutton, first published in the *Political Quarterly*, can be found in A. Gamble and T. Wright (eds), *The New Social Democracy*, Oxford, Blackwell, 1999, p. 99. The rebuttal by Ruth Kelly MP in that same collection ('Response to Will Hutton') rests on New Labour's possession of what she terms 'New Keynesian growth theory' (p. 103). She is right. The New Labour project is underpinned by such a growth theory. But so is Hutton. Whatever else that growth theory is, it isn't anti-capitalist.

44. Representative pieces from the Blair wing of the party that do this are Alan Milburn's 'Shift the political geography to the Left' and Peter Mandelson's 'Forget New Labour – here comes even newer Labour': respectively the *Guardian*, 26 September 2003, p. 23 and 7 July 2003, p. 24.

45. Tony Blair, to the Labour Party conference, Brighton, 28 September 2004.

46. Tony Blair, to the TUC at Brighton, 9 September 1997.

47. For a timely critique by the man who coined the term 'meritocracy', read Michael White's 'Down with meritocracy', *Guardian*, 29 June 2001, p. 17.

48. Roy Hattersley, 'It's no longer my party', *Observer*, 24 June 2001, p. 25.

49. Bill Morris, BBC News, 9 December 2002.

50. Martin Kettle, 'Hartlepool, not Brighton, will decide Blair's fate', *Guardian*, 28 September 2004, p. 22.
51. Gordon Brown, to the 2004 Labour Party conference, Brighton, 27 September 2004. And it does not appear to be pure rhetoric. After all, the first public scrap between Roy Hattersley and the New Labour leadership over their toleration of what Hattersley later termed 'the widening gap between rich and poor' was not with Blair, but with Brown: and drew from Gordon Brown a rejection of 'equality of outcomes ' as 'neither desirable nor feasible', and an explicit defence of 'equality of opportunity' as both ethically and economically desirable (*Guardian*, 2 August 1997, p. 9). Brown characterized his own position as one committed to 'equality of opportunity and fairness of outcome' (in his address to the CPAG, 15 May 2000).
52. Lest this seem wisdom after the event, this from 2000: 'That may be electorally popular within the successful economy, but it is neither socially progressive at the level of the world economy as a whole nor free from its own internal propensity to be undermined by similar initiatives elsewhere, whose cumulative effect is to leave individual economies persistently prone to the crises of competitiveness, unemployment and social retrenchment that re-skilling was meant to avoid. You cannot get off the treadmill simply by running faster. All you can do by that mechanism is temporarily pass others, until they respond by running faster too, with the long-term consequence of having the whole field increase their speed just to stand still. The victor in such a race is not the runner, but the treadmill' (David Coates, *Models of Capitalism*, p. 254).
53. This is entirely to be expected from a growth strategy of the 'progressive competitiveness' kind. As Bryan has argued, 'a predictable policy consequence is to shift onto labour the costs involved in the pursuit of national competitiveness....Although advocates of competitiveness extol the possibilities of high wages associated with working for high profit companies in high productivity industries...benefits accrue to labour only for relative productivity...for it is only productivity converted into profitability that supports wage growth. Hence the prospect is that penalties in the form of wage cuts and/or work intensification are the likely dominant outcome of global competition for most of the world's workers. National policies of competitiveness for collective gain thereby secure the complicity of labour in a policy program in which the gains are private, and the collectivism is a rhetorical construction based on statistical aggregation' (cited in Leo Panitch and Sam Gindin, 'Euro-capitalism and American empire', in Coates, *Varieties of Capitalism, Varieties of Approaches*, pp. 141–2).
54. Ruth Lister, 'Doing good by stealth', *New Economy* vol. 8(2), June 2001, p. 66.
55. I am grateful for both these points to Joanne Cooke and her colleagues, in their article 'The evolution of active welfare policies as a solution to social exclusion in Britain', *Journal of European Area Studies*, vol. 9(1), 2001, p. 16.
56. D. Piachaud and H. Sutherland, 'Child poverty in Britain and the New Labour government', *Journal of Social Policy*, vol. 30(1), 2001, p. 115.
57. Charles Clarke, to the Labour Party conference, Brighton, 29 September 2004.
58. Polly Toynbee, *Guardian*, 29 September 2004, p. 22.

59. The Commission argued for child care to be treated as a public priority alongside education and transport (*Guardian*, 30 January 2001). The Treasury reportedly found the proposals 'extremely expansive', but they were fully in line with the findings of the *Guardian*'s own survey of the needs of young working mothers: that child care costs should be subsidized for mothers wanting to return to work (10 March 1998, p. 6).

60. M. Bunting, 'It's all about the opt-out', *Guardian*, 27 September 2004, p. 19.

61. For one valuable if sanguine discussion of the scale of policy-resetting required, see C. Lloyd and J. Payne, 'On the "political economy of skill": assessing the possibilities for a viable high skills project in the UK', *New Political Economy*, vol. 7(3), 2002, pp. 367–96.

62. Stephen Byers, 'I was wrong. Free market trade policies hurt the poor', *Guardian*, 19 May 2003.

63. Michael Kitson, 'Measuring capitalism: output, growth and economic policy', in Coates, *Varieties of Capitalism, Varieties of Approaches*, p. 33.

Index